A HISTORY OF THE WORLD IN 21 WOMEN

A HISTORY OF THE WORLD IN 21 WOMEN

A PERSONAL SELECTION

JENNI MURRAY

ONEWORLD

A Oneworld Book

First published by Oneworld Publications, 2018

ISBN 978-1-78607-410-2
eISBN 978-1-78607-411-9

Typeset by Hewer Text UK Ltd, Edinburgh
Printed and bound in Great Britain by Clays Ltd, Elcograf S.p.A.

Oneworld Publications
10 Bloomsbury Street
London WC1B 3SR
England

Stay up to date with the latest books,
special offers, and exclusive content from
Oneworld with our newsletter

Sign up on our website
oneworld-publications.com

CONTENTS

INTRODUCTION

OK, Thomas Carlyle, famous and greatly respected nineteenth-century Scottish philosopher, I'm going to quote you again, with the purpose this time of completely demolishing what are probably the best-known few words you ever said: 'The history of the world is but the biography of great men.' Wrong, wrong, wrong! And this time I have the whole wide world with which to prove how utterly mistaken you are and were, even in your own time. I wonder that a man of such erudition was so blind to the presence of all those great women, from the past and from his present, who spent their lives in defiance of the conventions that for centuries and across all cultures attempted to confine them to hearth, home and domestic servitude.

Perhaps it's simply been convenient for you and for many men like you to ignore the fact that women the world over are, like men, people and not some sort of enslaved lower life form with no purpose other than to breed your children, cook your food and make and mend your clothes. How strange, Mr Carlyle, that at the very time you took up your pen you should have remained oblivious to women across the globe questioning and challenging the status quo. In your own time a woman stood up and asked why it was that, even though she worked, as so many had to or chose to, and was expected to contribute to general taxation, she didn't have the right to vote and decide what kind of government ruled her. Had you, Mr Carlyle, not heard that other familiar saying 'No taxation without representation'? Or, as Susan B Anthony, one of the American leaders of the suffrage movement, put it during its campaign for the vote: 'Men their rights and nothing more. Women their rights and nothing less.' Women of the nineteenth and early twentieth centuries, after a long and hard battle, finally forced the agreement that, as citizens, we must be acknowledged to have won the right to vote and take a full part in democracy.

In the UK, universal suffrage for all women and men over the age of twenty-one was granted in 1928. Britain was a good way down the list of countries that finally gave in to the fact that so many men, and indeed, some women, had found so difficult to believe: women and men are equal citizens. New Zealand was the first, in 1893, quickly followed by Australia in 1902 (although Aboriginal women were excluded and did not win the right to vote until 1962). Finland, Norway, Denmark, Canada, Austria, Germany, Poland, Russia, the Netherlands, the United States and Sweden all came before Great Britain. Other countries you might have expected to be quick off the mark lagged behind well into the twentieth century; women in Switzerland won the right only in 1971.

Saudi Arabia came to its senses regarding the vote in 2011, and in 2018 the country's young Crown Prince, Mohammed bin Salman, heir to the throne, began his moves to drag the Kingdom into the twenty-first century. Women, who until now have been denied the right to drive a car, will be permitted to be behind the wheel later this year. There remains, however, a significant restriction on the free movement of what the Kingdom continues to regard as the lesser sex. In conversation with a Saudi professor of women's studies, Hatoum al Fassi, at a literary festival in Dubai this spring, I learned that the 'guardianship rule', which dictates that a woman must be accompanied by a man when she appears in public, still applies. It is, she told me, essential that the law be changed and written down clearly so there can be no argument or debate about a woman's right to personal freedom. This would, she said, be the most important step towards changing the culture. The Prince's plan to open theatres and cinemas, banned for the past thirty-five years, will also be significant in introducing more liberal ideas to the society. Art, she believes, will change women's lives.

All over the world, there is still a long way to go for women and girls. As Hillary Clinton, who has her own chapter in this book, said, 'Women are the biggest untapped reservoir of talent in the world.' In this collection of twenty-one of that reservoir – a tiny number when you trawl the entire globe, venture back in time and discover how many women have simply said no to the limits placed upon their hopes and dreams – I have tried to include as wide a range of clever, talented and determined women as possible. There must, I felt, be politicians, writers, artists, musicians, scientists and athletes, and there must be women of different ethnic backgrounds.

It's always necessary to emphasise that feminism and the fight for women's rights is not only the concern of white middle-class women. 'Intersectionality', the somewhat awkward word coined in 1989 by an American professor, Kimberle Crenshaw, means certain groups of women have to navigate multiple layers of discrimination. For instance, a black woman may have to deal with both sexism and racism, and the feminist movement has to account for class, race and gender when seeking to improve women's lives.

I have to admit that the word 'intersectionality' caused me one of the most embarrassing moments of my broadcasting career. I was interviewing Professor Crenshaw and asked her why she'd chosen such a difficult word to introduce what is, in effect, a pretty obvious concept. What exactly did it mean?

'Well,' she said, 'it's a crossroads, it's where these problems of race, class and gender intersect'.

'Of course,' I mumbled, blushing. 'We are indeed two nations divided by a common language.' The penny had dropped – Americans don't have roundabouts and their 'crossroads' are commonly called intersections. I really should have cottoned on quicker! What unites my chosen twenty-one is that each has faced seemingly insurmountable obstacles to achieve her ambition, regardless of her colour or class.

It's also important to emphasise that the women in this book are my personal choices and, inevitably, lots of truly great women will have been left out. In some cases, I have been privileged to meet the women, as a result of my thirty years as presenter of the BBC's radio programme *Woman's Hour*. They have impressed and influenced me beyond measure. Some have raised their heads so high above the parapet that they have faced ridicule, torture, and in some cases assassination, for having dared to pursue their beliefs and challenge male authority.

I hope this book will go some way to demonstrate how widely women's fight for justice and recognition of their human rights has spread, and how long it's been going on. In the twenty-first century, we often speak of role models. It is my passionate desire that others – male or female, young or old – should learn of the determination and courage of so many women throughout the history of the world. They should be known, remembered, cheered and emulated by we who follow them.

1

Pharaoh Hatshepsut

C.1500 BCE–C.1458 BCE

It was on a trip to Egypt in October 1988 that I came across the legendary figure of Hatshepsut, the first woman in recorded history to hold real power and certainly the first woman in ancient Egypt to have declared herself a Pharaoh – a regal position strictly restricted to men. A producer, Mary Sharp, and I had been asked to travel to Cairo to put together a *Woman's Hour* programme on gender issues in the country.

Hosni Mubarak took over as Egypt's President after the assassination of Anwar Sadat in 1981. He had outlawed the more extremist Islamic groups that had been pushing for stricter control of women's freedoms, so our programme examined what was going on in the lives of ordinary women. Why were so many beginning to wear the hijab, or head scarf? Was it a fashion statement or the return of a religious requirement? Why was the genital mutilation of girls still so common, even though it had been made illegal? Why was Egypt's family court described as the most backward in the world? And why was violence against women and girls a common occurrence?

Our best-informed commentator was Nawal El Sadaawi, a doctor, writer and activist who had long been a thorn in the side of Sadat's presidency. Nawal believed the country was facing a dark phase, and she fully expected women to be its first victims.

She described how, under Sadat, her feminist writings had been censored and how she had spent time in prison as a result of political campaigning against the increasing economic imperialism and geopolitical influence of America, genital mutilation, the rise in religious fundamentalism, the ever-present requirement for women to cover themselves and the common practice for a man to take up to four wives. She was not hopeful that Mubarak's regime would free women from what she described as 'those old issues'.

I remember asking her about a question that has long worried western feminists. Was it any of our business to poke our noses into the way women in other cultures lived their lives? Not only were they women, with all the discrimination that brings, but they lived with religious and cultural expectations that we could barely comprehend. Should we simply leave it up to women like her, on the ground, to develop feminist politics and fight for women's rights in their own way? Her response has stayed with me. 'When I was in jail – afraid, deprived, in the dirt and the dark and the heat – I felt the influence of western feminism washing over my feet like warm, comforting waves. Never fear the impact you can have.'

From Nawal's flat in Cairo we travelled back in time to uncover the history of Hatshepsut. It meant a short flight from Cairo to Luxor, once the ancient city of Thebes, centre of the greatest of all early civilisations and home of the Pharaohs. From there we could travel easily by taxi to the great temple of Karnak, dedicated to the god Amon, and cross the Nile by car ferry to the Valley of the Kings, the burial place of the rulers of Ancient Egypt.

My memories of that trip are somewhat mixed. There was much pleasure and excitement in the anticipation of exploring the great temple of Hatshepsut, where the story of her rise to power was engraved in the stone. There was also a degree of pain in the unwise decision made by poor Mary to accept, with impeccable British manners, the small glass of tea offered by the charming taxi driver hired to take us across the river. 'Don't drink it,' I warned. 'Tip it out of the window when he's not looking. It'll be Nile water and it won't have been properly boiled.'

My tea never passed my lips. Mary, raised a strict Leicestershire Methodist, told me I was rude and ungrateful. She drank hers. I have never witnessed such a speedy onset of Cairo cramp; Mary's exploration of the great temples and the rest of our trip was quite the most miserable event I've ever witnessed. I add this merely as a warning should you decide to follow in our footsteps and seek out Hatshepsut.

We stepped out of the taxi into a blazing hot desert. Sheer limestone cliffs rose before and above us. In this stunning and peaceful atmosphere, we found the extraordinary temple of Hatshepsut, cut deep into the rock. At the height of the summer heat there were few tourists around; we were able to spend as much time as we liked examining the temple's engraved walls. There was, in 1988, no thought of terrorist attack, although nearly ten years later, in 1997, Hatshepsut's name echoed around the world when fundamentalist terrorists attacked a group of sightseers visiting the terraces of her temple. Some thirty people from Japan and Switzerland died in the massacre.

Hatshepsut was the only surviving child of Pharaoh Thutmose and his wife Ahmose, but as a girl, had no right to inherit the throne. She married her half-brother, Thutmose II, the child of one of her father's lesser wives. On the death of her father, when she was around twelve years old she became Queen and her husband the Pharaoh.

Her husband died only four years after their marriage, but by a lesser wife he had a son, who did not have Hatshepsut's royal status. This toddler was named as the next Pharaoh, Thutmose III, and his stepmother, the teenaged Hatshepsut, was appointed as his regent. Within seven years she had decided she would be Pharaoh and declared herself the ruler. A wonderful picture of her carved in the stone of the Karnak temple shows her sitting at her desk; I could almost hear her saying, 'I can do this job!'

Egyptologists have achieved intellectual miracles with often contradictory, patchy sources; it's amazing that we know so much about this incredible civilisation. But, as ever, there are gaps. It's impossible to know whether Hatsheput took such a step from personal ambition or because of her determination to preserve a dynasty that was still young. I prefer to think it was ambition and an assertion of her belief that a woman could be as effective as a man, if not an even more successful ruler. She clearly believed in the capabilities of women; during her rule, she made a sustained effort to have her daughter, Neferure, empowered to succeed her. She failed: her stepson Thutmose III was to take what he considered to be his rightful place as Pharaoh when Hatshepsut died.

The story of Hatshepsut's claim to the throne of ancient Egypt is told in pictures and hieroglyphs in the stones of her temple. Egypt became one of the world's first nation states and it's no exaggeration to describe it as a cradle of civilisation. At every corner are iconic monuments, whether it's the pyramids, the last surviving Ancient Wonder of the World, the Sphinx or the stunning treasures discovered over the years by Egyptologists. They've uncovered the riches of the burial places of leaders such as Tutankhamun and deciphered the words and pictures of the art and architecture of a wonderful culture.

With the aid of an interpreter, Mary and I followed the elaborate fiction Hatshepsut created to convince her people that she had as much right to rule as any man, in a time of fierce and vicious warfare between competing tribes. First, she told of an invented conception: the god Amon, she claimed, was her real father, not Thutmose I. In a very detailed tale she described what had taken place:

He found her [Queen Ahmose] as she slept in the beauty of her palace. She waked at the fragrance of the god, which she smelled in the presence of his majesty. He went to her immediately. He imposed his desire upon her. He caused that she should see him in the form of the god. When he came before her she rejoiced at the sight of his beauty. His love passed into her limbs, which the fragrance of the god flooded. All his odours were from Punt.

The land of Punt is described in ancient Egyptian texts as 'the land of the gods'; in Hatshepsut's time it was a place famous for its riches. It's thought the location corresponds to what is now Somalia.

The pictures of the event are unusually graphic. Two figures are shown facing each other and very close. The first figure, to the left, is the god Amon, distinguished by a crown of feathers. He's seated, and, as our interpreter put it, is 'giving her the spirit of life or his seed'. Queen Ahmose is on the right, touching the god, knees to knees, feet to feet. In the words of the interpreter: 'he's giving her the key of life by touching her hand and nose as well, twice. She will be getting pregnant with her daughter Queen Hatshepsut.'

The picture that follows is highly unusual as it shows Ahmose is pregnant – an unfamiliar image even today. The series of pictures is very explicit, making it clear beyond doubt that Ahmose became pregnant as a result of being given the 'key of life' by the god. Then come the pictures of the birth of Hatshepsut. Even though it's known she was born as a girl, she is portrayed as a boy and later in the series, as a man.

It's now believed she would never have been accepted as ruler of Egypt had she not commissioned this extraordinary gender-bending fiction to be carved in the stones of her palace. In later drawings she is portrayed as a man, with a beard, male headdress and open, flat chest, kneeling in the classic position adopted in such art by any Pharaoh of the period.

After we left Hatshepsut's temple we spoke to expert Egyptologists who had long been fascinated by the ascendance of a woman to the position of Pharaoh and by the way she had conducted her reign for twenty-two years. Dr Fayza Haikal, professor of Egyptology at Cairo University, and Angela Millward Jones, an Egyptologist with the American Research Centre, were both full of praise for the way Hatshepsut ruled Egypt.

At a time when cruel wars were commonplace, her reign was marked by peace. It's said that military campaigns were rare, and few enemies were prepared to challenge her might. She organised trade missions to Punt and greatly increased Egypt's wealth, using the vast resources she brought together to begin a nation-wide programme of development. She oversaw an extension to the Karnak temple complex and was responsible for the building of the Deir el-Bahari mortuary temple in the Valley of the Kings, one of the most beautiful monuments of the dynastic age.

It's clear that Hatshepsut could not have ruled so successfully, despite her 'fake news story' of the nature of her birth, had she not been supported by Egypt's aristocratic elite, who recognised her abilities as a ruler. Her treatment of her stepson, Thutmose III, is interesting. A more ruthless woman might well have had him dispatched; he embodied a permanent threat to her authority and to that of the daughter she hoped might succeed her. However, she took no steps to remove him, had him trained as a soldier and promoted him to general of her armies. The fact that he made no attempt at a *coup* would seem to suggest either that he recognised how much he owed his Pharaoh, or he made a *realpolitik* calculation based on his knowledge that Hatshepsut carried the people and the elite with her: a case of straightforward self-preservation.

As Angela Millward Jones explained, it was remarkable that Hatsheput survived as long as she did in a man's world and achieved as much as she did. It took courage for her to become and remain Pharaoh. That implies a strong will, political *nous* and religious power, not only inside Egypt, but also throughout Asia Minor, because she was determined to establish Egypt as a power in the region. 'To sum up,' said Angela, 'she was very successful artistically and politically – look at the wealth of that period and the peace that reigned. She was clever enough to invent a story, which meant the people accepted her as Pharaoh and as divine. The rulers of Egypt had to be divine, it's the sign that they are the heirs of the gods who created the world and ruled the world first.'

It was only after Hatshepsut's death in 1458 BCE, at the age of forty-nine, and her burial alongside her father in the Valley of the Kings with all the honour due, that her stepson and son-in-law revealed his true colours and exacted a posthumous revenge. At the Temple of Karnak, on the opposite bank of the Nile from the Valley of the Kings, Dr Mohammed El Sadir, director of antiquities for Upper Egypt, showed us how Thutmose III had attempted to wipe his step-mother from history.

Hatshepsut had ordered two great obelisks to be placed in the Karnak temple, on which the story of her reign would be told. One of the two was simply demolished on the orders of the new Pharaoh. Dr El Sadir believes his actions were the result of pique because he had long considered himself the true ruler of Egypt and was determined that there should be no record of Egypt having been ruled by a great queen who had kept the peace and boosted the economy. The second obelisk, the biggest in Egypt, was spared demolition, but was instead surrounded by high walls to cover the inscriptions in praise of Hatshepsut. Thutmose had not accounted for inquisitive Egyptologists, who came so many years later and uncovered the obelisk. In a – to me – delightful twist of fate, his high walls protected the hieroglyphs from damage and erosion and they now appear as some of the best-preserved examples of writings of the period.

Opinions vary on why Thutmose was so determined to scrub Hatshepsut from popular memory. Some believe it was because she had been his opponent, but, according to Angela Millward Jones, the fact that she had him trained as a soldier and appointed him to a senior role in her army suggests the animosity he felt towards her was unlikely to stem from rivalry. More probably, Thutmose moved to act because of the very fact Hatshepsut had been a woman in a man's role. She had falsified her origin and upset the cosmic order.

Thutmose not only tried to erase Hatshepsut from recorded history, with which, of course, the ancient Egyptians were obsessed, leaving their legacy writ large in stone throughout the land. It's also believed he had her mummy removed from the grave where she had been buried with her father – a step in the rewriting of history not unlike the actions of James I of England when he succeeded Elizabeth I. Elizabeth was moved from her prime position in the chapel of King Henry VII to a side chapel alongside her half-sister, Mary Tudor and James's mother, Mary Queen of Scots. James's positioning of those graves questions the primacy of Elizabeth and Mary Tudor, and, through the positioning of his mother's tomb, emphasises his right to inherit the throne. Similarly, Thutmose was obviously a man who understood the principle that 'Who controls the past controls the future; who controls the present controls the past.'

The British archaeologist Howard Carter discovered the tomb of Hatshepsut during his excavations in the Valley of the Kings in 1902. His further explorations in 1920, two years before he discovered the tomb of Tutankhamun, found two sarcophagi, one for Hatshepsut and one for her father. But both lay empty. A separate tomb, known rather unromantically as KV60, that offered no indication that royals may have been buried there, was found to contain the decaying coffins of two women, lying side by side. One bore the inscription of Sitre-In, Hatshepsut's wet nurse; the other had no name. In 2005, Zahi Hawass, said to be Egypt's foremost archaeologist, began research on the unidentified mummy.

The sarcophagus was taken to Cairo for a CT scan and a long investigation led Hawass to confirm that the mummy was that of 'an obese woman between the ages of forty-five and sixty who had bad teeth and had suffered from cancer, evidence of which can be seen in the pelvic region and the spine'. The mummy was unquestionably, he told the press, the remains of Hatshepsut and he described his work as the 'most important discovery in the Valley of the Kings since the discovery of King Tutankhamun and one of the greatest adventures of my life'.

I was rather sad to find the great and splendid Hatshepsut had suffered from obesity and bad teeth and died relatively young from cancer. I suppose it's true that – as Gray wrote of a later memorial – 'the paths of glory lead but to the grave' whether you're a man or a woman. Despite the colossal efforts the Egyptians made – pyramids, sarcophagi, mummification – to cheat death and to preserve their mortal remains, it all comes to this.

I prefer to end her story with the words of one of her greatest fans, Angela Millward Jones. 'She was beautiful. Her statues are so beautiful, with a smile that can be recognized. Many people say Egyptian statues are all alike. I could recognize Hatshepsut anywhere, she is so distinctive.'

2

Joan of Arc

1412–1431

Any young woman who has seen the likes of Gemma Arterton or Anne Marie Duff play George Bernard Shaw's *Saint Joan* can't help but see her as a feminist hero. There she struts, the Maid of Orleans, 'La Pucelle', with her short hair and armour, taking on the might of the English army in support of her French Prince. She's a tiny teenage girl, virginal and pure, in a world of big bullying men, yet she fights on horseback in chain mail and wields a sword as she commands several thousand soldiers. She endures imprisonment and censure, and argues her case in a cruel trial for her life.

But who has not been horrified at the sheer agony of her brutal punishment and death? Could anything be more terrifying than being burned at the stake? I remember seeing Jean Seberg's performance in the 1957 film, when I was far too young to understand what was really going on. I cried buckets at her tragic end, thought of her whenever I stood too close to my grandmother's open fire, had nightmares for weeks and vowed she would always be my number one idol. She is the ultimate girls' fantasy of a truly romantic role model.

There have, of course, been many such poetic, fantastical representations of Joan. To some degree myth has inevitably outstripped reality but there is a true story of courage and determination here and, rightly, she is greatly lauded by the French on both the left and the right. In January 2012, the six hundredth anniversary of her birth, she was claimed as an icon and symbol of the independence of France by both President Nicolas Sarkozy and his rival Ségolène Royal, while on the far right, the leader of the National Front Marine Le Pen made her most significant speech in the presidential election in Paris in front of the gold statue of Joan on horseback, holding her spear aloft.

Joan's significance as a patriotic French hero has long been taught to children from their earliest school days. Marina Warner, in her book *Joan of Arc: The Image of Female Heroism*, recalls her years at a French-speaking convent school in Belgium and the patriotic hymn they were required to sing as they filed into their classrooms. The song was *Marche Lorraine*, 'a paean to the young shepherdess who took up arms and walked out fearlessly to confront her king and restore him to his throne'. The narrative is irresistible; indeed, the song was adopted by the Resistance during the Second World War. Joan, who according to traditional history had thrown an occupying power out of France, became the patron saint of the movement to expel Germans from French territory. She was elevated as the perfect symbol as de Gaulle rallied patriotic French men and women against the Vichy regime and the Third Reich.

In the US and Canada, Joan has become a feminist icon; a symbol of girl power. In Latin America she is claimed by the revolutionary left as one of the first courageous leaders of a resistance movement, described as a female Che Guevara in chain mail. In the UK, she was adopted by the suffragettes. In 1920 she was made a saint by Rome. Her canonisation took place during a period when the French Roman Catholic Church was keen to promote its central role in the culture of France, countering a Republican secularism that was taking an ever-greater hold. Nothing like a popular saint to remind people where their loyalties should lie.

Shakespeare included her in *Henry VI Part 1*, Rubens painted her, Voltaire wrote a poem about her, Verdi and Tchaikovsky made her the subject of opera and both Elton John and Madonna sang about her. Elton's song asks 'Did Anybody Sleep with Joan of Arc?' Often a subject of fascination when any woman claims virginity, it's a rather prurient query, but one of which I am not entirely innocent. How many times have I said I would love to ask Elizabeth I: 'Virgin, really?' I like to think Elizabeth found some pleasure with Leicester or Essex. As for Joan, she died far too young for the opportunity to have presented itself, at least by her own choice.

You may not have seen *Henry VI Part 1*. It's not one of Shakespeare's best-known plays, and is rarely staged, but his portrayal of Joan is perhaps the most surprising representation of a woman famed for her virginity. Shakespeare's Joan claims to be pregnant by one of two different men, repudiates her father and says she has noble blood. Shakespeare was drawing on a rumour, put about by her English captors, that she was no virgin and was with child; a rumour recorded in 'The Chronicles of England', compiled by Caxton and circulated around 1480. In Shakespeare's interpretation, Joan hopes a pregnancy will save her at her trial from the two interrogators, the Duke of Gloucester and the Earl of Warwick, who are keen to despatch her as quickly as possible, although Warwick calls for a little clemency: 'And hark ye, sirs; because she is a maid, Spare for no faggots, let there be enow: Place barrels of pitch upon the fatal stake, That so her torture may be shortened.' We shouldn't forget that Shakespeare's history plays are loaded with propaganda and were to be played before the English crown. He's hugely influential in our perceptions of historical figures – most famously Richard III. Nevertheless, Joan's legacy is so powerful she even manages to trump the influence of the Bard.

Her claim of being 'with child' is an obvious and perfectly calculated ruse to save her life. Even the most brutal regimes have consistently refrained from hanging or burning a pregnant woman. But it has no impact on the English lords. 'Well, go to', says Warwick, 'we'll have no bastards live.' In the final part of the scene she denies the pregnancy but not the lovers, and the rumours of her impurity persisted for some time in England and in France. As is so often the case where women of distinction are concerned, throughout history and even up to Elton John, their sexual behaviour rather than their intelligence and competence preoccupies the men who recorded their version of history.

Other writers have given Joan a rather more respectful deal. In the work of George Bernard Shaw, Mark Twain's *Personal Reflections of Joan of Arc* and Jean Anouilh's *The Lark*, she's a virginal, illiterate teenager with extraordinary courage and the mental strength to stand up to malevolent inquisitors when she comes to trial before the English. In Bertolt Brecht's *Saint Joan of the Stockyards* she's a member of the Black Straw Hats, a Salvation Army-type organisation in twentieth-century Chicago. She battles on behalf of the workers in a meat-packing plant who have been made redundant by ruthless capitalists, but dies heart-broken, having discovered that corruption and cruelty are not remedied by praying to God. Each generation appears to have invented its own Joan.

Who was the real Jeanne d'Arc? She was born around 1412 in Domrémy, a village in north-east France. Her father, Jacques d'Arc, was a tenant farmer. Her mother, Isabelle Romée, was a pious housewife. Joan was taught the domestic duties expected of a girl by her mother, but she never learned to read or write.

At the time of her birth France and England were seventy-five years into the Hundred Years War, which had begun in 1337 because of a dispute over the succession to the French throne. Edward III had laid claim to the crown of France. He and his son, the Black Prince, scored a number of successes, notably at Crécy and Poitiers. Henry V claimed to have won the war after the

Battle of Agincourt. (He's the one who encouraged his troops with: 'Once more unto the breach, dear friends, once more, Or close the wall up with our English dead . . . Cry "God for Harry, England and St George!"' Yet again, Shakespeare permeates our view of history.) Henry married King Charles VI's daughter, Catherine, and was proclaimed the rightful heir to the French crown by the King. It looked for all the world as if the long war was at an end and the great monarchies of England and France would be united. The big loser was Charles VI's son, also Charles, Catherine's brother. He lost his title of *Dauphin*, the name given to the next in line to inherit the throne. (Why the French should choose to call the heir 'the Dolphin' is beyond me – but I suppose it's more poetic than 'the Prince of Wales'.) Enter Joan, at a time when France was utterly demoralised. The English had operated a scorched earth policy during the war and the crops were virtually ruined. France's population had not bounced back after the calamity of the Black Death, the French had failed to achieve any major victories and the King and the Dauphin were weak, indecisive and in constant conflict with the Burgundians, the Princes of the Blood, and the English, with whom the Duke of Burgundy formed an alliance. The King was known as Charles the Mad; in his frequent bouts of insanity he believed he was made of glass or denied he had a wife and children. Rumours abounded that he had iron rods sewn into his clothes so that he would not break. In a time when the power and prestige of a country rested in the person of the monarch, France was cursed.

In 1422, King Charles VI died in Paris. The Dauphin was nineteen and had acted as regent during his father's bouts of illness. He was unable to go to Paris for his coronation, as the city was occupied by the English and the Burgundians. Young Charles stayed in Chinon in the Loire Valley, where he set up the French court. Henry V, who had expected to inherit the French crown, also died in 1422, at the age of only thirty-six. His and Catherine's son was only nine months old when his maternal grandfather and his father died; he duly succeeded, becoming King of England and France. Would his inheritance survive?

Joan claimed to have begun hearing voices at the age of thirteen. She said her visions included Saint Michael, Saint Catherine and Saint Margaret and their message was clear: it was her duty to fight the English and bring the Dauphin to Reims to be crowned as King Charles VII. The little girl held to her belief that she had been given a message from God to save France from the English invaders.

She was granted a military escort to visit the court in Chinon. Initially she was refused entry, but after correctly predicting that the tide of the campaign was beginning to turn in favour of the French, she gained growing support from the soldiers. It was agreed she should be accompanied across enemy territory to meet the King. She was dressed as a male soldier, presumably for protection from any passing rapist.

In 1429, at the age of only seventeen, she met the Dauphin, who ordered that she should be questioned by theologians. They seemed convinced by her claim that she had been sent by God to save France. Charles was impressed, gave her armour, a military household, a squire, allowed her brothers to join her and gave her permission to accompany the army on a relief mission to Orléans.

Most historical accounts of Joan's brief time as leader of the Dauphin's troops against the English paint a picture of her actually leading the army, dressed in the famous chainmail covered in a white shift and riding a white charger. They tell of how she broke the siege of Orléans, created a sense of French nationhood and changed the course of the Hundred Years War. Then came the tragic endgame: betrayed by French traitors and burned by the English as a heretic and a witch.

It is, though, rather in the nature of revisionist history to debunk the myths that form such an important part of a nation's nostalgia. Recent French historical studies have questioned the veracity of the traditional narrative. It's now believed that Joan never really led the French armies and was merely a mascot in armour. Maybe Charles was well aware of the PR value of a fit and fearless young woman riding out for his cause. It has been confirmed that she was sent by the Dauphin, later King Charles VII, to relieve Orléans in April 1429 as part of a food convoy. Contemporary reports speak of her galvanising effect on the defenders of the city, but they were, in reality, under no real threat of capture, facing only a small English military force. A few English outposts were attacked and their soldiers retreated across the River Loire. Joan was wounded but returned to the front.

Joan and her followers then escorted Charles across enemy territory to Reims where he was crowned in July 1429. Joan set about trying to persuade Charles to march on Paris, but courtiers were now whispering poison into Charles's ear, warning that Joan was growing too powerful and was dealing out bad advice. Charles hesitated and the Anglo-Burgundians fortified their position in Paris. Without the strong support of the King, Joan set herself up as an independent guerrilla leader.

Despite the way the wind was blowing in Charles's court, Joan was something of a heroine for the French forces; the previously demoralised troops did indeed win a couple of serious battles. Persuaded by Joan, Charles finally plucked up the courage to march on Paris but was completely routed. Joan never wavered in urging him to boot out the English but Charles firmly rejected the idea, opting for a diplomatic solution. Joan continued her battle, conducting her brief guerrilla war with a small group of devotees.

In 1430 she led an attack on a Burgundian group at Compiègne in northern France, was thrown from her horse and captured by the Burgundians on 29 May. Her military career had lasted only a year. King Charles showed no sympathy nor did he offer any thanks for her efforts and support. He refused to ransom her. The English paid £10,000 pounds to get their hands on her – a considerable sum for what was clearly a significant propaganda prize.

Joan was taken to Rouen and imprisoned under the supervision of the English commander. To the French troops she was a fallen national heroine and her captivity did nothing to enhance the reputation of the French King. There's no doubt that Charles was blamed for his failure to offer support to the young woman who had defended him with such passion and commitment. Personally, I harbour a suspicion that his abandonment was motivated by his shame: intolerable to his pride to be seen as a monarch who owed his position to a mere girl.

It's now, as her trial begins, that I believe we learn that this was not, as some have suggested, a mad, anorexic, possibly schizophrenic young woman with ideas far above her station. The transcripts of her trials are there to read, and Joan's voice and personality have survived across the centuries. She is calm, obstinate, determined, intelligent and driven; far from a crazy fanatic.

Joan faced seventy charges at her trial, including witchcraft, heresy and dressing as a man. First, she was examined by the Duchess of Bedford, who confirmed she was a virgin. Then, representatives of the judge were sent to her home town of Domrémy to enquire into her habits and virtue. A number of witnesses were questioned but the man commissioned to compile reports of the testimony found nothing to support any of the charges against her. Nicolas Bailly said he had found nothing concerning Joan that he would not have liked to find about his own sister. The judge was so angry at this 'unhelpful' report that he refused to pay Bailly his promised salary.

Everything was stacked against Joan. But at her first appearance in court she was described as showing 'great humility and simplicity of manner, this poor little shepherdess'. Nevertheless, the tone of the charges reveals exactly what the court intended: 'This woman, utterly disregarding what is honourable in the female sex, breaking the bounds of modesty, and forgetting all feminine decency, has disgracefully put on the clothing of the male sex, a shocking and vile monstrosity.' There was no hope of a fair trial.

Reading through the records of the questioning Joan had to undergo, I'm reminded of those trials in the twenty-first century in which barristers representing a group of alleged abusers put teenage girls through a barrage of complex questions designed to trip up and confuse a young victim. For instance, when Joan was asked whether or not she was in God's grace she answered: 'If I am not, may God put me there; and, if I am, may God so keep me. I should be the saddest creature in the world if I knew I were not in His grace.' A clever response to a question designed to entrap, since Church doctrine held that no one could be *certain* of being in God's grace, and yet answering 'no' could have been used against her; the judge could have spun it as a tacit admission of sin. Joan's response, according to one of the notaries, left the court stupefied.

Joan held her own through fifteen of these sessions during March 1431, answering questions about her voices and visions, which she never denied had taken place. 'I was thirteen when I had a Voice from God to help me govern my conduct. And the first time I heard this Voice, I was very much afraid.' As for her patriotism, she was never afraid to insist that the English should leave France:

You men of England who have no right in this kingdom of France, the king of heaven orders and commands you through me, Joan the Maid, to abandon your strongholds and go back to your own country. If not I will make a war-cry that will be remembered forever.

And in that she was right!

Ultimately, it was the wearing of men's clothes that seems to have ended everything for her. Throughout her imprisonment she had begged to be allowed to attend mass but refused to wear women's clothes to attend church. She held throughout her trial that her guards had tried to molest her sexually and it was only when wearing men's clothes that she could feel safe from their unwanted attentions. On 24 May she was taken to the scaffold and told she would be burned immediately unless she signed a document renouncing her voices and visions and agreed to stop wearing soldiers' clothing. She agreed to sign the document, presumably in the hope of avoiding that terrible fate, or at least to grasp the chance to attend mass before her execution.

There is no evidence that Joan was allowed to attend mass. On 28 May, she recanted her confession, went back to wearing men's clothing, again arguing they protected her from rape. On the 29th she was sentenced to die, on charges of heresy and dressing as a man.

On 30 May, at the age of nineteen, she was led to the Market Place in Rouen, crying 'Alas! That my body, clean and whole, [which has] never been corrupted, today must be consumed and burnt to ashes.' Then Joan was burnt alive. There is no evidence that she was given the privilege of strangulation before the flames took hold, a method of release sometimes accorded to people undergoing such a vile method of execution. The English raked the coals to expose her body so no one could spread rumours that she had escaped. They then burned her body twice more to reduce it to ashes so no one could collect relics, and threw the remains into the River Seine.

In 1452, when Charles VII re-entered Rouen after the end of the Hundred Years War, he ordered an inquiry into Joan's trial. The verdict was reversed and she was declared innocent.

It's impossible to know whether Joan really heard those voices that instructed her to go to the assistance of the Dauphin and remove the English invaders of her country, or if she was simply an ambitious, clever girl who answered the call when she saw her country embroiled in a war, in a land where food was scarce and brutality commonplace, regardless of your sex. She was certainly let down by the Dauphin, who did nothing to rescue her and by the God who left her to suffer an agonising death after, as she had claimed, promising to save her. She admitted herself that her voices had deceived her. She even attempted suicide by hurling herself from the window of her tower cell.

What is most infuriating about this whole story is that, in the end, it was not Joan's contribution to thwarting the English conquest of France, nor her defiance of the medieval Church with her claims of a hot line to God that did for her. It was wearing the trousers. Please, in her memory, wear yours with pride and breathe a sigh of relief that you will not be punished for it.

3

Isabella of Castile

1451–1504

In my choice of women to celebrate, remember and introduce to a wider audience, I've generally tried to confine myself to those I instinctively like and admire. After all, to tell their stories I have to spend a great deal of time in their company. So it was kind of difficult to include Isabella, whom I've always perceived as a fanatically devoted Roman Catholic and, not for nothing, an icon of the fascist regime of General Franco, whose brand of right-wing ideology encapsulated the kind of racial purity and religious piety to which Isabella herself devoted her life. She was the instigator of the Spanish Inquisition and, as I saw her, an anti-Semite and Islamophobe.

It is perhaps anachronistic to use such modern terms when it's considered historically correct to judge people only by the standards of their time and the context of the world in which they lived. As I look back, though, I can't help feeling what I feel. After all, one of the elements that unites all the women in this book is that they refused to fall in with the expectations and mores of their day.

Isabella came to power in a time when Catholic Europe and the Muslim Ottoman Empire struggled for territory and dominance, and the religious chasms that were to give birth to the Protestant reformation were just a short generation in the future.

Yes, it was Isabella who set about expelling the Jews and Muslims – then known as the Moors – from Spain. Those who wished to, or tried to, stay without converting to Christianity were to be executed. *Auto-da-fé* is the term most readily associated with her reign. It literally meant 'act of faith' for condemned heretics or apostates but in popular use came to mean victims of the Inquisition burning at the stake.

Yet Isabella is described by her biographer, Giles Tremlett, as 'Europe's First Great Queen', although he does also say of her: 'the line between strong rule and tyranny was wafer thin, and there is no doubt that Isabella crossed it.' Yes, a tyrant; nevertheless, throughout the twentieth century and even at the beginning of the twenty-first there have been moves to have her canonised. It hasn't happened; the Vatican, according to Tremlett, has filed away the documents arguing for her to be named a saint – clearly too controversial a move in today's religious and political atmosphere. She does, though, have a great many admirers and her influence continues. She was responsible for bringing unity to Spain and, as the person who made the decision to fund Christopher Columbus's sea-faring adventures, she's the fundamental reason why a considerable part of the population of the new world was converted to Catholicism.

Catholic historian William Thomas Walsh said: 'Isabel the Catholic was a woman with the soul of a crusader that not only changed the course of civilisation, but also the aspect of the entire world.' Another distinguished Spanish historian, Hugh Thomas, said: 'No woman in history has exceeded her achievement' and, equally, Luis Aponte Martinez, the only Puerto Rican to have become a cardinal in the Catholic Church, said of her, 'Considering her Christian impact on two continents and twenty nations, it can be argued that she, and no other, merits the title of "history's greatest evangeliser".'

So, who was this superwoman? She was born on 22 April 1451 in Ávila in Spain to John II of Castile and Isabella of Portugal. She had an older half-brother, Henry, who was twenty-six when she was born and first in line to inherit the throne of Castile. Castile and Aragon were the two largest territories in the north of Spain; the south was occupied by the Moors. Two years later a younger brother, Alfonso, arrived so she dropped to third in the succession. Her father died when she was only three and Henry duly took the throne. Isabella and her younger brother were eventually taken from the care of their mother – who was sliding into insanity – to live with the new King and his family. The young Princess was not cared for in a manner that fitted her station, being forced to play second fiddle to the King's daughter, universally regarded as illegitimate. When she was fourteen her brother the King attempted to marry her off to his brother-in-law, Alfonso of Portugal. It's then that we first see the true mettle of this young girl. She refused the match, an extremely rare occurrence at a time when girls were used as pawns in the foundation of political alliances and generally given no choice. Royal and aristocratic marriages were purely dynastic. Love did not come into it.

She was subsequently promised to no fewer than six suitors. Some were quite unsuitable and seemed to be recruited solely so that Henry could shunt Isabella out of the way. One of the potential fiancés, when Isabel was only fifteen, was Pedro Girón, a man of forty-three. He had no royal blood and a terrible reputation as a scoundrel, though he was a powerful regional magnate and military leader. Again she resisted, locking herself in her room and fasting for three days. She knelt almost continually in front of her crucifix, repeating over and over, 'Dear God, compassionate Saviour, do not let me be given to this man! Either let him die or let me die.'

Her half-brother, the King, was furious at her behaviour, and with King Henry's connivance, Girón set off from his home in Andalusia for the palace and the wedding, apparently boasting to everyone that the Princess would soon be his. On the first evening after his departure he became violently ill and died. Isabel, on hearing the news, went straight to her chapel to thank God for hearing her prayers!

In 1468 her younger brother, Alfonso, died, so she again moved to second in line. In her negotiations with Henry she agreed she would not marry without his consent if in return he named her as his heir, but maintained she would not marry against her will. She outflanked him completely: she rejected all other offers of marriage and instead entered a secret arrangement to marry Ferdinand of Aragon, heir to the second great kingdom in northern Spain, to whom she'd been betrothed as a six-year-old. Then it had come to nothing, but Isabella decided she would have the boy she described as the one 'with the laughing eyes'. She, unusually, was taller than her husband, and, as second cousins, they had to obtain special permission from the Pope to marry (which Ferdinand's father promptly faked). The marriage had to take place discreetly.

Isabel eloped from Henry's home, Ferdinand crossed Castile disguised as a servant, and the historic union took place. The marriage, unusually for the time, seemed to be a love match and, despite Ferdinand's consistent wandering eye and frequent affairs, they seem to have worked and lived together happily and efficiently. There was, though, no doubt who metaphorically wore the trousers. By a prenuptial agreement, Ferdinand was not allowed to visit his kingdom without his wife's permission, and she foiled his attempt to usurp her throne as the nearest male heir.

They certainly forged an important political bond; through their marriage, they united Aragon and Castile. They did not, though, share a moral compass. Isabella was faithful, pious and greatly valued honesty. Ferdinand did not. He once stated rather proudly that 'the King of France complains that I have twice deceived him. He lies, the fool: I have deceived him ten times and more!'

Five years after Isabella's dramatic marriage, in 1474, Henry died. On 13 December, disregarding the claims of her supposed niece, the 23-year-old Isabella marched through the streets of Segovia to take her place as Queen of Castile. A soldier led the procession, carrying the royal sword, with its point towards the ground. Isabella followed, dripping with magnificent jewels. She had grown up in a world of ritual and performance and was instinctively aware of the importance of symbols. The jewels and the sword spoke volumes about the power and riches she brought with her and emphasised her willingness to exercise her power in a way her forebears had not. One contemporary reported, 'Some of those in the crowd muttered that they had never seen such a thing.' An early visitor to her court, seeing the fear and loyalty she inspired among both the Castilian peasantry and the mightiest nobles, said that Isabella was indeed a queen who had had no equal. Isabella was, of course, a predecessor of that other great European queen, Elizabeth I of England. Isabella's daughter, Catherine of Aragon, had married Elizabeth's father, Henry VIII – a union that, famously, did not end well, when Henry divorced Catherine in favour of the mother of Elizabeth, Anne Boleyn, who was beheaded for alleged infidelity. It's interesting to compare the way these two great queens presented themselves. Elizabeth, when rousing her troops, dressed as a soldier and mounted on horse-back, cried out that she might 'have the body but of a weak and feeble woman, but I have the heart and stomach of a king'. Isabella proudly sewed shirts for her husband and often referred to herself as 'a weak woman'; but she left the men who served her in no doubt that she was more daring and warlike than they.

Ferdinand and Isabella divided their duties, embarking on their plan to clean up what was a violent and impoverished part of the world, ruined by decades of weak kingship, anarchy and civil war, to bring Spain together as a unified entity. He would lead the army while she would raise troops, look after the reserves and act as the army's quartermaster general, making sure the soldiers were armed and fed. It was Ferdinand's success in battles, particularly in assisting his wife's conquest of Granada in southern Spain – completing the 700-year *Reconquista* and restoring Europe to Christian rule – that led Machiavelli to use him as an 'admirable example of the New Prince who dazzled his people with great projects, keeps his subjects in line and gives the appearance of great power and invulnerability which guards against rebellion'. The two monarchs formed a fearsome partnership. Ferdinand did the fighting; Isabella, as happened when rebellion broke out in Segovia in 1476, tended towards diplomacy. She was a ruthless ruler, but not afraid of negotiating with the rebels and achieving successful compromise.

And so we come to the difficult question of the expulsion of Jews and Muslims from Spain. Isabella had reduced the power of the mighty warring grandees, reformed a Church infamous for its loose morals, instituted early policing and judicial structures across the land, licensed prostitution (presumably for the protection of the women involved), and made use of new technologies such as the printing press and artillery. She began her reign adhering to the traditional tolerance towards Jews, Muslims and Conversos (Jews who had converted to Christianity). She said, 'All the Jews in my Kingdom are mine and are under my protection and safe keeping and it falls to me to defend, protect and provide them with justice.' Early in her marriage, she had consulted a Jewish doctor about how to get pregnant and, when the Muslims of Granada surrendered after the invasion of 1492, a treaty was signed which guaranteed that both Jews and Muslims would be allowed to live there in peace and keep their properties and laws.

Later that same year Isabella was persuaded by Ferdinand – or vice versa – that they should all be required to leave Spain; that the united and expanded country should be a wholly Christian, Catholic nation. It would mean that in the next half century Spain would not be affected by the battles between Protestant and Catholic that caused such upheaval as the Reformation spread across Europe. *Un roi, une loi, une foi* was the basis of the

European medieval civilisation but Isabella was the only monarch with the determination to impose what would now be seen as ethnic cleansing. It was not until 1992 that Spain said sorry, when King Juan Carlos formally apologised for his predecessor's expulsion of the Jews, and contemporary Sephardic Jews, many of whom still speak a language rooted in fifteenth-century Spanish, were offered special immigration rights.

Even in her time Isabella faced severe criticism for the brutality of the Inquisition, set up in 1478 with the sole aim of retaining Spain's Catholic religion and, I think one can say, racial purity. The Inquisitor General, a Dominican friar called Tomás de Torquemada, became a watchword for cruelty and torture in his questioning of those who had claimed to have converted to Christianity. Isabella may have been reluctant to expel the 'infidels'; she did intervene at times, with a respect for the rule of the law and the arrangements made in the Treaty of Granada, and personally threw out some of the false testimony against conversos, and she demanded that Jews and Muslims should not be harassed as they left her kingdom. But even the Pope said of the Inquisition that:

> . . . many people have been unfairly and deliberately jailed, without proper observance of the law; they have been subjected to terrifying torture, unjustly declared to be heretics . . . The Inquisition has for some time been moved not by zeal for the faith and the salvation of souls, but by lust for wealth.

Machiavelli himself, the notorious cheerleader of amoral politics, was amazed at her 'pious work of cruelty' of expelling Muslims who would not convert. 'There could not have been a more pitiful or striking enterprise.'

Once Granada, the last stronghold of independent Islamic power on the peninsula, fell to Isabella and Ferdinand, the two set about stretching their horizons with a phase of imperial expansion, driven by the ambition of becoming a world power. Soon after the Alhambra decree was issued, expelling Jews and Muslims, Isabella agreed to fund Christopher Columbus and his expeditions to seek out what would become known as the New World. Clearly she hoped for rich discoveries but her declared intent was not so grasping. She claimed that her principal intention in the discovery of the lands and islands in the 'West Indies' was 'the evangelisation and conversion of the natives of those places to the Catholic faith'.

In her dealings with the inhabitants of the New World Isabella showed rather more humanity than had been the case in her ejection of Jews and Muslims from her country. It was frequently debated throughout Europe whether indigenous peoples could be considered full human beings. The argument centred on whether such people, not exposed to the corrupting influences of European civilisation, were somehow other than human and could be described as noble savages or prelapsarian souls – the term applied to people who might have existed before the Fall of Man. Isabella was having none of it and insisted that the natives of those lands were her subjects and should be treated justly.

When the first shiploads of Indians arrived in Spain in 1495, Isabella ordered that the 'sale of slaves must be absolutely suspended'. When Columbus, after his third voyage, gave each of his men an Indian as his personal servant, Isabella's response was 'Who authorised my admiral to dispose of my subjects in this manner?' She sent them all back to the Americas.

The riches Isabella had hoped for were not immediately forthcoming. After Columbus's first voyage he reported to her that, as far as he could see, there was not much promise of material wealth in the lands he had visited. He told her there were no mountains of gold or other precious metals to be seen. Her response was 'Although there would be nothing but stones, I would continue there while there may be souls to save.' She may have been disappointed at the lack of immediate financial gain but she agreed to continue to sponsor Columbus, even saying she would sell her jewels if necessary to pay for the enterprise. It was her zeal to spread the Catholic faith that seems to have been her true motivation.

As the contemporary Catholic historian Nemesio Rodríguez Lois points out, North and South America:

> ... will soon be home to more than half the Catholics of the whole world. This is the reason for which recent Popes have baptized these lands with the significant name of 'The Continent of Hope'. Truly, the great hope that this continent holds can be traced to the extraordinary virtues of Queen Isabel; her hope of bringing Christ to new peoples; her charity in making laws to protect these peoples from exploitation and enslavement; and her great faith, whose legacy still lives in South and Central America, Mexico, the western United States, the Canary Isles and the Philippines, among other places.

Some may not be quite so convinced that Isabella's activities in building an empire were an entirely good thing. There were terrible Latin American genocides as a result of her expeditions. She urged that her explorers should 'Treat the Indians well and lovingly without upsetting them in any way.' But conquering other people's lands and imposing a culture and religion from afar rarely results in a humanitarian project without conflict. In the Canary Islands, according to Giles Tremlett, it took five years to conquer Gran Canaria alone, even though its inhabitants fought only with sticks and stones. Estimates suggest that up to 85% of the more than 60,000 islanders were killed or exiled.

On an even larger scale, in the early sixteenth century, following the explorations of Columbus and the expansionist policies of Ferdinand and Isabella, came the infamous conquistadores. The most famous is Hernán Cortés, the man who led the dismantling of the Aztec empire and the Spanish plundering of a continent. Cortés and other successors of Columbus then destroyed the Incan civilisation, carried out the effective genocide of Native Americans, began the first phase of the colonisation of the Americas and paved the way for heavy Spanish involvement in the slave trade.

Personal happiness and queenship rarely go hand in hand but Isabella's domestic life seems to have been good as far as her marriage is concerned, notwithstanding her bouts of extreme jealousy when Ferdinand strayed. His last will and testament suggests a lasting love match. He requested they should be buried together, 'so that, just as we have had a singular love and marriage in this world, so we will not be separated in death'.

Isabella was not so lucky when it came to her children. Her only son and heir, John, died in 1497 while on his honeymoon. Rumour has it that overindulgence in sex led to his demise. His doctors had suggested that he should be separated from his wife for a short time to give him a break. Isabella's religious mania may have contributed to the tragedy. She refused to allow the separation, quoting the Bible and saying, 'Those whom God has joined, let no man put asunder.'

Her eldest daughter, Isabella, died in childbirth in 1498. Her daughter Juana went mad after the death of the husband she adored and was locked up by her father and then her son for fifty years. Maria had ten children and died at the age of only thirty-four. And, of course, her youngest daughter, Catherine of Aragon, married the English Prince of Wales, Arthur, who promptly died. She was engaged, then married, to Arthur's younger brother, who became King as Henry VIII. Catherine lost five babies and succeeded in producing 'only' a mere daughter, Mary Tudor. The passion for her Catholic faith, inherited by Catherine from her mother, was passed on to Mary Tudor. Mary's half-sister, Elizabeth I, was a confirmed Protestant, but that's a different story.

In 1504 Isabella officially withdrew from government, though it was said she had been in decline since the death of her son seven years earlier. In November of that year she died and was buried in Granada alongside her husband and some of her children.

I can't help but admire a woman of that period who from her earliest years was courageous enough to make her own decisions about her future, choose her own husband and rule alongside him on an equal basis. Against every possible institutional and cultural prejudice, she successfully ruled a great country, forming and steering Spain's destiny. I have not, though, grown to like her for that ruthless piety, or for her determination to achieve world dominance.

I did discover that she had a surprising and pretty impressive impact on the game of chess – and all as a result of the way she ruled. Until the fifteenth century, the queen on the chessboard was a relatively weak figure, able to move only one square at a time. In 1495, when Isabella's rule and influence spread far and wide, the laws of chess were changed. The queen was allowed to move in all directions, and as far as she liked, striking from afar. She became, and remains now, the most powerful piece on the board. As indeed was the woman who inspired her.

4

Artemisia Gentileschi

1593–1652

I've long been a fan of a great crime story, whether in book form or as a television series, and a recent favourite has been *Endeavour*. It's inspired by Colin Dexter's character Morse, the Oxford detective who loves a vintage car, listens to opera, is classically educated and partial to a good pint of beer. In the original television series John Thaw played the detective from middle age to his death, and he was never anything but 'Morse'; his first name was never revealed. *Endeavour* is the young Morse, played by Shaun Evans, learning his trade as a detective constable, then sergeant, and already quite brilliant at solving Oxford's many murders.

Only a couple of weeks ago, as I was buried in research for this book, I switched on the television on a Sunday evening to enjoy an hour or so's relaxation with Morse. Three murders of men – a taxi driver, an academic and an art dealer – followed in quick succession and the methods of killing were brutal. The first victim was shot and then had a metal bar drilled into his ear; the second, a history don, was stabbed in both eyes with a steak knife; the third was decapitated. The body was left in his bed, the head concealed under a silver cloche.

Morse solved the mystery thanks to his great interest in art. The *eureka* moment came as he was flicking through a book of the paintings of Artemisia Gentileschi. It turned out the murders had been committed by a latter-day Gentileschi (the story is set in the 1960s). The murderer, Ruth Astor, was exacting her revenge on the men, who had been at a Bullingdon-style private members' club where she and a friend were waitresses. The men had become drunk and violent; Ruth had been thrown across the table, gang-raped and had wine poured over her face and head.

The rape, and the desire to avenge herself, were a parallel to what we know was the inspiration for so many paintings by the extraordinary Baroque artist Artemisia Gentileschi. She didn't actually murder the man who violated her, but she turned the horror of her own life into scenes of women's vengeance on the men at whose hands they had suffered. She used biblical stories to portray, in exquisite paintings, her fury at the sexual violence she herself had endured. I was delighted to see her marked and celebrated in an acclaimed television programme.

Artemisia was well known as an artist of the Italian Baroque in her day and was considered one of the most accomplished painters in the generation that followed Caravaggio. In an era when it was tough for a woman to become anything other than a wife or a nun, she was the first woman admitted to the prestigious Accademia delle Arte del Disegno in Florence, and she counted dukes, princes, cardinals and kings among her clients. She wrote of her success to her friend, the astronomer Galileo, in 1635. 'I have seen myself honoured by all the kings and rulers of Europe to whom I have sent my works, not only with great gifts, but also with most favoured letters, which I keep with me.'

But, as has happened to so many great women of the past, she disappeared from public consciousness, from museums, catalogues and exhibitions for some four hundred years. Ripe for rediscovery, she was put back in her rightful place by the women's movement in the twentieth century. *Endeavour* is not the only popular work in which Artemisia has appeared in the twenty-first century. After centuries of neglect there came articles about her in the *New York Times*, a popular novel (*The Passion of Artemisia*, written by Susan Vreeland), a play, *Lapis Blue, Blood Red*, appeared on Broadway and one of her paintings appeared in a play, *Painted Lady*, starring Helen Mirren.

Perhaps the most important signal of her appreciation as a great artist by a modern audience was the exhibition in 2002 at New York's Metropolitan Museum of Art. She shared the billing with her father, Orazio but it was Artemisia's art that inspired the *New York Times* to describe her as 'this season's "it" girl'.

Artemisia was born in July 1593. She was the eldest child of Orazio Gentileschi, a Tuscan painter, and his wife Prudentia Montone. She was only twelve when her mother died in child-birth in 1605. Her father harboured no artistic ambitions for his only daughter; he fully expected she would become a nun. As a lone father, he had to keep the children with him in his studio while he worked, and Artemisia showed herself a quick learner. Under her father's tutelage she displayed a precocious talent for drawing, mixing colour and painting and, like him, she was drawn to Caravaggio's dramatic style. By the time she was fifteen it was obvious to her father that his daughter demonstrated a much greater natural talent than the brothers who served the same apprenticeship in their father's workshop.

Nevertheless, Artemisia was only too well aware that she would have to fight for her father's support if she, rather than her brothers, was to become a professional painter rather than a dabbling amateur. She was clearly conscious that she had to resist any traditional attitudes and psychological submission to what she saw as brainwashing and jealousy of her obvious talent.

Her first painting is testament to her awareness of the sexual politics of the position in which she, and indeed any woman who attempted to break away from convention, might find herself. Her paintings are often inspired by biblical stories; this first one, completed when she was only seventeen, followed this source.

Like Caravaggio, she chose not to paint in an idealised style but to make the people in her work look real, fleshy and passionately involved in the events being portrayed. She used live models and, in the case of *Susanna and the Elders*, it's likely she included a self-portrait, looking at her own face reflected in a mirror.

The painting depicts the story of Susanna, from the book of Daniel. She's a virtuous wife who is sexually harassed by the elders in her community. It was common for all painters of the period to use the same run of biblical stories as their inspiration. In works on a similar theme by male artists, Susanna is generally depicted as 'asking for it', appearing flirtatiously coy and seductive. In Artemisia's painting, Susanna sits naked apart from a white cloth across her lap. Above her are two old men, lasciviousness oozing from every pore. She twists her head away from their pointing fingers, her hands raised in a gesture that clearly indicates, 'Go away and leave me alone.' Her face shows fear and vulnerability as the men lean over the wall towards her, whisper to each other and leer. No one who stands before this painting could doubt that the men's attentions are unwelcome.

No other painting I've seen on the subject contains any hint that the uninvited lecherous attentions of two nasty old men might have been traumatic for Susanna. Isn't it interesting that it took until the twenty-first century for women to come together and say 'Me too', as the similarly disgusting behaviour of the film producer Harvey Weinstein came to light. Artemisia Gentileschi got it in 1610 and wasn't afraid to make it known that treating women as sexual objects was really not on.

This painting was to prove somewhat prophetic. Artemisia's father, as might be expected, kept his daughter confined to the house and often left her at home alone as he went about his business. As the house doubled as his studio it was not unusual for friends and fellow artists to pop in from time to time. One fateful day Orazio left his seventeen-year-old daughter in the care of a family friend, Tuzia Medaglia, who was there with her infant son.

Artemisia was raped. The man responsible, a fellow painter, Agostino Tassi, was tried for his crime. The court report of the case brought by Orazio in 1612 describes what happened from his perspective:

> Agostino, having found the door of Artemisia's house open, entered the house as an ungreeted guest and went to Artemisia. He found her painting and with her was Tuzia, who held her son on her lap. As he approached Artemisia he ordered Tuzia to go upstairs because he wanted to speak to Artemisia in private. Tuzia stood up immediately and went upstairs. On that very day Agostino deflowered Artemisia and left.

Artemisia was questioned at home by two magistrates who ordered her to swear to tell the truth. She told them what happened in staggering detail. She had told Agostino that she was a virgin and that any rumours about her having been engaged in sexual activities were untrue. Any man who desired her, she said, would have to marry her and put a ring on her finger. He continued to press his case even though he was already married:

> When he found me painting he said, 'Not so much painting, not so much painting' and he grabbed the palette and brushes from my hands and threw them around, saying to Tuzia 'Get out of here.' And when I said to Tuzia not to go and not leave me as I had previously signalled to her, she said, 'I don't want to stay here and argue. I want to go about my own business.' . . . As soon as she was gone he took my hand and said 'Let's walk together a while, because I hate sitting down.' . . .
> After we had walked around two or three times, each time going by the bedroom door, when we were in front of the bedroom door, he pushed me in and locked the door.

He then threw me onto the edge of the bed, pushing me with a hand on my breast, and he put a knee between my thighs to prevent me from closing them. Lifting my clothes, which he had a great deal of trouble doing, he placed a hand with a handkerchief at my throat and on my mouth to keep me from screaming. He let go of my hands, which he had been holding with his other hand, and, having previously put both knees between my legs with his penis pointed at my vagina he began to push it inside.

I felt a strong burning and it hurt very much, but because he held my mouth I couldn't cry out. However I tried to scream as best I could, calling Tuzia. I scratched his face and pulled his hair and before he penetrated me again I grasped his penis so tight that I even removed a piece of flesh. All this didn't bother him at all, and he continued to do his business, which kept him on top of me for a while, holding his penis inside my vagina. And after he had done his business he got off me. When I saw myself free, I went to the table drawer and took a knife and moved towards Agostino saying 'I'd like to kill you with this knife because you have dishonoured me'. He opened his coat and said 'Here I am,' and I threw the knife at him and he shielded himself, otherwise I would have hurt him and might have easily killed him. And the said Agostino then fastened his coat. I was crying and suffering over the wrong he had done me, and to pacify me he said, 'Give me your hand, I promise to marry you as soon as I get out of the labyrinth I am in.' . . . This is all that happened between Agostino and me.

In the seventeenth century rape was considered more of a crime against the family's honour than as the violation of a woman, and it was only when Tassi went back on his promise to marry Artemisia that her father decided to bring the charges against him to court. When Artemisia appeared in the court to give her evidence she was tortured with thumbscrews – a primitive form of lie detector test. As they were tightened around her fingers she cried out to Tassi: 'This is the ring you gave me and these are your promises.'

Clearly she passed the test and was believed. Not always the case even today when a woman gives details of her sexual assault. Tassi was convicted and sentenced to be banished from Rome for five years, although there's no evidence the punishment was ever carried out. Artemisia's father's response to the scandal was to marry his daughter off to a minor Florentine painter, Pierantonio Stiatessi. The couple moved to Florence, bearing a request for patronage for the talented young painter, written by her father, Orazio and addressed to the grand duchess of Tuscany. He wrote '[She] has in three years become so skilled that I can venture to say that today she has no peer; indeed she has produced works which demonstrate a level of understanding that perhaps even the principal masters of the profession have not attained.'

Her time in Florence made her famous, and by her late twenties she had painted at least seven works for the Grand Duke Cosimo II de Medici and his family. As a family and as patrons of the art, the Medici of Florence need no introduction.

Artemisia then made the difficult decision to quit the Tuscan capital, which under the Medici had been the cradle of the Renaissance and was still, a hundred years after its flowering, a key artistic hub. She explained her decision in a letter to her father, describing 'troubles at home and with my family'. She had had four children, but only one, her daughter Prudentia, had survived. Her husband was unfaithful, jealous and extravagant and in 1621 he walked out on his wife and daughter.

It was a struggle for a single mother to find commissions for her work in Rome, so she moved again. In Venice she received the patronage of Philip IV of Spain, who commissioned a painting of Achilles. Soon Artemisia found herself having to move again, this time to flee the plague, which in 1639 wiped out a third of the population. She moved on to Naples, then under Spanish rule, and had some success in painting an altarpiece and a public commission for a major church. She often complained, though, about how difficult it was for a woman to find work when she was competing in an almost exclusively male arena. A brief scan over Vasari's *Lives of Artists*, regarded as the first definitive book on Renaissance art, reveals how few female artists there were. Of the numerous painters and sculptors listed in his text, only four are women – Properzia de' Rossi, Sister Plautilla, Madonna Lucrezia and Sofonisba Anguissola. Artemisia was born some forty years after the publication of Vasari's work but this was the background and culture against which she had to make her way.

She wrote to her last major patron, Don Antonio Ruffo, angry at always having to haggle and beg for a decent wage for her commissions, 'You feel sorry for me because a woman's name raises doubts until her work is seen. If I were a man I can't imagine it would have turned out this way.' The question of unequal pay was obviously as much of an issue in the seventeenth century as today!

Her best-known paintings – the ones spotted by Endeavour Morse as his clue to the murders in the story of Ruth Astor – are *Judith and her Maidservant* and *Judith Slaying Holofernes*. The biblical story is set in the time of King Nebuchadnezzar, who sent his general, Holofernes, to subdue his enemies the Jews. Judith, a beautiful widow, hears that her people are on the brink of capitulating to the invaders and makes up her mind to deliver her city from the enemy. She creeps into the Assyrian camp, seduces Holofernes, waits until he is drunk and cuts off his head. The Jews regain their courage and drive the enemy away.

How much of the artist can one really read into a work of art? Some critics have argued that Artemisia's graphic depictions of two women beheading a man and conspiratorially carrying off his head in a bloody basket were nothing more than gory examples of a subject popular with painters of the period, simply designed to appeal to wealthy patrons with a taste for violence and eroticism. Given her difficulties in getting decent payment for her work it would not be surprising if Artemisia had indeed decided to make horror an important part of her portfolio. But I don't believe it for a second.

Her first two versions of the Judith story were painted early in her career, in 1612 and 1614, not long after she was raped. You have only to look at the expressions on the faces of the women and the power of Aremisia's brushstrokes to know that anger and revenge were her motivations. Her Judith is not the pretty pretty, rather delicate woman seen in work painted by her male contemporaries. She's strong and powerful woman, not unlike the Susanna of *Susanna and the Elders*, thought to have been painted using Artemisia's own image in the mirror.

Artemisia had been let down by the woman, Tuzia, left by her father to chaperone her before the attack by Tassi. In these paintings she imagines a sisterhood among women as the two work closely together. In *Judith Slaying Holofernes*, the strong arms and hands of her maid hold down the man lying on his back on the bed. He has no chance of pushing her away, although he tries. Judith wields the sword like a hefty professional. Neither woman appears remotely shocked or horrified as the blood pours from their victim's neck. They are just determined to get the job done.

In *Judith and her Maidservant* we see the same two powerful women conspiring to carry away in a basket the head of the man they have assassinated. For me this is the manifestation of the endless hours a once-powerless woman spent asking what she might have done to save herself. She expressed her fury and what she might have liked to have done in the way she knew best – with her paintbrush.

In 1638 Artemisia was drawn to London and the court of Charles I. Her father Orazio was already there as a court painter, so he and his daughter were again in harness after a seventeen-year separation. She was, though, not there only to help him. She had been invited by King Charles himself, a request based not on her father's reputation but rather on her eminence as an artist. It was in London that she painted one of her best-known and most beautiful works, *Self-Portrait as the Allegory of Painting*. It hangs in the Royal Collection.

Her father died in 1639. Artemisia had left England by 1642, just as the Civil War was beginning. In 1649 she was back in Naples, working again with her former patron, Don Antonio Ruffo, and, no doubt, still complaining about the lack of equal pay for work of equal value. *Plus ça change!*

The date of her death is not certain. Some have placed it in 1652 or 1653, others have speculated that she died in the Naples plague of 1656, but there are no works dated during this period and no records I could find of her death.

I'm no professional art critic. I only know what I see and what excites me but I know in my heart she's a truly great painter and, thank goodness, there are critics who agree with me. Roberto Longhi, an important Italian critic, described her in 1916 as 'the only woman in Italy who ever knew about painting, colouring, doughing, and other fundamentals'. And, of her style in the portrayal of women, he wrote, 'There are about fifty-seven works by Artemisia Gentileschi and ninety-four per cent (forty-nine works) feature women as protagonists or equal to men.' Another critic said of her in the nineteenth century, 'No one would have imagined it was the work of a woman. The brush work was bold and certain, and there was no sign of timidness.' It may seem surprising that it should be assumed that the work of a woman would somehow have a distinctly feminine style that's softer, prettier and more hesitant than work that's painted by a man. When I compare Artemisia with Caravaggio, whose realistic style influenced her, I simply can't see it. There's strength and brutality in the work of both artists. Maybe I would have to concede the focus is somewhat different, although it's not Artemisia who gives the impression that a woman is weaker than a man.

In Caravaggio's painting of Judith and her maidservant slaying Holofernes a pretty, slim and rather delicate Judith looks barely capable of wielding the sword with which she's slicing off the still-screaming head. Her maidservant, who looks on from behind, is portrayed as a bit of a wrinkled old hag. In Artemisia's depiction of the same subject the two powerfully built young women work together to complete their task.

I have no doubt that much of her work was inspired by events that could only have happened to a woman, particularly the terrible sexual violence she experienced as a teenager, but it would be wrong to assume her fame and appreciation was purely a result of her notoriety and vengefulness. Yes, she was a victim who fought back through her work but as an artist she is wonderful. She may have complained about equal pay but patronage came to her thick and fast. Michelangelo, supported by the Medici, had established the Renaissance principle that great wealth should support great art. Like her contemporaries, Artemisia was a considered a real artist, worthy of financial backing and not merely a jobbing tradeswoman.

What I love about her is the way she painted other women as she saw them: courageous, resourceful, rebellious and strong. And she painted them beautifully. While her Susannas and her Judiths have delighted me for precisely those reasons, I have to confess one of her more tender portraits is my favourite. Her *Madonna and Child* shows us a rather buxom Mary, dressed in pink rather than the traditional blue, halo around her head and her feet somewhat inelegantly wide apart, to balance her solid little boy on her lap. She gazes down lovingly on her golden-haired child and offers her nipple as he reaches up and touches her face. It's a picture of an adoring mother preparing to breastfeed, with no hint of salacious intent for the titillation of the viewer. It's captivating and, I think, could only have been painted by a woman. As she once declared herself, 'The works will speak for themselves.' They do!

5

Catherine the Great

1729–1796

In early autumn 2017 I made my first-ever trip to St Petersburg. It was the hundredth anniversary of the Russian Revolution. To stand outside the Winter Palace, stormed by the revolutionaries in one of the key moments of 1917, was genuinely thrilling. It is a spectacularly beautiful place and you quickly realise what phenomenal wealth was held by the Romanov dynasty. The waterfront of the Neva River is lined by exquisite buildings commissioned by Peter the Great in the late seventeenth and early eighteenth centuries, displaying his passion for the work of the great European architects.

The Hermitage museum has a collection of art that would take months if not years to view. There is so much gold inside and outside the churches, palaces and monuments that your eyes are simply dazzled. Across the river from the Winter Palace rises the towering Cathedral of St Peter and St Paul. There lie all the Romanovs, including, in a small side chapel, the remains of Nicholas II, the last Tsar, and his family, murdered by the Bolsheviks in Ekaterinburg.

Most curiously, considering the history of their marriage, are the remains, close together, of Peter III and his wife, Catherine II, known as 'the Great'. I could just about make out the Cyrillic script of her name, from my scant memory of learning to read

Russian at school. The marriage lasted for seventeen years but it was Catherine who forced her husband's abdication and most probably arranged for him to be murdered by one of her lovers.

After Catherine's death, her son, Paul I, brought the coffin of the man he believed to be his father, unlikely as that seems given his mother's amorous history, from its first resting place in the Alexander Nevsky Monastery to the Winter Palace, where his body was laid in state next to Catherine's. From there, they were carried together across the frozen Neva to be buried alongside each other near the tomb of Peter the Great. The dates of their births and burial are inscribed on their marble tombs, but not their dates of death, giving the impression they ruled together. A classic example of an heir rewriting history on a monument to secure his legitimacy and family respectability. One which Paul promptly followed up not just by re-establishing the principle of male primogeniture but by barring females from the throne altogether.

The royal line of descent that leads to Catherine the Great is slightly complicated. Please bear with me for a moment. Peter the Great (1682–1725) ruled jointly with his brother Ivan for the first fourteen years of his reign. He was famously tall and, improbably, trained in shipbuilding in the London docks. He ruthlessly reformed and expanded the Russian Empire but his cruelty towards his son and heir is legendary. Alexei developed a hatred of his father and plotted to overthrow him. He fled to Finland, was persuaded to return, but was eventually tortured to death on his father's instructions. Peter claimed the right to name his own successor but failed to do so. A surprising number of women ruled Russia after his death. The Supreme Privy Council of Imperial Russia evidently thought they would be easy to control. How wrong they were.

Peter's illiterate second wife became Catherine I, succeeded by her young great-nephew, Peter II, at which point Peter the Great's daughter Elizabeth I staged a *coup* with a pocket army of only three hundred and eight soldiers. The new Empress then began to search for a capable bride for her unpromising nephew, who would become Peter III.

Catherine the Great was not Russian but German. She was born to members of minor German nobility as Sophie Augusta Fredericka of Anhalt-Zerbst in Stettin in the Kingdom of Prussia. She would later say of her birth: 'I was born on April 21st 1729 . . . I was told later that, a son having been more desired, my arrival as first-born had given rise to some disappointment.' Things did not improve as she grew older: 'My mother did not pay much attention to me . . . I was merely tolerated and often I was scolded with a violence and anger I did not deserve.'

She grew up with no sense of sisterhood with other women, of whom she often spoke as a 'weak, frivolous, whining species'. But she had little opportunity for the company of other women, saying:

> There are no more than two women in the world to whom I can talk for half an hour at a time. From fifteen to thirty-three years old I had no women to talk to and only dared have chambermaids with me. If I wanted to talk I had to go into another apartment where there are only men.

Nor did she appreciate the sound of cannons announcing the birth of her fifth granddaughter. 'Do they have to make so much noise for a rotten girl?' No feminist leanings then!

Sophie was raised a Lutheran and as a child had tussled with her religious instructor over the question of whether 'all the great men of antiquity' could really be eternally damned. Her instructor was forbidden to flog her for her refusal to accept his dogma. Instead, he tortured her mentally with threats of her eternal damnation. It was something of a relief when, in 1744, Sophie was received into the Russian Orthodox Church in anticipation of her marriage to that 'unpromising nephew', now Grand Duke Peter of Holstein-Gottorp, grandson of Peter the Great and heir to the Russian throne. She was the young woman Elizabeth had chosen to fit the bill as wife to the Tsar-to-be.

Sophie disliked Peter from the outset. She had met him first when she was only ten and wrote that she found him detestable. She hated his pale skin, and he was already keen on a drink or three. But she dutifully spent time before the wedding learning Russian. She wrote in her memoirs that she had settled in her own mind that, when she came to Russia, she would make a success of her role: she would believe, do and say whatever was required to wear the crown.

The couple married in 1745. Sophie, now *Catherine*, moved into her new home at the Russian Royal Residence of Oranienbaum on the Gulf of Finland, west of St Petersburg. It was a miserable union. Catherine, who once said 'Above all I love the truth, and you must feel free to say it, without fear', was not shy in telling, with a brutal honesty, of the unhappiness she endured. 'I am one of those women', she said:

> ... who believe it is always the fault of the husband if he is not loved, for in truth I would have loved mine very much, if it had been possible to do so, and if he had the kindness to want it . . . I said to myself, 'if you allow yourself to love that man, you will be the unhappiest creature on earth' . . . I admit frankly that I was often worn out by his visits, walks and conversation, which was of an insipidity beyond parallel. When he left me, to read the most tedious book seemed a delightful pastime.

I don't think I've ever read so frank or elegant a description of a wife's inescapable boredom with a dullard husband. She did, though, use her time wisely, spending it educating herself and reading widely, particularly the work of French philosophers.

The marriage was not consummated for nine years. Catherine described the humiliation she suffered as her husband spent every night in her bed playing with his toy soldiers and regaling her with tales of his infatuation with one woman after another. He was violent, sometimes towards Catherine, taking great pleasure in bizarre acts of brutality such as hanging a rat that had eaten his cardboard soldiers. No wonder she looked elsewhere for love and affection.

Catherine's Chamberlain, Count Andrei Shuvalov, knew the diarist James Boswell (of Boswell and Johnson fame) well. According to Boswell, Shuvalov was rather indiscreet when it came to intimate gossip about the two monarchs. Peter took a mistress, Elizabeth Vorontsova, while Catherine conducted liaisons with Sergei Saltykov, Grigory Grigoryevich Orlov, Alexander Vasilchikov, Grigory Potemkin, Stanislaw August Poniatowski and others. (An impressive list, but not all at once, and mostly after her husband's death!) It is unlikely that Paul and Anna, recorded as the children of Peter and Catherine, were actually sired by her husband, though Paul did share many of the less fortunate traits of his 'father'. Orlov is the most likely candidate. Had DNA testing been available at the time, the crowned heads of Europe might have looked very different indeed.

Catherine, unlike her silly husband, was a woman of great intelligence, with ambition to match, as were the men with whom she chose to spend her time. Most came from distinguished families and had outstanding political careers. While none of them, except for Grigory Potemkin, was allowed by Catherine to use their status to interfere with government policy, she never acted with anything other than generosity when a relationship ended. Poniatowski, for instance, was rewarded for his attentions with the Crown of Poland in 1764. (And robbed of said crown by Catherine when he showed signs of independence.)

When Empress Elizabeth died in December 1761, her nephew Peter was proclaimed Emperor Peter III and Catherine became the Empress. Catherine was warned by friends that she might not sit on the throne for long, because her husband was plotting to divorce her and marry one of his mistresses. She was advised to flee Russia for her own safety. She ignored them, continued to cultivate relationships among the elite of the court and to watch her husband make a mess of things. He offended the leaders in government, the church and the military. Catherine was made aware of plots to remove him. One plan was to make the seven-year-old Paul Tsar and ask Catherine to become his regent until he came of age. Catherine had a different idea.

As part of my St Petersburg trip I was advised to visit the palace at Peterhof. It's a beautiful series of small imperial homes, with the most exquisite gardens and a Grand Cascade of fountains leading down to the sea. It was built by Peter the Great in a defensive position on the gulf opposite the warring Finns and became known as the Russian Versailles. It became one of Catherine's favourite haunts; a series of paintings hanging in the great hall is testament to her love for art and her determination to give the artists she favoured whatever help they needed.

The paintings tell the story of the Battle of Chesma, a naval victory in the Russo-Turkish War (which took place between 1768 and 1774). The paintings were made in the early 1770s by the German artist Jacob Philipp Hackert but his early attempts were criticised by people who had witnessed the actual battle. The eyewitnesses punched holes in Hackert's approach – those exploding ships just didn't look like that! Not nearly enough flying timbers, flames, smoke and fireballs. Cutting to the heart of the problem, Catherine ordered a frigate to be blown up in the harbour of Livorno in Italy so that Hackert could paint his scenes from life. What a privilege to find yourself in a position of absolute power and wealth. And such a delight to be able to dish out thrones to your lovers and explode warships to inspire your favoured artists!

There's a wonderful painting hanging in the palace, completed in 1762, apparently showing Catherine on her way to Peterhof once she had achieved her ambition of taking the throne from her husband. Catherine is a young, attractive woman with a strong, determined expression. She sits astride her exquisite grey warhorse, Brillante, wearing knee-high riding boots with her feet perfectly positioned in the stirrups. Her green long coat and trousers and her tricorn hat are the uniform of the Life Guards and she holds her sword pointing to the sky. It could not say more clearly, 'Do not mess with me! I'm a match for any man'.

On 28 June 1762, with the aid of her lover Grigory Orlov, she rallied the troops of St Petersburg to her support and declared herself Catherine II, the sovereign ruler of Russia, naming her son Paul as her heir. She ordered her husband to be arrested and forced him to sign an act of abdication. He begged her permission to leave the country, but she refused and had him imprisoned. She said it was her intention to keep him in prison for life. There is no proof that Catherine was directly involved in his murder but, only a few days after he was incarcerated, he was killed in what's been described as 'a fight with his captors'. Orlov was suspect number one.

Some aspects of Catherine's life as the ruler of Russia rather remind me of Margaret Thatcher, the 'Iron Lady' who ruled the UK in the late 1970s and '80s. Catherine worked incredibly hard and mapped out her days in five-minute increments; a schedule she maintained until her death. At the height of her reign she woke every day at 5am, allowing herself to lie in until 6am as she grew older.

Catherine had plans for foreign policy and the expansion of her power, but her early years were spent consolidating her position. She dealt harshly with those influential people who considered her ascent to power illegal and would happily have overthrown her in favour of her son. She was aware that she could be deposed in a *coup* every bit as easily as she had been brought to power by one, so she took great care to cultivate friends and supporters among the nobility and military.

She understood that Russia needed a period of peace and stability during which she could concentrate on domestic affairs. At the end of the seventeenth century, Russia was a vast, backward, feudal country where the nobility wielded great power and influence and completely ruled the daily life of their serfs, even dictating whom they should marry and allowed to exile them to Siberia on a whim. Russia stood outside the political affairs of Europe, and its customs and culture were more influenced by eastern than by western traditions. Agriculture – the mainstay of the economy – was primitive and the military was out of date. As far as expansion and civilisation were concerned, Peter the Great had looked to Europe for culture, manners and economic development but the country could not escape its geography, hemmed in by Sweden and Finland on the Baltic and the Ottoman Empire on the Black Sea. Russia had no warm-water ports and, consequently, limited opportunity for sea-borne trade.

Catherine approached foreign policy with caution, appointing Count Nikita Panin, an able diplomat, as her foreign secretary. By the mid-1760s she felt secure enough to set her plans for reform into motion. Her behaviour during this period earned her the title of 'enlightened despot'. She was influenced by the ideas of the Enlightenment, writing frequently to friends such as Voltaire, and purchasing a library from Diderot, with whom she ran famous salons in the early 1770s. She aimed to become a wise and generous ruler who, through living and ruling by reason, could improve the lives of her people.

Her first major reform addressed the country's legal system. She drew up the '*Nazak*' (Instruction), a voluminous legal treatise, inspired by Enlightenment ideals, in which she analysed Russia's old and inefficient Code of Laws and put forward her suggestions for reform. Her modern biographer, Isabel de Madariaga, claims the *Nazak* was 'one of the most remarkable political treatises ever compiled and published by a reigning sovereign in modern times'. Voltaire raved about it and called it 'the century's most beautiful monument', even though it must have been clear to him that Catherine had drawn heavily on the work of the French lawyer and philosopher, Montesquieu.

She called for a system – way ahead of its time – in which there would be equal protection under the law for everyone, and emphasised that criminal acts should be prevented rather than punished harshly. She had written in her journal, before taking power, 'Liberty, the soul of all things, without you everything is dead. I want the laws to be obeyed, but I don't want slaves.' She hated being described as a despot. 'While despotism may work for the Ottomans or Persians', she wrote, 'it ill suits a European nation like our own.' In 1767 she created the Legislative Commission, which comprised delegates from all levels of society except the serfs. It was at the first meeting of the Commission that she was offered the title 'Catherine the Great'. She declined, but it stuck, despite her disapproval.

Catherine made some efforts to improve the lives of serfs, establishing a special commission to improve their treatment in the country's foundries and other workplaces but her reputation for being enlightened was perhaps a little exaggerated when compared to her actions. She declared herself strongly opposed to serfdom but didn't dare work to abolish feudal slavery; she needed the support of the nobility and could not afford to upset them. When she set up the Russian Statute of National Education in 1786, some free primary and secondary schools became available to both boys and girls but the doors were closed to the children of serfs.

By the end of 1768 Catherine's enthusiasm for the Commission, and the progress towards representative and inclusive government that was its intention, rather waned. Her attention turned to imminent war with the Ottoman Empire and she postponed its sessions. She never reconvened the Commission, even after Russia emerged a somewhat battered victor of the long and expensive Russo-Turkish War that ended in 1774. She managed the expansion of the Russian empire in Poland and the Ottoman Empire, but what did she achieve at home with her enlightened views on the legal system? The millions of indentured serfs gained nothing from her. There were recurrent spasms of peasant revolts and their lives remained grim. But Catherine made certain that a number of her principles, particularly those dealing with crime and punishment, found their way into Russian law and helped prepare the ground for the emancipation of the serfs a century later in 1861. She was not unaware of the difficulties of translating ideas into practical policies. She wrote to Diderot, 'While you write on unfeeling paper, I write on human skin, which is sensitive to the slightest touch.' Her humanity shines through.

The only significant internal threat to her reign was a revolt organised by a Cossack, Yemelyan Pugachev. He claimed that Peter III's death certificate had been fabricated and said *he* was, in fact, the deposed Emperor. He gathered support from the Cossacks, the sabre-carrying, independently ruled people (from what is present-day Ukraine) who were known for their horsemanship and ferocity. Napoleon described them as 'the best light troops among all that exist. If I had them in my army, I would go through all the world with them.' Thousands followed Pugachev and the uprising came dangerously close to the gates of Moscow. The imperial forces mounted several major counter-expeditions, and Pugachev was defeated and captured in 1774. Catherine was deeply alarmed by the revolt and decided to strengthen the local administrative authority of the aristocracy rather than concentrating on measures to improve the conditions of the lower classes.

There were, though, significant improvements during Catherine's reign. The territory and economic power of Russia increased greatly. The population of the country almost doubled, she ordered 144 new towns and cities to be built and strengthened the army and navy. She founded the Hermitage, which would become one of the world's greatest collections of paintings and sculpture, and vastly increased the artistic and educational life of her empire, even introducing some free health care and a home for orphaned children.

The best summary of Catherine's success comes in the words that would be carved on her tomb. Catherine being Catherine, she wasn't going to let anyone but herself write them:

In the year 1744, she went to Russia to marry Peter III. At the age of 14, she made the threefold resolution to please her husband, Elizabeth, and the nation. She neglected nothing in trying to achieve this. Eighteen years of boredom and loneliness gave her the opportunity to read many books.

When she came to the throne of Russia she wished to do what was good for her country and tried to bring happiness, liberty, and prosperity to her subjects.

She forgave easily and hated no one. She was good-natured, easy-going, tolerant, understanding, and of a happy disposition. She had a republican spirit and a kind heart.

She was sociable by nature.

She made many friends.

She took pleasure in her work.

She loved the arts.

No mention, you will note, of her ruthlessness in despatching the husband who had so bored her. But I don't think, selective amnesia aside, she exaggerates her determination to do her best by the country and the people she led. It's curious that she describes herself as having 'a republican spirit' when she, a crowned monarch, held so tenaciously to her throne and ruled a vast empire so effectively when kings and queens in other parts of the world were losing their heads or their empires.

It is, of course, her love life for which she is most often remembered in popular imagination. As so frequently happens to a woman who has no qualms about enjoying her sexuality with whoever takes her fancy, Catherine was often gossiped about and made the subject of horrible rumours. The most persistent has been that she died on 6 November 1796 as a result of intercourse with her horse. Absolutely not true. She simply had a stroke.

6

Clara Schumann

1819–1896

Why might it be that, when the name of Clara Schumann is mentioned, it's generally to point to how passionately she loved and how assiduously she cared for her husband, Robert? The clue lies in something she said herself. 'I once believed that I possessed creative talent, but I have given up the idea; a woman must not desire to compose – there has never yet been one able to do it. Should I expect to be the one?' In that one question she echoes the voices of hundreds of talented women who were pressured into believing that composing music was really not a job for a woman.

It's an attitude that's persisted well into the twentieth and twenty-first centuries, even though the earliest composer in the western canon whose name we know is Hildegard of Bingen, who lived in the twelfth century and was . . . well, yes, a woman! Yet I clearly recall listening to an interview in the *Woman's Hour* archive dating from the late 1940s, long before I became involved with the programme. The interviewee was Elizabeth Lutyens, best known for the terror-inducing chords for her Hammer Horror film scores, who expressed with absolute clarity what she called 'the tyranny of choice'.

Lutyens was talented in music, loved to compose and wanted it to be her profession, but she also wanted to have a husband and children. 'If I were a man', she said, 'I would not have to make a choice. As a woman I would not be expected to do both. My husband and children would always have to take precedence.' And that's the atmosphere in which Clara had found herself a hundred years earlier.

She was born Clara Josephine Wieck, on 13 September 1819. Her father, Friedrich Wieck, was a Leipzig salesman of pianos and a piano teacher. Single-mindedly, and on his own, he taught his daughter to play. So talented was she, and so insistent was he that she practise, practise and practise some more, that he turned Clara into a child prodigy and performing phenomenon.

Wieck was so obsessed with his daughter and her career as a pianist that his neglected wife, Clara's mother Marianne, left him for another man when her daughter was only four. Marianne was a famous singer of the time and performed regularly at the Gewandhaus concert hall in Leipzig. She had an affair with Adolph Bargiel, one of her husband's friends. The Wiecks were divorced in 1824 and Marianne and Bargiel married.

The law then allowed a divorced woman to have custody of her child only until the child's fifth birthday. Friedrich wrote in Clara's diary, in the girl's voice but his own hand, that her father 'had the legal right to take possession of me beginning in my fifth year'. The word *possession* is instructive. On one occasion, when he allowed the six-year-old Clara to visit her mother for a short time, he told his former wife Marianne to say nothing to Clara about the fraught marital history of her parents and gave strict instructions as to how she should be cared for. 'You will give the child little pastry and make sure you do not condone any naughti-ness . . . When she practises do not allow her to rush. I expect the most rigorous adherence to my wishes; if not, my anger will be incurred.'

Despite his chillingly controlling manner – he wrote her diaries as if in her voice until her late teenage years, and pieces of music he claimed she had composed as a child had in fact been written by him – his work as Clara's teacher paid off. He taught her everything she needed to know about the music business and how to conduct herself as a professional musician. As, at the age of nine, Clara began her professional career at the Gewandhaus in Leipzig, he instructed his second wife, Clementine Fechner, to ensure that her stepdaughter's performances appeared in the Leipzig newspaper. He also asked a young student, Robert Schumann, an occasional journalist, to do what he could about publicity.

Friedrich's treatment of his daughter was often brutal. When her little half-brother, Clemens, whom she adored, died suddenly at the age of three, her father ensured she had not a second to grieve. She'd been booked to give two concerts close to home in Leipzig; Friedrich cancelled them and promptly packed her off to Dresden, an unfamiliar and forbidding city to the young Clara. She played with supreme professionalism.

She wrote that she had learned to withstand the pressures she faced from her father: 'I am a girl within my own armour.' Although for the rest of her life she described acute physical symptoms of stage fright before or even during a performance, she never failed to do anything other than her best. And her best was generally agreed to be brilliant.

As a very little girl, at the age of five, before she learned to read music, she played by ear. Her father encouraged her to improvise her own themes or riff off ideas he gave her. When she was ten Clara began to learn formal harmony, counterpoint and composition. Her style of performance fitted perfectly with the style of music of the time. The classical movement had waned; the nineteenth century ushered in the romantic period, with artists such as Beethoven, Brahms, Liszt and Tchaikovsky. Critics and audiences loved her romantic mystique; when she played in Weimar, the tutor of its young duke wrote:

She has a look of unhappiness and of suffering which distresses me; but she owes perhaps a part of her fine talent to this inclination to melancholy; in examining closely the attributes of the Muses, one could almost always find there some traces of tears.

It seems appalling now that a childhood destroyed by a fanatically ambitious father, and her evident misery, should actually have been admired. It's interesting too that Clara's capabilities as a performer should be so approved and lauded when there would no doubt have been severe criticism had she been sold to the public as a composer. The thinking of the time held to the idea that it was perfectly acceptable for a girl to be allowed to *interpret* the work of great men, but far from OK for her to assume she possessed the creativity and ability to innovate required of a true composer. These were traits believed to be present only in the male of the species.

It's clear from what Clara wrote that she loved performing, although we have to bear in mind that much of what she appeared to have written was either composed, or at least edited, by her father. She showed off proudly about 'four curtain calls after *every* piece' at a concert in Prague; in Dresden, Felix Mendelssohn wrote that he thought her the best interpreter of one of his own works, *Capriccio*, because she played like a 'little devil'. Her father had been worried – not without reason – that Dresden, with its racier lifestyle, would corrupt his little girl. Her sixteenth birthday party was attended by a host of young men, including Mendelssohn and her father's pupil, Robert Schumann. There was dining, dancing and a late-night walk. It also the first occasion on which Schumann kissed her. 'It was marvellous', she wrote to a friend.

Even though 'female composer' was considered something of an oxymoron, Clara's talents in composition did not go unnoticed. It was common practice for a performer to improvise brilliantly during a performance, and even to play their own compositions, as had been heard in the legendary performances of other young prodigies such as Mozart and Mendelssohn. As a result of simply following the fashion of the time, Clara Wieck became not only a child prodigy at the piano, but also a child prodigy composer for the piano.

Her *Piano Concerto Opus 7* was begun when she was thirteen and first performed soon after her sixteenth birthday. One reviewer wrote: 'If the name of the female composer were not on the title one would never think it were written by a woman.' Another critic was not so impressed: 'If, in their cherished domestic and matrimonial circumstance, the daughters of Eve would make no other, larger leaps, deviations or evasions than such a teensy half step, then everything would be just fine.' Ah well, Clara, where prejudice abounds it seems you can't please all of the people any of the time.

It was around this time that what has been called the most feted romantic love story in the history of western music began to flourish. Clara and Robert Schumann first met towards the end of 1828 when Robert moved into the Wieck household as Friedrich's piano student. Clara was eight and Robert eighteen. Robert later wrote to her that he remembered her as 'an odd little child with a stubborn streak, beautiful eyes, and you liked cherries more than anything'. He confessed he became romantically interested in Clara when she was thirteen or fourteen, long before their first kiss at her sixteenth birthday party.

It's doubtful that the young Clara was aware of Robert's other carryings-on. At the same time as his early involvement with Clara, he was engaged to a young woman called Ernestine von Fricken. He was also intimate with another woman in the early 1830s. Known only as 'Christel', she gave him syphilis, the sexually transmitted disease that would eventually destroy both his mind and his body. He was told by a doctor that medicine could not help him, but that what he needed was to find a woman – at once – who would cure him.

It may seem strange advice from a doctor, even in the early nineteenth century, although Robert's condition occurred long before penicillin was found to be a cure for sexually transmitted infections. Mercury would have been tried but was ineffective. I think the doctor's advice was similar to some of the crazy ideas about curing HIV/AIDS that were put about in the twentieth century in parts of Africa: that sex with a virgin or a baby would make a man better. It's a myth that goes back a long way. Hanne Blank, in 2007, published a book called *Virgin: The Untouched History*, in which she describes how in eighteenth-century London, one in every five rape cases involved children under the age of ten. The rapists, suffering from syphilis or gonorrhoea, commonly cited the virgin cure myth in their defence.

Robert later wrote gratefully to Clara:

> You have brought me back to life again and I want your heart to lead me to ever greater purity. I was a poor beaten man who could no longer pray or cry for eighteen months. My eyes and my heart were cold and as hard as iron. And now? How different everything is, like being reborn through your love and your faithfulness.

Quite what convinced a doctor that the love of a good woman would cure a man's syphilis remains a mystery. Nor can it be understood why a man would risk sharing his affliction with a woman he claimed to love. But Robert did; in 1837, when Clara was eighteen, he asked Friedrich's permission to marry his daughter.

Friedrich was a great admirer of Robert's work but furious at the suggestion of marriage. I'm sure his objection was partly fanned by jealousy; he didn't want to lose his power over his daughter's career. She was, after all, his meal ticket. He would also, no doubt, have been aware of Robert's other sexual escapades and possibly of the disease that threatened his mental stability. Friedrich said no, threatened Robert with a gun and insisted the young couple should never see each other again.

I guess Friedrich was neither the first nor the last father to discover there's nothing so powerful as parental opposition in fanning the flames of young love.

Clara and Robert began a secret correspondence. Eventually, they decided to go to court and sued Friedrich, in a long and protracted case. The judge found for the young couple and allowed the marriage. The two were wed on 12 September 1840, the day before Clara's twenty-first birthday. One day later, she would have achieved her majority and been able to marry without permission.

For a time it seemed the musical match made in heaven would fulfil its promise. The two geniuses worked together at composition, encouraging and inspiring each other, and Clara continued her profitable career as a renowned concert pianist throughout Europe. In 1837 so many people flocked to hear her play at a concert in Vienna that police were needed to restrain the frantic crowds. Robert had reassured her that, after their marriage, she would not need to sacrifice her talent to his because, as a fellow artist, he understood her needs: 'I think we will continue to improvise for one another, as we used to, and compose the most wonderful operas together, and I'll often listen to the music coming from your room and think, "Why, the one who's playing is your Clara".'

With the benefit of hindsight it's easy to see that his enthusiasm for their shared musical projects in the early part of their marriage was somewhat tempered by the expectations of a conventional husband. He promised 'You will want to remain an artist . . . you will want to be supportive, work with me, share joy and sorrow with me,' but it seems he was more keen on the supporting and sharing part than on her need to remain an artist in her own right. Thus, she develops the reputation which has been written about so often and continues to be spoken of today by musicologists: 'Clara's influence over Schumann's piano music cannot be overestimated, either as creative muse or as performer.'

Ah, yes, that old chestnut; the woman is merely a muse to the great artist and when she plays his work, she is, again, performing the acceptable role of a woman, 'imitating genius'!

Within three years of their marriage the Schumanns had two daughters, Marie and then Elise. As a present for their first Christmas together Clara composed three songs that delighted her husband. He said that, 'in the songs, she gushes like a young girl'. A modern critic was a little more positive in his analysis of the work. 'Seldom has such happy, breathless excitement been portrayed in music, with such intensity from the very first note.' The songs were published in a joint collection soon after Marie's birth.

It wasn't long before Robert began to assert his authority in the marriage. His behaviour, as a result of the disease that had NOT been cured by his sexual relations with a virgin, became increasingly irrational and melancholic. When Clara complained that she was afraid she would now have to bury her heart if she were not allowed to get on with her creative work, he threatened suicide. He wrote of her efforts to set her songs and several piano pieces in order but 'Marie is grasping her dress on the one side, Elise also creates much to do, and the husband sits deep in thoughts of *Peri* (his oratorio)'. He even tried to restrict her performances, although goodness knows what the family would have lived on without them, as her parents were no help with money. But Robert wrote that his 'dearest wish was that Clara would have no further appearances in public'. What he wanted from his wife was exactly what she had feared: an artist 'with a bonnet on her head and a bunch of keys at her waist'. Her role, he said, was to stimulate and encourage her husband because 'Men stand higher than women.' When a plaster relief was made of the couple six years after they were married he insisted that he should be portrayed in the foreground since the 'creative artist has higher status than the performer'.

Clara's angst is reflected in her diaries:

My piano playing is falling behind. This always happens when Robert is composing. There is not even one little hour to be found in the whole day for myself! If only I don't fall too far behind. Score reading has also been given up once again, but I hope it won't be for long this time.

Through several years of giving birth to children and dealing with her husband's drinking, gambling, and mental and physical deterioration, Clara found help with childcare from Robert's brother and his wife, and continued her career as a performer. During this period she managed to find the time and energy to compose what's described as her greatest work: *Piano Trio Opus 17*. Some years after its publication Joseph Joachim recalled his incredulity at the authorship: 'I . . . remember that Mendelssohn once had a big laugh because I would not believe that a woman could have composed something so sound and serious.' Mendelssohn had, of course, been strongly influenced by his sister, Fanny Mendelssohn, also a composer, who had managed to convince him that a woman was as perfectly capable as a man of composing well.

Pregnancy and childcare did not stop Clara's performances altogether, despite the difficulties of juggling them with her role as a mother and as the wife of an increasingly difficult husband. When three months pregnant with her first child, she returned to the concert hall and continued through seven more pregnancies, at least two miscarriages, the death of her first son, Emil and the institutionalisation of her second son, Ludwig. She managed it because servants were cheap and one of her piano students, Emilie Steffens, was often happy to take over her duties at home.

As her husband's illness grew worse and worse, Clara's fortitude was spectacular. She wrote some music, performed endless concerts, befriended Brahms and a young musician with whom she often performed, Joseph Joachim. Both men were considerably younger than Clara but adored and supported her.

By February 1854 Robert Schumann was lost to her. He threw himself into the Rhine, was rescued, and asked to be taken to the asylum at Endenich. George Eliot, the novelist, was an admirer of the way Clara handled her woes. 'Clara Schumann is a melancholy, interesting creature. Her husband went mad a year ago and she has to support eight children.' During Robert's treatment at Endenich, the doctors thought Clara's presence would worsen Robert's condition and banned her from visiting. She disobeyed; in July 1856 she insisted on seeing him. He died two days later.

In a diary entry she described how she had prayed for him: 'All my thoughts went up to God with thanks that he is finally free ... It seems as if a magnificent spirit was hovering over me ... ah, if only he had taken me along.' Her wish was not granted. She lived for another forty years and died after a stroke in 1896 at the age of seventy-seven. She continued her career as a performer until 1891 but never composed again after Robert died, apart from one deeply romantic piece, *Romance in B Minor*, written in 1856. I've often wondered whether it reflects her heartbreak at the death of her husband or if there were stirrings of some new love after the misery of Robert. Perhaps Brahms or Joseph Joachim got her creative juices flowing just once more.

Clara once wrote: 'Composing gives me great pleasure ... there is nothing which surpasses the joy of creation, if only because, through it one wins hours of self-forgetfulness when one lives in a world of sound.' There is, though, very little output after her thirty-sixth birthday. Given the nightmare of her domestic life, it's hardly surprising her earlier passion for composing waned. I've listened so often to the last major work she composed, the *Piano Trio Opus 17*, the one Mendelssohn had described as 'so sound and serious'. I've always found it an intensely feminine work but not at all in a soft, sweet or romantic way. For me it's the piece of music in which every woman who's tried to juggle children, home, husband and a demanding job will hear her own life reflected; at once tender and loving and stomping about in a frustrated fury. No wonder she just couldn't manage everything any longer. It was composition that had to go. Her husband was only too well aware of the pressures of being a woman trying to keep all her balls in the air but, as is so often the case, a little complacent about his contribution to her stress:

> Clara has composed a series of small pieces which show a musical and tender ingenuity such as she has never attained before. But to have children, and a husband who is always living in the realm of imagination, does not go together with composing. She cannot work at it regularly, and I am often disturbed to think how many profound ideas are lost because she cannot work them out. Clara herself knows her main occupation is as a mother and is happy in the circumstances and would not want them changed.

Not disturbed enough, though, to take on his share of the childcare and the housework and the endless performances she gave to keep the family finances afloat. And there you have it. Two great composers living in the same household but only one of them faced with that 'tyranny of choice'.

7

Dowager Empress Cixi

1835–1908

L ook to the People's Republic of China in the twenty-first century and you'll be hard pressed to find a female face in the higher echelons of political power. Since the Communists came to power in 1949 no woman has sat on the party's highest body, the seven-member Politburo Standing Committee, currently led by President Xi Jingping. At the time of writing, the 25-member Politburo has only two women, and that's the highest number since the Cultural Revolution, when the wives of Mao Zedong and Lin Biao were given seats in 1969. The constitution is committed to gender equality but discrimination is widespread, summed up by a familiar saying that a woman with power is like 'a hen crowing at dawn'; a sign that family and state will collapse.

Cheng Li, director of the John L Thornton China Center at the Brookings Institution in Washington said recently, 'It would take a miracle for a woman to become head of the People's Republic in China in the near future.' Interest in this vast country, so closed to western tourism for so long, is now increasing as China opens up. As its economic power and global influence become ever more significant it's time we all began to look east to uncover the wonders of Chinese civilisation and understand that there's much more to be discovered than the Great Wall, pandas, the Forbidden Palace and the Terracotta Army. We may well be living in what will be called China's century.

In the nineteenth and early twentieth centuries one woman broke through the fear of the 'hen crowing at dawn' and gained absolute power, sometimes by fair means and often by foul, but her intention was always to try to bring medieval China into the modern age. One of her most significant successes, in the context of this book, was to liberate women from foot binding.

Imagine what it must have been like to have been born into a culture in which you take a little girl – your own daughter – crush her feet and strap them up tightly, condemning her to the life of pain you, her mother, have also suffered. Victims of this appalling 'beauty treatment' were barely able to walk. And all because men found dainty, tiny feet irresistibly sexy. As a Manchu from a well-off, upper middle-class family, Cixi was spared foot binding, which had gone on for a millennium among the indigenous Chinese, the Han. She cringed at the sight of bound feet and eventually banned the practice.

In the seventeenth century the Manchus, native to the north-east, broke out of their homeland and, even though they were outnumbered a hundred to one by the native Han, they prevailed and conquered China, establishing a dynasty of absolute monarchs. The whole of China was closed off to the rest of the world, with only one port, Canton, open for trade. This policy began in 1757 and was a major factor in China remaining a medieval, gender- and race-segregated empire. It also resulted in the Opium Wars. Britain fought for greater access to China, to open up trade and import silk, tea and, importantly, opium. The first trade war broke out in 1839. China lost and Britain increased trade relations, as well as taking Hong Kong as part of its war reparations.

Cixi was born into her Manchu family four years before the wars broke out in November 1835. Her father was a government official. The first hints of an extraordinary personality contained in a rather short and not particularly beautiful girl of limited education came in 1843, when she was only seven. China had to pay a large amount of money in reparation when the first Opium War was lost. The Emperor, in turn, demanded money from government officials suspected of stealing cash from the treasury. Cixi's grandfather was a suspect and was imprisoned until a hefty fine was paid. He would only be released when his son, Cixi's father, could pay the fine.

As Cixi was the oldest child in the family her father turned to her for help and advice. She took in sewing to raise money and, by the time she was eleven, had dreamt up so many schemes that the family had collected enough to pay the fine. Her father gave her the ultimate compliment in a society that generally valued only boys: 'This daughter of mine is really more like a son!' As a result, Cixi was not treated as a girl could expect. She became involved in long conversations with her father about state affairs and gained a considerable amount of confidence in her own abilities.

She and her father had raised a phenomenal amount of money to pay her grandfather's fine, and her father was rewarded with a more important job. He became the governor of a large Mongolian region and so Cixi left crowded Beijing for the first time, travelled beyond the Great Wall of China and encountered the wide open spaces of the Mongolian steppes. She became passionately fond of the countryside.

In February 1850, only a few months after the move to Mongolia, the Emperor, Daoguang, died and his nineteen-year-old son, Xianfeng, succeeded. The new Emperor, who was born prematurely, had not been a healthy child. He also walked with difficulty, the result of a fall from a horse. He was nicknamed 'the Limping Dragon' by the gossips in Beijing.

After Xianfeng's coronation a search began across the country to find him consorts, as tradition dictated. The listed candidates had to be Manchu or Mongol teenagers of a reasonably high rank; their parents were required to register them for selection as possible royal concubines when they reached puberty. The girls were paraded before the Emperor in March 1852. The chosen few (actually not so few – emperors liked to have a wide range of sexual playthings) would become the imperial concubines and live in the harem at the Forbidden Palace in Beijing. Others would be given to royal princes. The ones not chosen in the royal court would be sent home to marry someone of their parents' choice.

The girls entered the Forbidden City by the rear entrance. The front one was for men only. Years ago, when I walked through the enormous halls of the City, I remember thinking that my generation of women were probably the first to be allowed to enter through the front gate. The women in Cixi's time not only had their own entrance but were also forbidden from entering any part of the palace except the rooms at the rear where the harem was situated, and where no men apart from the Emperor and several hundred eunuchs were allowed.

Cixi played the seduction game well. She was beautifully dressed, walked with the required upright poise and fluttered her eyelashes to attract the Emperor's attention. People often mentioned her eyes. From her first appearance in royal circles, and right through her political career, she used them to smile at, flatter and bewitch any official who was reluctant to accept her ideas. Generally, this succeeded. If officials continued to disagree or displeased her in any way her eyes would flash in fury. A future President of China, General Yuan Shikai, said her gaze was the only thing that could unnerve him. 'I don't know why', he said, 'but the sweat just poured out. I just became so nervous.'

Cixi was one of the chosen ones, and moved into her new home in the Forbidden City as a concubine on 26 June 1852. She'd made it, but Cixi was not a high-ranking concubine. The imperial harem placed every consort on one of eight rungs of a ladder; Cixi found herself on the sixth. Another girl, named Zhen, who entered at the same time as Cixi, was on the fifth rung, but she was soon promoted to the top rank and became the Empress. She was apparently not picked because she was particularly beautiful but because she had a reputation for possessing good managerial skills. The Emperor was only too well aware that he needed such a woman to head the harem and keep the women under control, preventing any bitchiness or backbiting.

There's no evidence that Cixi was a favourite. For six years a frenetically sexually active Limping Dragon had a wild old time. The concubine he'd selected for the night would be brought to his bed, lying naked underneath a silk drape, then be whisked away when he'd had enough of her. His sexual activities were meticulously recorded, including liaisons with the Han prostitutes who were smuggled in. He had a particular liking for their bound feet which, of course, none of his Manchu concubines had.

Cixi made a terrible mistake during her early years as a level six concubine. The Taiping peasants' rebellion of 1850 created a huge convulsion in the state, resulted in widespread famine, and was so serious that it led to an opposing state being set up in Nanjing. Cixi tried to offer the Emperor advice on how he might deal with the upheaval and raise funds for the treasury. After all, she'd done it before to help her family. He was furious. It was strictly forbidden for a Royal Consort to play any role in state affairs. He told Empress Zhen to do something about Cixi's 'crafty and cunning' behaviour and wrote a note ordering that, if Cixi tried to interfere in the affairs of state after his death, the Empress was to show his edict to the royal princes who would follow his orders to have Cixi 'exterminated'.

The Empress protected Cixi and tried to persuade the Emperor that she had only been expressing her love and loyalty. The two women were devoted to each other for the rest of their lives. Later, after the Emperor's death, Zhen showed Cixi the note ordering Cixi's 'extermination'. Cixi burned it. It may have been Zhen who arranged Cixi's promotion to the fifth rank on the concubines' ladder. She had learned her lesson and never again, while in that role, tried to involve herself in politics. Instead she made it her business to share the Emperor's interest in art and music. They were particularly fond of opera and developed a close relationship as a result. On 27 April 1856 she gave birth to a child. It was a boy.

He was the Emperor's first-born son. A previous pregnancy with another concubine had produced only a daughter. Cixi's boy was called Zaichun and his mother quickly became the undisputed number-two consort, second only to her ally, Empress Zhen. She had achieved that ultimate success for a woman, which exists in China even now: the production of a male heir. It was to determine her future for the best part of the next forty years.

When her son was five years old, his father, the Emperor, died. On his deathbed Xianfeng set up an eight-man regency to run China, designed to keep Cixi under control. Together with her friend, Empress Zhen, Cixi succeeded in mounting a *coup* against the appointed regents before their husband's funeral. Cixi accused the regents of forging the Emperor's will and ordered the suicide of the two men who'd been the most powerful of the eight.

Disposing of those who stood in her way became something of a habit, despite her claim that 'All I desire is peace under Heaven.' Her boy was crowned Emperor Tongzhi and his mother became regent. As a woman she could never sit on the throne herself, so her political career depended on the Emperor being a child for whom she could rule as regent. In this, the dynastic lottery played out well for Cixi. Her own son died as a teenager in 1875 and her three-year-old nephew, Guangxu, succeeded him. Cixi adopted him, demanding that he address her as 'My Royal Father'.

The death of her co-ruler, Zhen, believed, despite their long friendship, to be at the hand of Cixi, left Cixi in sole charge of the young Emperor. She reluctantly handed over the reins of power when he reached maturity and she went into temporary retirement in 1889, devoting herself to re-building the summer palace outside Beijing. One visitor to the completed structure and its surrounding gardens said: 'I have never seen such splendid buildings and such luxurious decoration.'

Her retirement did not last long. She returned to state affairs in 1894 to help heal the wounds of the traumatic lost war against Japan and she readied herself for the next political move. In 1898, Guangxu launched a radical reform plan under the guidance of two imperial scholars, Kang Youwei and Liang Qichao. Kang persuaded the Emperor that Cixi was an obstacle to his plans and advised that she should be neutralised.

The reform plan was not a success; conservative forces in the court expressed such violent objections it almost led to civil war. Cixi made her move. By September of that year she had deposed and imprisoned Guangxu and re-taken power. The reformers who failed to escape were executed, as were two men who were completely innocent of plotting against her. Cixi had stopped their trials, to prevent the Emperor's role in the plot to assassinate her becoming public.

The last few years of Cixi's career make for a dramatic history. She committed a grave error in encouraging the Boxer Rebellion, a xenophobic and anti-Christian movement, which ended in a bloody siege of the foreign legations in Beijing. The rescue of the foreigners cost China and Cixi heavily. Huge indemnities had to be paid to the countries concerned. She had to flee the capital, pausing, according to her biographer Jung Chang, to order the killing of Guangxu's favourite concubine, allegedly thrown down a well for suggesting negotiation rather than flight. When she returned to the capital she apologised for her support of the Boxer rebellion, 'I let down our ancestors and I let down our people', and began to make friends with the wives of the resident diplomats in an attempt to restore her reputation in the wider world.

It was in 1902 that she made her ceremonious return to Beijing and within two years she had launched her own programme of sweeping reforms, based on the suggestions of Kang Youwei, the scholar who had worked with Emperor Guangxu, but had escaped to exile when the plot to assassinate Cixi was discovered. Curious that she instigated the very reforms devised by the men against whom she'd fought.

There are a number of conflicting opinions about Cixi's ruthlessness and her success or otherwise as the ruler of China. Keith Laidler, in *The Last Empress: The She-Dragon of China*, blatantly accuses her of murdering her co-empress Zhen by sending her poisoned cakes, murdering her daughter-in-law, possibly faking her pregnancy and the birth of her son Zaichun by buying him from a peasant woman, and deliberately ensuring he became infected with syphilis. Jung Chang, the author of *Empress Dowager Cixi: The Concubine Who Launched Modern China*, is considerably more sympathetic to the aims and practice of the woman once described by a European diplomat as 'the only man in China'.

Jung Chang, in her carefully researched work, seeks to rehabilitate the woman who, she claims, was slandered by the willingness of men to believe the worst of her. She describes the changes Cixi made as 'dramatic and yet gradual, seismic and yet astonishingly bloodless'. Of her disposal of her enemies and those who threatened her power, Chang says, 'In some four decades of absolute power, her political killings – whether just or unjust . . . were no more than a few dozen, many of them in response to plots to kill her.'

Not so bloodless then, but there can be no doubt that she was an extraordinary figure. From squalor and bankruptcy, and as a semi-literate woman, she rose first to become a sixth-rank concubine and then, instead of dutifully starving herself to death to join her late husband, she became the ruler of a third of the human race for almost half a century, albeit from behind a curtain. Yes, many of her actions were cruel. It's really not very nice to have your adopted son's favourite concubine thrown into a well and drowned, nor to end the life of the Emperor Guangxu, the nephew you had adopted as a child, by sending him cakes laced with arsenic. Nor to terrify emperors into wetting their pants. Guangxu succumbed on 14 November 1908 and Cixi herself died unexpectedly, of natural causes, the following day, having installed Guangxu's toddler son, Puyi, as Emperor. I guess she'd been planning another term as regent to another child. As it was, after her death, Puyi was to be the 'Last Emperor'.

But Cixi did bring about important reforms. She defeated the Taiping Rebellion – the largest peasant revolt in Chinese history – in which twenty million people perished. She imported vast quantities of food to aid those who were starving during a number of natural disasters and conflicts. She ended the slave trade in China, unveiled China's first national flag, doubled the country's revenues and drew up border treaties that remain in place. She ended gender segregation and the apartheid between the Manchu and the Han, prohibited torture and banned the common method of execution by a thousand cuts, that notorious practice in which bits of the body were systematically sliced away while the victim was conscious.

Jung Chang, in the epilogue to her biography, says of Cixi:

[Her] legacy was manifold and towering . . . she brought medieval China into the modern age. Under her leadership the country began to acquire virtually all the attributes of a modern state: railways, electricity, telegraph, telephones, Western medicine, a modern-style army and navy, and modern ways of conducting foreign trade and diplomacy. The restrictive millennium-old educational system was discarded and replaced by Western-style schools and universities. The press blossomed, enjoying a freedom that was unprecedented and arguably unsurpassed since. She unlocked the door to political participation: for the first time in China's long history, people were to become 'citizens'. It was Cixi who championed women's liberation in a culture that had for centuries imposed foot-binding on its female population – a practice to which she put an end. The fact that her last enterprise before an untimely death was to introduce the vote testifies to her courage and vision.

For me, I go back to those women with their broken and bound feet, and I can't help but continue to find that my main reason for praising and celebrating the Dowager Empress Cixi is the sight of all those twenty-first-century young women in Beijing who march about in their high heels, boots or trainers – whatever they choose to wear – without any pain or discomfort. China, as I said, still has no women in the higher echelons of political power, but a woman prevented from walking out into the world has no opportunity to make her way. Women all over China have Cixi to thank for their first steps towards liberation.

8

Marie Curie

1867–1934

As a non-scientist I can't begin to pretend a deep understanding of Marie Curie's work on the discovery and
application of radium. I can only acknowledge that, on
the numerous occasions I have fetched up in hospital with a
suspected broken limb (both wrists – twice, both ankles, the
humerus, a finger – yes, I am known to be accident-prone) I have
had good reason to be grateful to the woman who gave us the
X-ray as a tool to be used in hospitals. I didn't have radiotherapy
after a mastectomy, just chemotherapy, but all of us who've had
tumours blasted have her to thank too. The German physicist,
Röntgen, and the French physicist, Becquerel, are credited with
first observing X-rays in the late nineteenth century, but it was
Marie, together with her husband, Pierre Curie, who continued
to investigate radioactivity and its practical application. And all
that is a mere hint at part of the towering achievements of this
scientific genius.

As she told audiences on her speaking tour of America in 1921,
Marie had no idea when she began the work how it might be
useful:

We must not forget that when radium was discovered no one
knew that it would prove useful in hospitals. The work was

one of pure science. And this is proof that scientific work must not be considered from the point of view of the direct usefulness of it. It must be done for itself, for the beauty of science, and then there is always the chance that a scientific discovery may become, like radium, a benefit for humanity.

Yes, there has been great benefit to humanity but we can't ignore the fact that scientific advances often have unintended consequences. Her work would eventually lead to the development of nuclear weapons. The potential danger was not unacknowledged by Curie and her husband Pierre, who said:

> One can imagine in criminal hands radium could become very dangerous, and here one can ask if humanity is at an advantage in knowing nature's secrets, if it is mature enough to make use of them or if this knowledge might not be harmful . . . I am one of those who believe with Nobel that humanity will derive more good than harm from the new discoveries.

Neither Marie nor Pierre lived long enough to witness the carnage brought about by the nuclear bombs in Hiroshima and Nagasaki in 1945 at the end of the Second World War. Marie was a lifelong pacifist. Recalling her experience of the First World War, she said:

> To hate the very idea of war, it ought to be sufficient to see once what I have seen so many times, all through those years: men and boys brought to the advanced ambulance in a mixture of mud and blood, many of them dying of their injuries, many others recovering but slowly through months of pain and suffering.

Her daughter, Irène, often said she was glad her mother had not witnessed the terrible destruction and harm done to innocent civilians in Japan but would it have deterred this woman who was utterly dedicated to her scientific work? Somehow I doubt it. 'Radioactivity', she said, 'is a very young science. It is an infant that I saw being born, and I have contributed to raising with all my strength. The child has grown. It has become beautiful . . . Nothing in life is to be feared, it is only to be understood. Now is the time to understand more so that we may fear less.' If only we could be certain that those in power in the twenty-first century have understood enough of nuclear war to fear it for all our sakes.

Marie was born Maria Skłodowska in Warsaw in Poland in November 1867, during one of the frequent Russian occupations of the country. She was the youngest of five children. Her father was a teacher of science and her mother died of tuberculosis when Maria was only ten. Maria was sent to boarding school and then a Gymnasium for girls, where she proved to be something of a prodigy in both literature and maths, graduating in 1883 with a gold medal.

She moved back to Warsaw to live with her father and work as a tutor. She also, together with her older sister Bronisława, enrolled at a clandestine establishment known as the 'Flying University'. It was the only academic establishment that would admit women. Physics and natural history were taught, as well as the forbidden subject of Polish history and culture. Its location changed frequently, to stay one step ahead of the Russians.

In 1886 Maria got a job as a governess in Szczuki with a family called the Zorawskis, wealthy relatives of her father's. The intention was to earn enough money to help finance Bronisława's studies in Paris. Her father was not well off enough to pay for his girls to be educated, although he encouraged them in their work. The deal was that Maria would work to pay her older sister's university fees and the favour would be returned at a later date. I find this example of a younger sister's sacrifice so endearing.

Sisters are often portrayed as jealous and horrid to each other. This is what I like to think we early feminists meant when we talked of a sisterhood between women; that we would help and support one another.

Maria hated her 'nightmare' job as a governess, saying 'I shouldn't like my worst enemy to live in such a hell. My soul is worn out. Ah, if I could extract myself for a few days from this icy atmosphere of criticism.' It didn't help that she fell in love with the son of the house, who after years of torment obeyed his parents and omitted to marry his 'inferior'. She persevered, to pay her sister's way through medical school. Bronisława was one of only three women in the thousand students studying medicine at the Sorbonne, but she graduated successfully. When Bronisława was in a position to repay her debt to her little sister, Maria seemed to suffer a crisis of confidence and decided not to take up her own studies in Paris. She explained it away as a determination to carry out her filial duty, returning to Warsaw to live with her father to 'give him a little happiness in his old age'. Later she said, 'I have been stupid, I am stupid and I shall remain stupid all the days of my life . . . I have never been, am not and shall never be lucky. I dreamed of Paris as of redemption, but the hope of going there left me a long time ago.'

In Warsaw, Maria continued to study at the Flying University, worked as a tutor giving a basic education to local peasant children – work for which she could have been imprisoned or deported to Siberia had it been discovered – and eventually began work as a scientist in a chemical laboratory at the Museum of Industry and Agriculture.

At the age of twenty-four, in 1891, Maria had finally, with a little help from her now married sister, saved enough money to buy a train ticket to Paris, find herself somewhere to live in the Latin Quarter and enrol at the Sorbonne. She immersed herself in learning French and studied maths and physics, earning a meagre income by cleaning glassware in the university's laboratories. She was often so short of food she fainted from hunger in her classes but she was thrilled by the science. After only two years she was awarded a Master's degree in physics and began working in the industrial laboratory of Professor Gabriel Lippmann. A year later she had a Master's degree in maths.

In 1894 she met Pierre Curie, a 35-year-old physicist teaching at the Paris Municipal School of Physics and Chemistry, specialising in studying crystals and magnetism. More than a decade earlier he and his brother, Jacques, had discovered piezoelectricity, an electric charge produced in solid materials under pressure. The breakthrough would prove useful in Marie and Pierre's collaborations. The couple fell in love, drawn to each other's passion for their scientific work. He proposed marriage. 'It would be a beautiful thing', he wrote, 'to pass through life together hypnotised in your dreams: your dreams for your country; our dream for humanity; our dream for science.'

Maria refused Pierre's first proposal but eventually agreed. The two were married on 26 July 1895. She was completely uninterested in her appearance, as seen in her characteristic practicality when she wrote to her brother about what she might wear for their wedding: 'I have no dress except the one I wear every day. If you are going to be kind enough to give me one, please let it be practical and dark so that I can put it on afterwards to go to the laboratory.' She wore blue cotton at the civil ceremony attended by family and a few friends.

The couple determined that they would live what they called 'an anti-natural path'. One of the key choices was a 'renunciation of the pleasures of life'. They lived the plainest possible lifestyle in their flat on the rue de la Glacière, within walking distance of the dilapidated shed with broken windows and poor ventilation where they carried out their experiments. Marie effectively took charge of the work; Pierre admitted, much later, that had he been left to his own devices he would never have embarked on the research in radium in which she led and he followed. He was always supportive of her plans, even offering to move to Poland with her – she missed her home country very much – and abandoning his own crystallography research to follow her interests.

The Curies' first daughter, Irène, was born in 1897. It was a difficult pregnancy and Marie was forced to cut down her laboratory time, just as she was gathering data for a doctoral thesis. When her mother-in-law died only weeks after Irène's birth, her father-in-law, a retired physician, stepped in to provide childcare. Marie faced censure from colleagues and friends for handing her child over to someone else and failing to be the hands-on parent that was expected of a woman. No such critique was directed at Pierre, of course.

Soon after Irène's birth, she became pregnant again, but suffered a miscarriage. She was devastated. 'I am absolutely desperate and cannot be consoled', she said. 'I must admit that I have not spared my strength. I had confidence in my constitution and, at present, I regret this bitterly, as I have paid dear for it.' Marie thought seriously about having no more children after the miscarriage. 'Existence is too hard, too barren. We ought not to inflict it on innocent ones.' But in 1904, when Irène was seven, their second daughter, Ève, was born. Still, criticism of her maternal tendencies came from disdainful colleagues who thought she spent far too much time in the laboratory and not enough in the nursery. One friend and collaborator, Georges Sagnac, confronted her. 'Don't you love Irène?', he asked, 'It seems to me that I wouldn't prefer the idea of reading a paper by [Ernest] Rutherford to getting what my body needs and of looking at such an agreeable little girl.' Ah, yes, the tyranny of choice again and the pressure an ambitious, driven woman always has to endure when she, like a man, wants both to have a family and use her talents for her work.

Marie ignored her critics and spent a good deal of time reading scientific papers on the new and surprising phenomena that were being uncovered by Röntgen (who in 1895 had discovered X-rays) and by the mathematician Henri Poincaré. They were delving into the mysteries of these luminescent rays, which could pass through a hand and produce a ghostly image on treated paper. Henri Becquerel, meanwhile, had published his findings on the emission of a different kind of mysterious ray that came from uranium salts. JJ Thomson discovered the negatively charged particles now known as electrons. It was a golden period of scientific endeavour; these new discoveries were throwing up fundamental questions about the real nature of our world. What created these strange energies? Of what did they consist? Were they waves or particles?

Marie focused on the implications of Becquerel's observations of uranium. At first confusion reigned: what on earth could be the source of those high-energy emissions? 'The uranium', she wrote in 1900, 'shows no appreciable change of state, no visible chemical transformation. It remains, in appearance at least, the same as ever, the source of the energy discharges remains undetectable.'

Crikey, I wish I'd concentrated harder during basic physics at school but, as my maths and physics teachers agreed, I was spending far too much time reading Jane Austen, learning poetry and appearing in the school play to retain any of what took place in the lab. But I think what Marie had discovered was that the atom, which had previously been thought to be unsplittable (if that's a word, if not bear with me) could in fact be split. This theory startled the scientific world. She explained her findings by saying that the number of detected rays varied according to the weight of the uranium, forcing her to conclude that the emissions came from the element's atom rather than from interaction with light or external substances. The radical implications of her theory are described by Trish Baisden, a senior chemist at the Lawrence Livermore National Laboratory in California, as a shocking proposition:

It was truly amazing and a bold statement at the time because the atom was thought to be the most elementary particle, one that could not be divided. It further meant that atoms are not necessarily stable. Curie's hypothesis would revise the scientific understanding of matter at its most elemental level.

Splitting the atom, see!

Marie used an electrometer, which had been invented by Pierre and his brother, to measure the intensity of the rays from the uranium, and was puzzled by the results. It's a classic example of Isaac Asimov's famous remark: 'The most exciting phrase to hear in science . . . is not "Eureka", but "That's funny!"' The intensity of the rays emitted by the uranium she tested was greater than she expected. 'There must be, I thought, some unknown substance, very active, in these minerals', she said. 'My husband agreed with me and I urged that we search at once for this hypothetical substance, thinking that, with joined efforts, a result would be quickly obtained.'

In 1898, one of the substances yielded its secrets. Curie called it 'polonium', after her beloved homeland of Poland. Five months later, she discovered a second element, which she called radium. She described the elements she was studying as 'radio-active'. Pierre's electrometer would later be developed into the Geiger counter; a machine for detecting radiation.

Radium was present in the source minerals in such minuscule amounts that isolating a pure sample was almost beyond the bounds of what was technically possible in Curie's day. In 1902, using a tonne of uranium's chief ore, pitchblende, the Curies managed to produce one-tenth of a gram of radium chloride. It took Marie until 1910 to isolate pure radium in its metallic state. She found her work had an extremely important medical application; not only had she made it possible to use X-rays to detect broken bones or worn-out hips, she'd also found a way of treating cancer. She discovered that tumours shrink when exposed to the substance and, throughout the rest of her life, she called it 'my beloved radium'.

Pierre and Marie were constantly plagued by ailments, burns and fatigue that we now know were caused by constant exposure to high doses of radiation. Blithely, Marie had wandered around with unshielded vials of radium in her lab coat pocket. Neither she nor her husband ever accepted that their illnesses might be caused by their research, but her notebooks, more than a century on, remain too radioactive to be handled without wearing a special protective suit.

As busy as she was with her research in the laboratory, Marie still found time to pursue her academic work. In 1903, she became the first woman in France to be awarded a PhD in physics. The professors who reviewed her doctoral thesis, on the subject of radiation, proclaimed it the greatest single contribution to science ever written. When rumours began that she was to be awarded the Nobel Prize in physics, some members of the French Academy of Sciences claimed that the brilliance of the work was not hers, but that of Becquerel and Pierre. A whispering campaign began, for the prize to be split between the two men. Pierre defended his wife to influential people on the Nobel Committee, assuring them that it was indeed Marie who had originated the research, set up the experiments and formulated the theories about the nature of radioactivity. In 1903 the prize was shared between the three of them.

It was the first Nobel Prize to be awarded to a woman, but the President of the Swedish Academy, which awarded it, couldn't resist questioning Marie's role. At the award ceremony, he quoted the Bible: 'It is not good that a man should be alone, I will make a helpmeet for him.' We know that it was Pierre who was help-meet to Marie and not the other way around, but the insult damaged her reputation for some time. Marie's friend, the British physicist Hertha Ayrton, said: 'Errors are notoriously hard to kill, but an error that ascribes to a man what was actually the work of a woman has more lives than a cat.'

The prize inevitably enhanced Pierre's reputation; he was offered a full professorship at the Sorbonne. But the knock-on effects of the Nobel Prize's prestige didn't, for some reason, extend to Marie: no promotion for her. Pierre took on more assistants to work with her and made her the official head of his laboratory. She was free to conduct whatever experiments she chose and, for the first time, was paid for her efforts.

Her promotion to full professor at the Sorbonne came as a result of tragedy. In April 1906, Pierre absent-mindedly walked into the busy traffic in the Rue Dauphine. He was hit by a carriage and killed instantly. Privately, Marie was heartbroken, saying: 'I will not kill myself, I don't even have the desire for suicide. But among all those carriages, isn't there one which will make me share the fate of my beloved?'

In public she showed no sign of mourning. She refused a widow's pension from the Sorbonne, instead taking over Pierre's job as Chair of Physics, becoming the first woman to teach at the university. Hundreds queued up outside the university on 5 November 1906, in the hope of attending her first lecture. She made no reference to her husband in her address, simply beginning by summarising the recent breakthroughs in physics research: 'When one considers the progress of physics in the last decade one is surprised by the changes it has produced in our ideas about electricity and about matter.'

Perhaps it was her lack of open emotion that led Albert Einstein to say of her, 'Madame Curie is highly intelligent, but has the soul of a herring, which means that she is poor when it comes to the art of either joy or pain. Almost the only time she shows emotion is when she's grumbling about things she doesn't like.' Privately, she addressed her diary of this period to her late husband, explaining how she was continuing with her work. 'I am working in the laboratory all day long. It is all I can do: I am better off there than anywhere else.' In 1910, after she had published a 971-page treatise on radioactivity, she applied for membership of the French Academy of Sciences. Pierre had been a member, but she was rejected by two votes. One Academy member, the physicist Émile Amagat, said that 'women cannot be part of the Institute of France'. The misogyny was far from concealed.

It was around this time, in 1911, that rumours of an affair with the well-known physicist Paul Langevin began to circulate. He was five years Marie's junior and had been a student of Pierre's. Langevin's estranged wife discovered what appeared to be love letters from Marie to her husband and gave them to a tabloid newspaper. The headlines screamed 'A Romance in a Laboratory'. While a widower would have caused no scandal by having an affair with a woman separated from her husband, Marie was reduced to wandering the streets 'like a beast being tracked', her reputation in tatters despite five duels being fought in her honour.

For both Marie and Langevin, their private lives were just that. Marie dismissed one of her critics with a smart, 'I believe there is no connection between my scientific work and the facts of private life', but mud sticks. The newspaper coverage of the rumours threatened to overshadow the next big news story about Marie Curie: her second Nobel Prize. A Nobel Prize has always been, was then, and remains, the ultimate accolade for a scientist. So to win two of them? Incredible!

The Nobel Prize in Chemistry was awarded in her name alone 'in recognition of her services in the advancement of chemistry by the discovery of the elements radium and polonium, by the isolation of radium and the study of the nature and compounds of this remarkable element'. She went to Stockholm to receive her prize. In this speech she did make reference to her husband but emphasised the differences between her work and his, dwelling on the discoveries she had made since his death.

At the end of 1911 she grew very ill and was forced to undergo an operation to remove lesions from her uterus and her kidney. Her recovery dragged on, but in 1913 she returned to her laboratory bench. She opened and headed a new research facility in Warsaw; her loyalty to the country of her birth had never waned. As she was setting up a second Institute in Paris, the First World War broke out. This extraordinary scientist found a way personally to put her discoveries to work in the field to help the hundreds of thousands of young men wounded in battle. She took on the responsibility of installing twenty X-ray vehicles at the front. And she was not afraid to get down into the mud and the blood of the field hospitals. She operated and repaired the machines, and brought comfort to the patients and expertise to the medical staff grappling with the terrible injuries sustained in the trenches.

A trip to America in 1921 saw the first attempts to romanticise the story of the woman who was, above all else, a committed scientist. An American journalist, Missy Maloney, spotted a good tale when she discovered the Curies had never patented the process for purifying radium; instead it had been taken up commercially by other scientists and chemical companies for cancer treatments and military research. They were not the only great inventors to fail to patent their work. Jonas Salk, who discovered the polio vaccine, was asked to whom his patent would belong. 'Well, the people, I would say. There is no patent. Would you patent the sun?' I suspect the Curies may have had a similar attitude.

Radium was selling for $100,000 a gram. Maloney started the Marie Curie Radium Fund to raise money to purchase radium for Marie's continued research. The stories about her visit to America to collect the radium were headed 'That Millions Shall Not Die' or 'the Jeanne d'Arc of the laboratory'. Marie hated the publicity and was always at pains to point out that her work was 'pure science ... done for itself ... rather than with direct usefulness in mind'. She returned to Paris with her gram of radium, which had been presented to her by President Harding at the White House, and got on with her research, opening, with her sister, the Marie Skłodowska Curie Oncology Centre, which still exists today.

Marie became a fellow of the French Academy of Medicine, as well as a member of the International Commission for Intellectual Cooperation of the League of Nations. She worked in her laboratory until her death in 1934 at the age of sixty-six. She had developed aplastic anaemia, as a result of her prolonged exposure to radiation. In 1995 her ashes were enshrined in the Pantheon in Paris. She was the first woman to be honoured at the memorial dedicated to the 'great men' of France.

After her death the image popularised by Missy Maloney, of the 'modest self-effacing woman who . . . embodied in her person all the simpler, homelier and yet most perfect virtues of woman-hood' began to take hold. The portrayal of her in books and films, notably MGM's 1943 *Madame Curie*, emphasises the devoted wife, mother and humanitarian. We can, at last, give her the credit that is her due. She was a brilliant scientist, utterly devoted to her work who made sure she had good childcare to enable her to get on with her job.

Neither of her two daughters suffered in any way from their mother's single-mindedness. Ève became a journalist, and wrote the definitive biography of her mother, *Madame Curie*, published in 1937. Irène qualified as a scientist and, with her husband, Frédéric Joliot-Curie, her mother's former assistant, won the Nobel Prize for synthesising new radioactive elements. It was the first time a parent and child had won the Nobel Prize on separate occasions.

Not only did Marie Curie lead the way in the new science that has had so much impact on the twentieth and twenty-first centuries, but she made it possible for any girl who sees science as her life's ambition to say, 'If Marie Curie could do it, so could I.' She had no wealth or class advantage behind her, and she worked at a time when it was considered impossible for a woman to have a husband, children *and* an utterly absorbing job. She did it and the patriarchy had to admit, finally, that a woman, like a man, can indeed have it all.

9

Coco Chanel

1883-1971

I guess we tend to associate Chanel with the very highest end of the fashion scene. She's the ultimate in Parisian *haute couture*. She's the woman who created some of the most exquisite and expensive garments ever worn. She gave us the most hankered-after perfume in the world, Chanel No. 5, and even her handbags would bankrupt the majority of us. The most famous garment that carried her label was that worn by the fashion icon of the early 60s, Jacqueline Kennedy: the rose-pink Chanel suit she was wearing as she cradled the head of her husband, President Jack Kennedy, as he lay dying after being shot in Dallas in 1963.

But Chanel's influence has spread far and wide. Even though you may not be aware of it, for those of us who like our clothes to be comfortable, sporty or made from soft, easy-care fabrics, it was Chanel who made this possible. I honestly can't remember the last time I wore a skirt, and for the permission to abandon what for so long was required clothing for women I have to thank Coco Chanel. Then there's the little black dress. She introduced it, saying: 'I imposed black. It's still going strong today, for black wipes out everything else around.'

Thanks to her, every woman knows that black hides a multitude of sins as it skims the figure and slims you down. But it was the trousers that scandalised the world when she introduced them in the 1920s as leisure wear as she relaxed on the Riviera or, a little later, when she joined the English aristocracy, including Winston Churchill, for their countryside pursuits. Even in my lifetime, even around the time of Chanel's death in the early 1970s, trousers on a woman were considered rather shocking. And jersey as a material? Oh dear! Weren't women supposed to wear silks and satins? But for Chanel, easy-to-wear comfort went hand in hand with chic.

There's a well-known story of a young studio manager who turned up at Broadcasting House around 1972 wearing trousers, a tunic that ended just above her knees and a white polo-neck sweater. In the lift she was berated by her line manager, who told her women were not allowed to wear trousers at the BBC unless they worked in the Arab Service. The offending young woman promptly whipped off the trousers right in front of him – she told me the boss clearly had no objection to her wearing the tunic as a mini skirt. So, even in the 1970s a woman wearing trousers had the power to shock – and the story illustrates how important Chanel has been to the way we look now. In a photograph taken in 1930, she's sporting a short, slick haircut and wearing loose, soft trousers, a striped sailor's Breton shirt and a buckled belt, her hands tucked into pockets at the front of her trousers. It could be a picture of any young woman today. As Chanel said herself, 'Fashion passes, style remains.'

Chanel's early life is somewhat sketchy. She kept it shrouded in secrecy and lies and often told different stories about her background to different people. Not long before her death she told a friend, Claude Delay, 'People's lives are an enigma . . . I don't like the family. I don't know anything more terrifying than the family.' It is known that she was born on 19 August 1883 in the poorhouse in Saumur in the Loire Valley. She was the second daughter of Eugénie Jeanne Devolle and Albert Chanel. Her parents were not married.

The name on her birth certificate is Gabrielle Chasnel. Her surname was misspelt, probably because her mother was too ill to attend the registration of her birth and her father was simply not around. He is described on the certificate as 'travelling'. She was named after a nun at the hospital, Gabrielle Bonheur, who became her godmother. According to Chanel, she was baptised Gabrielle Bonheur Chanel.

There are doubts about the origin of the nickname Coco. She invented the story that her father didn't like Gabrielle and said, 'My father used to call me Little Coco until something better should come along.' It's more likely that she picked the name herself much later, from a popular ditty she sang during the short period when she worked as a cabaret singer.

She was often evasive about her past, telling Delay that the house she grew up in was large enough for the five children to live separately from their sick mother. Not so: they were, in fact, all crowded with her in one room in the railway town of Brive-la-Gaillarde, on the main line from Paris to Toulouse.

When she was around twelve years old her mother died. Chanel claimed her mother had tuberculosis. Justine Picardie believes it was a combination of poverty, pregnancy and pneumonia. What is certain is that her father was not prepared to take responsibility for the care of his children. He abandoned the boys with a peasant family and the three girls were left in an orphanage run by nuns in the Aubazine Abbey in Corrèze in Limousin.

There were no luxuries or creature comforts in this orphanage, and the rules were strict and strictly enforced. However, the place had a profound impact on Chanel's sense of style. The village of Aubazine is medieval and the abbey buildings are exquisite, with pure architectural lines and stone walls. Chanel learned to sew during the six years she spent there and the elegance of the simple fabrics and the colours of black, beige and white worn by the nuns would become her signature style as she developed her talent as a dress designer. There are intertwining letter C's on the abbey's stained-glass windows. It would become her logo.

Chanel lived at the abbey until she was eighteen, as did her sisters. Only girls who had a religious vocation were allowed to stay beyond that age, so Gabrielle was sent to the Notre Dame School in Moulins. It too was a religious institution, where her Aunt Adrienne was already being taught. Adrienne was only a year older than Gabrielle; the two young women became friends and were given more instruction in how to sew. The Mother Superior at Notre Dame found them jobs as shop assistants and seamstresses in a draper's shop on the rue de l'Horloge, popular for its wedding trousseaux, layettes for new-born babies and funeral outfits for the local gentry.

Adrienne and Gabrielle shared an attic bedroom above the shop and took in sewing at the weekends, altering trousers for cavalry officers for a local tailor. Two attractive young women were bound to attract the attention of their virile young customers. They soon found themselves invited to La Rotonde, a pavilion in the park in Moulins where audiences from the barracks drank and listened to concerts in the style of the music hall. Gabrielle decided to become a singer and found herself a regular slot. She did not have an extensive repertoire, just two songs. One was 'Ko Ko Ri Ko' and the other 'Qui qu'a vu Coco', about a girl who lost her dog. She was popular with the audience, who would call out 'Ko Ko Ri Ko' (cock a doodle do) or 'Coco'. My suspicion is the name Coco Chanel originated there and just stuck.

Chanel often denied that this musical performance part of her life had ever happened, and joked about the rumours of her humble origins, saying: 'My legend is based upon two indestructible pillars: the first is that I have come up from goodness knows where; from the music hall, the opera or the brothel; I'm sorry, for that would have been more amusing.' It was, though, in this period that she met a cavalry officer, Étienne Balsan, who became her lover. She lived with him at Royallieu, a former abbey in

Compiègne, where he kept a racing stable, and she made hats for his wealthy friends. He introduced her to a luxurious lifestyle and, while he may have been something of a roué, he proved a useful stepping stone from small-town life to Paris and the Belle Époque. The two remained friends until his death in 1953. He never married, and was always loyal to Chanel, never answering questions about their life together.

During her time at Royallieu Coco met Arthur Capel, known as Boy, said to have been the love of her life. He was wealthy, an accomplished polo player and shared with Étienne a fondness for fast horses and women. For some time, Coco entertained both men; the arrangement seemed quite amicable, with no obvious animosity between the two men while Coco sat pretty between them.

In 1909, when Chanel was twenty-six, she said she'd had enough of being piggy in the middle, decided Boy was the one with whom she was in love and determined to leave Étienne. She sent him a letter: 'My dear Étienne, I shall never be able to repay the kindness and comfort you have given me while I have been with you.' She followed Boy to Paris; three days later Étienne, uninvited, followed them. Years later, she admitted that she had eventually agreed to carry on seeing both of them and that Étienne had always declared his love for her. She claimed it was all rather torrid: 'We lunched and dined together, Étienne, Boy and I. Occasionally Étienne talked about killing himself and I wept. I wept so! You aren't going to let Étienne kill himself, I said to myself. You'll set them both free! Go throw yourself in the Seine.'

Neither Coco nor Étienne decided to throw themselves in the Seine. Instead Boy and Étienne discussed how they would split the financial responsibility of Coco between them. Eventually they agreed to share the cost of setting her up in business as a milliner. It was quite a leap for a young designer to go from creating hats for women in the countryside of Compiègne to setting up a boutique in the fashion capital of the world. How would the wealthy women of the Champs Élysées, used to the elaborate fashion of the Belle Époque, with its fine tailoring, corsets, tiny waists, elaborate embroidery, frills and furbelows, high necks, full long skirts and huge hats dripping with ostrich feathers, respond to this young upstart and her simple styles?

Her backers had every confidence in her ability to take Paris by storm. Étienne came up with the premises in Rue Cambon and Boy covered the running costs. Chanel was not afraid to turn the fashion world upside down, describing the big fancy hats of the period as weighing a woman down and being too cumbersome to let her think straight. Sometimes her designs were boyish Chanel originals, sometimes little straw boaters bought at Galeries Lafayette and decorated with ribbon or a few flowers. Soon she began to develop cheeky little styles with a rim cutely turned up above one eye, or the cloche, pulled down firmly on the head. She liked to dress herself in the style of a boy or a schoolgirl, saying 'Nothing makes a woman look older than obvious expensiveness, ornateness, complication.' Parisian actresses loved her work and where they led, others followed.

As Coco was beginning to establish herself as a milliner, she took on the responsibility of her six-year-old nephew, André Palasse. After the Chanel girls left the convent at Aubazine, Julia, the eldest of the three, became pregnant, never revealing the name of the man responsible. The boy's birth certificate registers him as André Palasse, but the surname could have been that of a boyfriend to whom she had not confessed or possibly a complete invention. It meant that, when Julia died at the age of 30 when her son was only six, he was an orphan. No father came forward to claim him.

Chanel rarely referred to her big sister and when she did the stories were often contradictory. Sometimes she would say Julia had loved the convent and been devoted to the religious life. At other times she would invent a husband and say her sister had loved him very much but had killed herself by slitting her wrists when she discovered he had a mistress. Whatever the truth of André's birth, Chanel, who was 29 when her sister died, took him on and brought him up as her own, leading to a lot of speculation as to whether the boy was Julia's or Gabrielle's. Coco ignored the gossip and became a devoted aunt. She paid for André's care and education at an English boarding school but didn't take him with her to her life in Paris.

There, she was going from strength to strength. Paul Poiret, who called himself the 'King of Fashion', said of her early days as a milliner, 'We ought to have been on guard against that boyish head. It was going to give us every kind of shock, and produce, out of its little conjurer's hat, gowns and coiffures and jewels and boutiques.' Chanel's business was growing, extending to clothes as well as hats. More boutiques were opened in Deauville and Biarritz, the most fashionable seaside towns of the period, where British royalty and French aristocracy enjoyed the sun and the sea air. For Chanel, work became her most pleasurable activity, rather than the racy lifestyle she'd enjoyed with her two playboys. She was not only a designer and a seamstress but also a businesswoman.

Her financial dependence irritated her. She was distressed to discover that Capel had deposited bank securities to guarantee her overdrafts. She wasn't, she realised, making the profits she thought she was. The following morning she went to the shop and told her head seamstress, 'I am not here to have fun or to spend money like water. I am here to make a fortune.' And make a fortune she did. Within a year she was earning enough to be independent from her benefactors. Her clothes, designed to be worn without corsets, were a huge hit. 'I was my own master, I depended upon myself alone', she said. 'Boy Capel was well aware that he didn't control me: "I thought I'd given you a plaything. I gave you freedom", he once said to me in a melancholy voice.'

We now take it for granted that a woman is perfectly capable of running her own successful business and there's continual growth in the number of female entrepreneurs in everything from beauty products, to fashion, technology and engineering. In Chanel's day there were very few women who could deal with both the creative side and the money side of their work. Veuve Cliquot had done pretty well in the champagne business but, as the name of her product suggests, she had taken over an established enterprise when she was widowed. Anita Roddick, who founded the Body Shop, told me that even in the 1960s, the bank manager wouldn't talk to her without her husband being present. Similarly, Stephanie Shirley, who set up her own software company in 1959, called herself Steve to get over the problem of appointments being refused if she presented herself as Stephanie. At the beginning of the twentieth century Coco Chanel and Elizabeth Arden were pioneers, who went it alone and made millions.

The relationship with Boy remained close until the end of the war in 1918. So close, it's thought the double C in the Chanel logo is not only for Coco and Chanel, but for Chanel and Capel: overlapping but facing away from each other. It didn't even end when Boy succeeded in his hunt for a suitable English aristocratic heiress and Diana Wyndham became his wife. Chanel responded to his admiration for the flat chest, no hips and short hair she thought typical of the beautiful aristocrat by perfecting the look for herself. But the final flourish came about by accident.

She had been invited to the opera. She had a white dress made, and wore her long hair tied up around her head. Just before leaving her flat, Chanel went into the bathroom to wash her hands. The gas burner exploded. Her white dress was covered in soot, her hair was burned and her face filthy. She washed her face, cut her hair short and changed her dress. 'I slipped on a black dress I had, crossed over in front – what a marvellous thing, youth – and caught in at the waist with a sort of minaret on top.' At the opera everyone was looking at the girl with the boyish hair and the little black dress.

In 1919 Boy Capel died, in a car accident. Twenty-five years after Boy's demise Chanel told the novelist Paul Morand: 'His death was a terrible blow to me. In losing Capel, I lost everything. What followed was not a life of happiness, I have to say.'

But the business continued to flourish. She moved her establishment in Paris from 21 to 31 rue Cambon and became a registered *couturière*. She was the toast of the city, and got to know everyone who was anyone in the capital's *avant garde*, at one of the most important and exciting periods in the artistic world of the city. She met the composer Igor Stravinsky (with whom it's believed she had an affair), knew Diaghilev, the impresario of the Ballets Russes, and acted as guarantor against financial loss when the project on which the two men had collaborated, *The Rite of Spring*, was first performed. It was just as well she came up with the cash. The ballet provoked a near-riot at its first performance in 1913. The *New York Times* reported that 'Parisians Hiss New Ballet'. It's now, of course, considered one of the great works of the twentieth century but it was a disaster when it burst on the scene. Chanel worked with the Ballets Russes for some years, designing costumes and working closely with composers such as Milhaud, writers such as Cocteau and great artists such as Picasso.

I doubt very many of us have ever been able to afford to wear Chanel unless we've splashed out on a pair of sunglasses, but I don't think there are many women in the world who haven't owned or longed for her most famous item; the perfume Chanel No. 5, first created in 1921. Marilyn Monroe famously endorsed the scent. 'You know, they ask me questions. Just an example: "What do you wear in bed? A pyjama top? The bottoms of the pyjamas? A nightgown?" So I said, "Chanel No. 5," because it's the truth . . . And yet I don't want to say "nude". But it's the truth!' When asked by a young woman where one should use perfume, Chanel said: 'Wherever one wants to be kissed'.

Throughout the late 1920s and 1930s there were more lovers, including the Duke of Westminster, the richest man in England.

Her frequent trips to Scotland with him brought tweed into her designs and lots of wealthy clients and influential friends, including Winston Churchill, to her door. By 1935 she had built a hugely lucrative enterprise employing 4,000 people, with five boutiques in rue Cambon. At the beginning of the Second World War she closed her shops, apart from the perfume boutique, which continued to be profitable as soldiers bought her famous scents to take back home. Nearly all her female employees lost their jobs. She kept her flat above the boutique, but spent most of the occupation living in the Ritz.

During the war she began an affair with a German officer, Baron Günther von Dincklage. He was a charming, handsome man, but inevitably Chanel was suspected of collaboration and even of acting as a Nazi spy. She was named as a suspect by the Prefecture of Police and was interrogated by the Free French Purge Committee but no documentary evidence suggested collaboration, so she was released.

Some have claimed that Churchill intervened on her behalf, thinking that, if she were forced to testify, she might reveal the pro-Nazi sympathies of some leading British officials and members of the royal family. What seems more likely to me is that Chanel was one of many thousands of French women who had affairs with German soldiers during the war. He was handsome, she was rich, and she didn't have a lot to do while Paris was occupied. They continued their relationship for some time, in Lausanne, after the war. (Chanel disappeared to Switzerland for a while following the allegations of collaboration.) In 1954 she came back to Paris, reopened her boutiques, launched a new collection and became the fashion icon her house continues to be.

Of her many relationships with men she once said:

It's probably not just by chance that I'm alone. It would be very hard for a man to live with me, unless he's terribly strong. And if he's stronger than I, I'm the one that can't live with him . . . I'm neither smart nor stupid, but I don't think I'm a run-of-the-mill person. I've been in business without being a businesswoman, I've loved without being a woman made only for love. The two men I've loved, I think will remember me, on earth or in heaven, because men always remember women who caused them concern and uneasiness. I've done my best, in regard to people and to life, without precepts, but with a taste for justice.

She died in the Ritz in January 1971, at the age of eighty-seven. That day she had gone through the motions of preparing the catalogue for her spring collection and gone to bed early after a long drive. She died in her sleep.

The funeral was pure Chanel. The front seats were occupied by her models and the coffin was covered with orchids, camellias, gardenias, azaleas and a few red roses. Her exit was exactly what she had said a girl should be: 'classy and fabulous'.

She truly created a fashion revolution, which contributed so much to the liberation of women from corsetry, voluminous skirts and tight, figure-hugging shapes. Thanks to her we can wear soft, malleable fabrics such as jersey, simple styles that are easy to wear and, of course, trousers, borrowing from the vocabulary of sportswear and menswear to create elegance and comfort for women. Her legacy is continued by designers such as Mary Quant, Barbara Hulanicki, Sonia Rykiel, Katherine Hamnett, Donna Karan and Stella McCartney. After Chanel no woman ever again wanted to be restricted by what she wore. We wanted to be able to move!

10

Golda Meir

1898–1978

I think it was Golda Meir who made me realise that, in the twentieth century, it was possible for a woman who had not inherited her role from her father or her husband to lead her country. She was not the first female leader. That was Sirimavo Bandaranaike of Ceylon, now Sri Lanka, of whom more later. For Meir the moment came when her nation, Israel, was in the midst of armed conflict and under the constant threat of terrorism. She was seen to manage her *macho* cabinet with aplomb and go on to sue for peace. Meir was doubly impressive because she had made it to the premiership entirely on her own merit, whereas Bandaranaike had taken over from her husband after he was assassinated.

I had gone to Israel as part of my year out between my second and third years at university. I lived there for six months. It was 1970, two years after the Six Day War, a year after she became Prime Minister, three years before the Yom Kippur War and four years before she resigned her premiership in 1974.

It was the period when second-wave feminism was beginning to take hold. The Miss America pageant in 1968 had seen protests from the Women's Liberation Movement. High-heeled shoes, bras, pots and pans were thrown into rubbish bins. Books such as Germaine Greer's *The Female Eunuch* were published and widely read, and Golda Meir became something of a poster girl for Women's Liberation. A picture of her, dressed in a smart black suit, with no adornment apart from a brooch, no make-up and no fancy hairstyle, was widely circulated. The ironic caption asked, 'But can she type?'

She was not, though, a keen follower of feminist politics. 'Women's liberation', she said, 'is just a lot of foolishness. It's men who are discriminated against. They can't bear children. And no one is likely to do anything about that!'

Her attitude to make-up and the fripperies of femininity was consistently dismissive. A CBS make-up artist, preparing her for a *Face the Nation* appearance on television in the early 1970s, asked Golda if, after she'd tidied her hair, she wanted make-up. 'No', said Golda, 'I'm a realist.' She was grateful for her looks. 'Not being beautiful was the true blessing. Not being beautiful forced me to develop my inner resources. The pretty girl has a handicap to overcome.'

Meir seemed to share a pragmatic attitude to the 'woman' question with Britain's 'Iron Lady', Margaret Thatcher. The two met in 1976, when Thatcher was leader of the Conservatives, before she became Prime Minister in 1979. Thatcher was asked if she had learned anything about being a female Prime Minister from Mrs Meir. 'No', snapped Thatcher, 'We had much more important things to discuss.' Meir consistently refused to be defined by her sex. When she was asked how it felt to be the only female foreign minister in the world, she would always say, 'I don't know, I was never a man.'

President Nixon said of Meir that, while Indira Gandhi acted like a man, with the ruthlessness of a man, but wanted always to be treated like a woman, Golda 'acted like a man and wanted to be treated like a man'. Meir was dismissive, though, of the rumour that Ben-Gurion, the first Prime Minister of Israel, had described her as 'the only man in his cabinet':

What amused me is that he (or whoever invented the story) thought that this was the greatest possible compliment that could be paid to a woman. I very much doubt that any man would have been flattered if I had said about him that he was the only woman in the government!

It's a bit depressing, isn't it, that even from these earliest examples of women who've taken power in global politics, right through to the current ones, it's still their sex, their handbags, their hair, their shoes, and their femininity or otherwise, that make the headlines. Maybe one day it'll be their intellect, their experience and their capabilities that will be the only topics for analysis of how suited they are to their role, just as it is for a man!

Golda Meir was born Golda Mabovitch on 3 May 1898, in Kiev in the Ukraine. Her father was a cabinet maker and, as a skilled craftsman, was allowed to live outside the Jewish ghetto. Anti-Semitism was a terrible fact of life, and the young Golda grew up under the shadow of pogroms; she consequently harboured a lifelong distrust of Russians. In her autobiography, *My Life*, she wrote:

I must have been very young, maybe only three and a half or four. We lived then on the first floor of a small house in Kiev, and I can still recall distinctly hearing about a pogrom that was to descend upon us. I didn't know then, of course, what a pogrom was, but I knew it had something to do with being Jewish and with the rabble that used to surge through town, brandishing knives and huge sticks, screaming 'Christ killers' as they looked for the Jews, and who were now going to do terrible things to me and to my family.

That pogrom never materialised, but to this day I remember how scared I was and how angry that all my father could do to protect me was nail a few planks together while we waited for the hooligans to come. And above all,

I remember being aware that this was happening to me because I was Jewish.

When she was asked during her tenure as Prime Minister of Israel how she had avoided direct contact with a pogrom as a child she said, 'Because my father and mother decided to get out'. It was, then, from her early childhood, that her understanding of anti-Semitism and deep commitment to the Zionist project – creating a homeland for the Jews – was formed.

The Mabovitch family moved to the city of Pinsk in Belarus, to be with her mother's family, when Golda was five. Soon after, her father emigrated to the United States alone to try and find work in New York. The time spent in Pinsk was terrifying for the family because, as she explained in an article in *Time* magazine, she witnessed mounted Cossacks jumping over Jewish children for sport and policemen beating anyone thought to be a Jewish socialist. Golda was not personally caught up in the Cossack activities, but she said her elder sister Sheyna was, as she was a staunch socialist. Nevertheless, Golda had witnessed enough anti-Semitism, even as a young child, to understand what Zionism meant to the Jewish people.

Eventually her father moved from New York to Milwaukee and found a job in the workshop of a railway yard. In 1906 he was established enough to bring his family to join him in the States. In only a few months, Golda mastered enough English to keep up with her studies by the time the school term began in September. After school she worked in the shop her mother ran, where they sold milk, cheese and butter, although her sister, Sheyna, refused to work in the shop because, she said, the capital-ist ethos clashed with her socialist principles.

Golda worked hard and was a good student. She attended a Talmud Torah school, which offered a secular and orthodox reli-gious education. She learned some Hebrew, although Yiddish was spoken at home. Both her parents became active in the

Zionist movement. They were members of B'nai B'rith, known as 'the Global Voice of the Jewish Community', an organisation that set out in the mid-nineteenth century to ensure the security and continuity of the Jewish people, combat anti-Semitism and bigotry and press for the creation of the State of Israel. Her father was also active in the American Jewish congress. When Golda was twelve she took on the family tradition of working at some form of social service. Her contribution was organising books for children whose parents couldn't afford to buy them.

During her early teenage years she decided she wanted to become a teacher, an ambition that was not supported by her parents, particularly her mother. The law in Wisconsin at the time banned marriage for anyone in the teaching profession. Mrs Mabovitch was doubly appalled. She was terrified her daughter would become an old maid and also disapproved of the mere idea of education for girls. Only men, she thought, should be educated and women should fulfil their roles as wives and mothers.

Golda profoundly disagreed. At the age of fourteen, she lowered a bundle of possessions out of her window to a friend and fled her parents' home. She went to live with her sister Sheyna, who was now married with children and established in Denver. It was there that Golda met Morris Myerson, a young man who quickly proposed marriage. Morris was an internationalist, a pacifist and a sign painter by profession. He was no match for the determined Golda, who by that time had stormed out of her sister's home in a huff at some slight to her independence; she left with nothing more than the clothes on her back. She agreed to become engaged to Morris only on condition that he would accompany her to Palestine.

She was nineteen when the two were wed in 1917. It was the year when the Balfour Declaration established that the British had accepted the principle of a Jewish National Home in Palestine and the year in which Ben-Gurion, the first Prime Minister of Israel, and Yitzhak Ben-Zvi, who would become the country's second and longest-serving President, visited Milwaukee, where Golda was studying at a teacher training college. She described the effect of that visit on her in an interview with the *Observer* in 1971:

> They came to America to urge young American Jews to go to Palestine and work on the collective farms – a call back to the land in both senses – and to build a labour-Jewish state. We heard their call of 'back to the soil' against the background of accounts pouring in about what millions of Jews were suffering in Europe from Austrian and Russian armies. I decided to go as soon as I could raise the money. Morris was dead against it, but he wanted to marry me. I told him that if he wanted me he had to come to Palestine. To be perfectly honest, if he could have had me without Palestine he would have been happier. But he couldn't, so he came.

In 1921 the couple sailed on a ship called the *Pocahontas*. It was not an untroubled trip. A passenger died, the ship's engineer was murdered, its engine and boilers were sabotaged by strikers, mutineers were clapped in irons, the engine room was flooded and supplies destroyed. After fifty-two days, they arrived in Palestine and settled in Kibbutz Merhavia, said, at the time, to be nothing more than a malarial swamp. Mrs Myerson, as she was then known, loved the communal, agricultural life of the kibbutz, but her husband hated it and they left after two years, to spend the next five years first in Tel Aviv and then in Jerusalem.

Golda ended her first pregnancy with a dangerous, illegal and expensive abortion. Her sister Sheyna was horrified to hear she had terminated the pregnancy because she was too busy looking forward to pioneering in Palestine to take care of a child. Sheyna berated her younger sister: 'Don't you know that your activities in comparison to motherhood are not worthwhile to speak about?

The woman that bears children and tries to bring them up properly does more towards humanity than you with your activities.' Golda did eventually give birth to two children, Menachem and Sarah, in Jerusalem, but it was already clear that the marriage was failing.

Nevertheless, the 'activities' were what drove Golda Meyerson forward. By 1928 she had shortened the family name, knocking off the 'son' part and spelling it Meir, and taken on her first public post as secretary of the Women's Labour Council. She was soon elected to the executive committee of the Histadrut, the General Federation of Jewish Labour. Throughout the 1930s and early 1940s she worked on health policy, trades union and labour relations and forged friendships and, at times, romantic relationships with the colleagues who, some forty years later, supported her rise to the premiership. Work was more important than family; Golda and her husband separated in the early 1930s. Morris returned to the United States and the single mother was briefly left in poverty even more crushing than that of her Russian childhood.

Late in 1940 she became chief of the political section of Histadrut and began to juggle the complex role of a Jewish official who had to co-operate with the officials of the British Mandate in Palestine while fighting its policy of restricting Jewish immigration. Thousands were trying to escape Europe and the Holocaust. In June 1946 the British arrested all the Jewish leaders in Palestine who had protested against the British Foreign Secretary, Ernest Bevin's, refusal to allow 100,000 Jews a month to enter Palestine, a recommendation made by the Anglo-American Commission of Enquiry. This was a moment that thrust Golda into a leadership position, as she was the only prominent Jew to remain at large. 'The British did not put me behind bars because I was a woman', she told the *Observer*, 'I was very annoyed . . . I was appointed acting head of the political department of the Jewish Agency – the body which officially represented and administered the Jews under the British regime.'

She remained chief of the agency when her predecessor was sent to the United Nations to lobby for the creation of the State of Israel. Although not a soldier, she was on the Haganah committee that led the resistance against the British. Between November 1947 and 14 May 1948, the day the state of Israel was established, she went twice at night, dressed as an Arab woman, to secret meetings with King Abdullah of Transjordan, in the hope of negotiating a peaceful transition from Palestine to Israel. She failed; Abdullah joined with the rest of the Arab world to wage war on the newly created state of Israel.

Golda was sent to America to raise money for arms and returned with pledges for $50 million, more than twice the amount anyone believed she could get. The Prime Minister, Ben-Gurion said of her, 'Some day when history will be written, it will be said that there was a Jewish woman who got the money which made the state possible.' The war was fought and won. Golda would say, of the hard, prolonged battles:

> We owe a responsibility not only to those who are in Israel but also to those generations that are no more, to those millions who have died within our lifetime, to Jews all over the world, and to generations of Jews to come. We do not rejoice in victories. We rejoice when a new kind of cotton is grown and when strawberries bloom in Israel.

This confirmed and passionate Zionist expressed little sympathy for the Palestinians, who had lost their homeland, staying to live as effectively second-class citizens or escaping to refugee camps in other parts of the Arab world. Of the Palestinians she said, throughout her political career, 'When peace comes we will perhaps in time be able to forgive the Arabs for killing our sons, but it will be harder for us to forgive them for having forced us to kill their sons . . . Peace will come when the Arabs will love their children more than they hate us.'

Soon after her return from America with the $50 million, she was sent to Stalin's Soviet Union as Israel's first Minister in Moscow. It could not have been a more difficult diplomatic job. Meir's memories of Russian anti-Semitism had rankled throughout her life. She had no Russian and it took her some time to recognise that Stalin's friendly approaches to the Jewish state and recognition of Israel were completely at odds with his view of any Soviet Jew who might be keen to emigrate to Israel. Russia's leader said Jews were thoroughly integrated in the Soviet Union. The 'active behaviour' of Russian Jews in their attempts to travel to Israel had, in Stalin's view, been encouraged by Golda. Her mission was not successful and throughout her political career very few visas were granted for Jews to leave Russia. The borders only opened under Mikhail Gorbachev in 1989.

In 1949 Mrs Meir became Minister of Labour in Israel's first cabinet, and had a hand in shaping every aspect of the new state, whether it be housing, jobs, social services, social security, pensions or maternity protection. Every so often she would have to take time out as she dealt with kidney stones, migraines, gruelling treatment for lymphoma, several assassination attempts and, in 1945, a near-fatal heart attack. Her doctor told her that her only chance of survival was to live a quiet rest-filled life, no more cigarettes and a lot less coffee. She continued to chain-smoke and always bounced back, ready for work.

Israel has periodically fought wars to ensure its survival. Conflict with the neighbouring states of Egypt, Jordan and Syria, known as the Six Day War, broke out in June 1967. Israel won a decisive victory and expanded her territory by occupying the Sinai Peninsula, the West Bank and the Golan Heights. The following year, 1969, when the Prime Minister, Levi Eshkol, died, Mrs Meir was invited to become Prime Minister. 'I, an old, weak woman – what are you talking about?' was her initial response, despite Eshkol mumbling on his death bed that the shrew was waiting for him to die. The polls had only 1% suggesting her as his successor, but who puts any trust in polls? At the age of seventy-one she took the job.

Life was never easy for the new premier. I remember during my time in Israel the fear of constant terror attacks. Indeed I narrowly missed a bomb in the Tel Aviv bus station. As my bus for Jaffa pulled away, the bomb exploded, shattering the windows. I had been on what I thought was a perfectly safe trip to the Arab market – the only place in Tel Aviv where you could buy bacon. It was a terrifying and shocking reminder of how randomly such incidents were occurring every day. None of us on the bus was injured apart from a few shards of broken class causing minor cuts but others were not so lucky. There were constant attacks on school buses and dozens of children died. Parents were invariably terrified as they sent their children off to their lessons. On both sides, Palestinian and Israeli, people lived with the daily fear that they or their children might be caught up in the violence.

Soon after my close encounter with a bomb, in 1972, the Prime Minister had to deal with the Munich Olympics massacre, when eleven Israeli athletes were murdered by the Palestinian terrorist group Black September. In response, she ordered the creation of an assassination team to hunt down and kill the perpetrators.

Then there was more war. On 6 October 1973, hoping to win back territory lost during the Six Day War, Egyptian and Syrian forces launched an attack on the holiest day in the Jewish calendar. When intelligence came through that showed suspicious movements of troops on the borders, Meir's gut instinct was to call up the reserves. She mistakenly allowed her instinct to be over-ruled by military men, including the forceful Defence Minister Moshe Dayan, who did not believe war could be imminent.

In the first week of October, when war seemed all but certain, she suppressed her instincts herself, deciding against the possibility of launching pre-emptive strikes against the massed Syrian and Egyptian forces. She was afraid the USA would consider Israel had initiated a regional war and potentially deny Meir's requests for vital military supplies. She said, of her lack of decision: 'I will never again be the person I was before the Yom Kippur war', although when her Defence Secretary suggested using nuclear weapons to prevent the country being over-run she firmly told him to 'forget it'.

Israel's victory came at the cost of heavy casualties and the Prime Minister was criticised for the government's lack of preparedness. She was exonerated by the inquiry into the war, described as acting 'fittingly, properly and wisely'. The American Secretary of State, Henry Kissinger, said of her: 'the lioness rallied herself for one more heroic effort to bring about an agreement with the hated Syrians'. Nevertheless, she felt it was time she resigned the premiership.

Although Egypt had suffered defeat, the initial Egyptian successes enhanced the reputation of Anwar Sadat, the Egyptian leader. At the end of the 1970s, Israel signed a peace treaty with Egypt and the Sinai was handed back. The West Bank and Gaza Strip have remained under military occupation ever since, although Meir had opposed their retention. She said: 'We don't want a million Arabs who don't want us.' She met King Hussein of Jordan several times in secret in the hope of reaching agreement over the West Bank and envisioned a union of Palestinian Arabs with Jordan. Thus, she bears no responsibility for the current battles over illegal settlements.

She lived to see the Nobel Peace Prize conferred on Sadat and the Israeli Prime Minister, Menachem Begin, for their efforts to negotiate the peace treaty between their two countries. At the time of her death in 1978, from liver failure resulting from lymphoma, Begin was in Oslo in Norway for the formal presentation.

The Zionism Meir embraced throughout her life is deeply controversial today, as the troubles between Palestinians and

Israelis continue to dominate the Middle East, but I have no doubt she died with the convictions from which she had never wavered. Meir lived through the agonies of the anti-Semitic pogroms of her youth, was part of the Jewish diaspora and watched millions of Jews being carried off and murdered in the concentration camps of the Holocaust. As we know today, politics is not free of anti-Semites even in a country as seemingly fair-minded as the UK. When she said, 'We Jews have a secret weapon in our struggle with the Arabs; we have no place to go', she spoke from bitter experience, and from her heart.

11

Frida Kahlo

1907–1954

I fell so in love with the work of the Mexican artist Frida Kahlo that I named one of my dogs after her. Well, there is an obvious connection. My Frida is a Chihuahua – also of Mexican extraction – and a very small one at that. When I first saw her, I was convinced I had seen the self-same dog in one of Frida Kahlo's paintings, *Itzcuintli Dog with Me*, painted around 1938. Those of us who surround ourselves with small animals are often accused of using them as child substitutes. I plead guilty, but only because my children are grown up and gone. For Frida I think the numerous paintings in which she painted herself with a dog, a monkey or a cat are precisely an expression of her longing to have a child to hold and to love. For her, sadly, the child never happened.

It turns out I was wrong about the breed. The dog in Frida's painting looks like a Chihuahua – tiny frame, long tail, pointed face and pricked up, alert ears – but, as the title of the painting might have suggested, if I'd been looking a little closer, it's a much rarer breed, a Xolo, a bald little creature, also of Mexican origin. So, I was on the right lines; there are a number of photographs of Frida, surrounded by what looks like a pack of the little dogs and another painting – *Self-Portrait with Small Monkey*, 1945 – where the dog sits in her lap and the wide-eyed monkey on her shoulder. I have no regrets about naming my Frida after her. I like to think she would approve.

Frida's significance as a painter has been summed up by two leading authorities. The Tate Modern Art Gallery in London described her as 'the most famous female artist in history'. Her husband, Diego Rivera, the artist she married, divorced and then married again, articulated perfectly why she is so important. He said she was 'the first woman in the history of art to treat, with absolute and uncompromising honesty, one might even say impassive cruelty, those general and specific themes which exclusively affect women'.

Just so. I doubt any artist has painted self-portraits that recount the story of their own difficult and damaged life as did Frida Kahlo's. In all her paintings of herself she is the delicate, beautiful woman with dark and elaborately decorated hair, the famous eyebrows that meet in the middle, the contrasting modes of dress, sometimes a masculine suit of shirt, jacket and trousers, sometimes a highly coloured traditional dress of Mexico, at times a simple white blouse and skirt and, most disturbingly, naked, in bed and in pain.

Frida was born Magdalena Carmen Frida Kahlo y Calderón in Coyoacán, Mexico on 6 July 1907. Her father was Guillermo Kahlo, a German-Mexican photographer; her mother, Matilde, was of Spanish descent. Three years later the Mexican Revolution began. For Frida's parents the revolution was a disaster. Her father's commissions from the Diaz government had made the Kahlos comfortably off, but the fall and exile of the dictator meant his work dried up and the family was forced to scrimp and save. Her mother was a fanatically religious woman who hired an alcoholic wet nurse to breastfeed Frida. She would paint that experience – a rare contemporary image of a woman breastfeeding – in *My Nurse and I* in 1937. It was, though, her father with whom Frida had a close relationship and it was presumably from him that she inherited her artistic talent and learned some of the tools of the artist's trade.

The tiny but chubby child grew to a mischievous, lively imp, but at the age of six she caught polio and had to spend nine months confined to her room. It was during this time that Frida invented an imaginary friend to keep her company, a companion who remained with her for much of her life. While there are theories that sensory deprivation can lead to great creativity, my suspicion is that her childhood experience of loneliness and pain, far from bringing her meditative relaxation as it is supposed to do, would have brought her anxiety, depression and possibly hallucinations. Much later in her life, in 1939, she painted the two friends as adults, their hearts exposed. The woman in white with the broken heart drips blood on to her skirt, the other holds her hand, and the two are tied by blood vessels. Both have the long skirts Frida usually wore to conceal her damaged leg. She called the painting *The Two Fridas*.

When she began to recover her father supervised a programme of physical exercise, recommended by her doctor, to strengthen her withered right limb. He encouraged her to play football, box, wrestle and swim, an unusual sporting regime for a girl. She wrote that she had enjoyed the activity, but friends were cruel, calling her 'Frida peg leg'. She said, 'The leg remained very thin. When I was seven I wore boots. In the beginning I supposed that the jokes did not injure me, but afterwards they did and, as time went on, more intensely.'

As Frida became a teenager, her father's influence stimulated his favourite daughter's intellectual curiosity. He loaned her books, introduced her to composers such as Beethoven and Strauss, and encouraged her to accompany him on photographic expeditions and help him with the fine brushwork needed to touch up the colour in the photos. There's no doubt that her artistic talent, like that of Artemisia Gentileschi, was fostered by her father.

In 1922, Frida joined the best school in Mexico, the National Preparatory School. She left behind village life in Coyoacán and found herself in the centre of Mexico City where modern Mexico was being invented; she was studying alongside the *crème de la crème* of Mexico's youth who would go on to become the country's leaders. It was during her time at the school, when she was fifteen, that she first came across the world-famous thirty-six-year-old Diego Rivera when he was painting a mural there. She spent three hours watching him paint. In his autobiography, *My Art, My Life*, he said of her:

> She had unusual dignity and self-assurance, and there was a strange fire in her eyes. Her beauty was that of a child, yet her breasts were well developed . . . When she left she said only 'Good night'. A year later I heard . . . her name was Frida Kahlo. But I had no idea that she would one day be my wife.

Of course Frida, who would go on to have a great many lovers, both women and men, had a boyfriend during this period. Alejandro Gómez Arias was a brilliant orator, an amusing storyteller, an erudite scholar and a good athlete. As far as his politics were concerned, he would often give speeches in school to encourage his fellow pupils to dedicate themselves to their nation's 'great destiny' in what he called 'my Mexico'. Frida began to associate herself so strongly with the Mexican Revolution that she claimed to have been born in 1910, when it began, rather than in 1907, her true birth date. Alejandro was handsome, charming and destined for great things. The two were very much in love and to most of their friends he was the perfect catch for beautiful, lively, politically engaged Frida. But Frida's parents were horrified at their daughter's passion for this young man and, as is so often the case for parents of a wayward teenage girl, did their best to ban the affair. Of course, Frida was not going to obey her mother and father. She was far too powerful a personality to play the obedient daughter and simply continued her great romance in secret.

All went well until 7 September 1925 when Frida was eighteen, the day after Mexico had celebrated the anniversary of its independence from Spain. Frida and Alejandro were travelling on a bus when it was hit by streetcar. Alejandro was thrown from the bus and suffered relatively minor injuries and scratches. Frida described what happened to her:

> It is a lie that one is aware of the crash, a lie that one cries. In me there were no tears. The crash bounced us forward and a handrail pierced me the way a sword pierces a bull. A man saw me having a tremendous haemorrhage. He carried me and put me on a billiard table until the Red Cross came for me.

Her rescuers found her naked – her clothes had been torn off in the accident – and, bizarrely, her body was covered in a golden powder that had been sprayed about during the crash.

She was taken to hospital, her condition so severe that the doctors didn't think they could save her. Her spinal column was broken in three places in her lower back. Her collarbone was broken, as were her third and fourth ribs. Her right leg, already withered by polio, had eleven fractures and her right foot was dislocated and crushed. Her left shoulder was out of its joint and her pelvis broken in three places. The steel handrail had skewered her body at the level of her abdomen, entering on the left side and emerging through her vagina. 'I lost my virginity', she said.

She left hospital a month after the accident and was taken home to her parents. Of her terrible pain: 'One must put up with it. I am beginning to grow accustomed to suffering . . . at the end of the day we can endure much more than we think we can.' Only three months after the accident she returned to Mexico City and took on part-time jobs to help the family finances and pay her medical bills. She and Alejandro drifted apart. But in the summer of 1926 she became too ill to care for herself and again went home to her family. There she made her first self-portrait and her first serious work of art. She's wearing a simple brown velvet wrap-over dress with an elaborately decorated collar. Her right hand is held across her left arm and her eyes look out seductively at the viewer. Sending it as a love token to Alejandro, she referred to it as 'Your Botticelli', though somewhat less poetically it was officially named *Self-Portrait in a Velvet Dress*.

After her polio her father had encouraged her to spend a lot of time doing physical activity and sport, which unquestionably helped to improve her mobility. For a child, her courage and determination had been quite remarkable but such physical effort was not possible given the severity of her injuries after the crash and she had to learn to be still. 'Without paying much attention', she said, 'I began to paint . . . I am not sick, I am broken. But I am happy to be alive as long as I can paint.' In a letter to the curator of a 1938 exhibition in New York she explained:

> I never thought of painting until 1926 when I was in bed on account of an automobile accident. I was bored as hell with a plaster cast so I decided to do something. I stoled [*sic*] from my father some oil paints, and my mother ordered for me a special easel because I couldn't sit down, and I started to paint.

Her correspondence with Alejandro continued throughout this period but eventually he was sent to Europe by his parents, apparently in an attempt to break the relationship with Frida. Obviously neither set of parents approved of the match. She continued to paint and recuperate to some degree and began to resume a more active life, although she was pretty constantly encased in various types of plaster casts to hold her broken body together. In 1927 she joined the Mexican Communist Party and by June 1928 her affair with Alejandro had fizzled out. And then came Diego Rivera.

There are lots of different stories about how the two finally got together but the most likely is the one told by Diego. He was painting a mural at the Ministry of Education when a girl called him down from his scaffolding to look at some of her own work. He confirmed she had talent and she invited him to her home to see more of her work. Her father warned him she was a devil. He said he knew, but was clearly attracted to her quick, unconventional mind and, of course, they shared their commitment to the cause of Communism. Of Diego, Frida said, '[he] showed me the revolutionary sense of life and the true sense of colour'.

In 1929 she and the world-famous muralist were married and became Frida and Diego, the Charles and Diana or Posh and Becks of their day. She was deliriously happy. Her parents were appalled at their daughter marrying an ugly, fat communist twice her age. It was, they said, 'like marriage between an elephant and a dove'. The post-nuptial party was quite an affair. Frida smoked a cigarette as the photos were taken and was reported to have downed tequila like a professional drinker. She described his behaviour: 'Diego went on such a terrifying drunken binge with tequila that he took out his pistol, he broke a man's little finger, and broke other things. Then we had a fight, and I left crying and went home. A few days went by and Diego came to get me and took me to his house at 104 Reforma.'

The drinking continued. Frida also became addicted to Demerol for her pain. I can't really imagine how she managed to function at all on the mix of pills and, apparently, a bottle of brandy every day. No wonder the marriage was volatile.

Frida laid down certain rules. She would keep her own name professionally, remaining Frida Kahlo rather than becoming Frida Rivera, as tradition would have expected, and she would stay financially independent of Diego by selling her work. Neither was remotely faithful. Diego continued his constant chasing of attractive women; at one stage he even had an affair with Frida's sister Cristina. In his autobiography he acknowledged the pain he had caused his young wife: 'If I loved a woman, the more I loved her, the more I wanted to hurt her. Frida was only the most obvious victim of this disgusting trait.'

Frida too had numerous affairs, with both men and women; Diego had no objection to the lesbian relationships but could never stand hearing about her heterosexual lovers. She apparently warned them all that their affairs must remain secret; Diego was capable of killing a rival because of his jealousy. Her most famous, and perhaps most curious, affair was with Leon Trotsky, whom she hosted at her home in Coyoacán in 1937 after he became a victim of Stalin's lust for power and was exiled from the Soviet Union. Strange that Frida was a fan of both Trotsky and Stalin. She was questioned by the police for twelve hours after Trotsky was assassinated by Ramón Mercader, who used an ice pick to smash Trotsky's skull. Frida knew the assassin but could throw no light on his motives.

Of her art, Frida said three concerns impelled her to paint: her 'vivid memory of her own blood flowing during her childhood accident; her thoughts about birth, death, and the "conducting threads" of life; and her desire to be a mother'. Frida's desire to be a mother was consistently thwarted. Her first pregnancy ended in abortion. She was unsure of Diego's commitment to becoming a father and she was afraid that she might pass on some genetic flaw, as her father had suffered from epilepsy, Then came the miscarriages and a degree of resignation to her fate. 'Since the accident changed my path and many other things, I was not permitted to fulfil the desires which the whole world considers normal.' To me there is no doubt that her desire for a child was genuine and not simply an attempt to fit the role expected of a woman. All the paintings into which she pours her affection into her animals are testament to her desire for a creature to love and care for.

So, why the termination? She was constantly conflicted. She longed to be a mother, but never stopped worrying about passing on imperfect genes to a child. As for Diego, she rightly assumed he was no model for devoted fatherhood:

> I do not think that Diego would be very interested in having a child since what preoccupies him most is his work and he is absolutely right. Children would take fourth place. From my point of view, I do not know whether it would be good or not to have a child, since Diego is continually travelling and for no reason would I want to leave him alone and stay behind in Mexico.

She travelled with him to San Francisco, and then to Detroit in 1932. It was there she painted her most moving work, *Henry Ford Hospital*, where she had had her first miscarriage. Diego, for his all his crass infidelities and appalling behaviour, was spot on when it came to the appreciation of her work and her need to express herself on the canvas:

> Frida began work on a series of masterpieces which had no precedent in the history of art – paintings which exalted the feminine qualities of endurance of truth, reality, cruelty, and suffering. Never before had a woman put such agonized poetry on canvas as Frida did at this time in Detroit.

The painting shows Frida naked in a hospital bed, blood pouring from between her legs on to the white sheets. Blood vessels connect her to a floating foetus, a broken pelvis, a snail, a salmon-pink torso on a pedestal with several sperm-like organisms. Her work is often described as surrealist, of which she said, 'They thought I was a Surrealist, but I wasn't. I never painted dreams. I painted my own reality.'

Her marriage to Diego lasted until her death in 1954, apart from a short hiatus between 1939 and 1940 when the couple divorced and then remarried. In *My Art, My Life*, Diego wrote:

> We still loved each other. I simply wanted to be free to carry on with any woman who caught my fancy. Yet Frida did not object to my infidelity as such. What she could not understand was my choosing women who were either unworthy of me or inferior to her . . . wasn't it merely a consoling lie to think that a divorce would put an end to Frida's suffering? During the two years we lived apart, Frida turned out some of her best work, sublimating her anguish in her painting.

It's true, it was during this time that she painted *The Suicide of Dorothy Hale*, a friend who had thrown herself from a high-rise building, *The Two Fridas* and, soon after the couple remarried, *The Broken Column*, depicting her unsuccessful surgery to straighten her spine. Her views on Diego and their marriage were wildly at variance. He was 'My Diego, my love of thousands of years' or 'There have been two great accidents in my life. One was the trolley, and the other was Diego. Diego was by far the worst.'

Frida died in her bed at home in 1954, officially from a pulmonary embolism, although no post mortem was carried out and suicide has been suspected; she had said in her diary 'I hope the exit is joyful – and I hope never to come back.' Diego managed to make her funeral sound suitably dramatic. 'At the moment when Frida entered the furnace, the intense heat made her sit up, and her blazing hair stood out from her face in an aureole . . . her face appeared as if smiling in the center of a large sunflower.'

Frida has become something of a star in the twenty-first century. Mattel have made her a Barbie doll and the British Prime Minister, Theresa May, wore a Frida Kahlo bracelet during a key conference speech (the infamous occasion when she suffered a terrible coughing fit). I find the combination of a Conservative politician and an avowed communist rather odd, and I dislike a great artist becoming such a commodity. One of the best testaments for Frida's art and her passion for Mexico comes from a group of fifty artists in a 'Day of the Dead' homage: 'Frida was portrayed as political heroine and revolutionary fighter, as suffering female, mistreated wife, childless woman and "Mexican Ophelia".' But one of the artists got to the bottom of her genius: 'Frida embodied the whole notion of culture for Chicano women. She inspired us. Her works didn't have self-pity, they had strength.'

The fact that Frida is a hero for Mexican women does not explain, though, why I felt a passionate connection with her when I first stood in front of an exhibition of her work at the Manchester Art Gallery and was simply blown away. I doubt there's a woman the world over who would not see some of her own life up there on the wall. It is tragically rare to see the universal experience of women included in any cultural conversation. Female bodies and their natural functions are too often deemed shameful, an embarrassing secret that should be hidden away. Either that or they should be portrayed as sexy and alluring, a feast for the male gaze.

In her self-portraits Frida gazes at the viewer with a determined and challenging look that says, 'Yes, I'm beautiful, but that's not the only thing about me to which you should pay attention.' She shows us pain and injury, the agony of loving a man who cannot be trusted, but most importantly, she demands that we see what a woman's body is like at its most vulnerable and its most creative.

The painting I found hard to leave behind was *My Birth, 1932*. On a huge wooden double bed, with pure white cotton sheets, a woman lies on her back, pubic hair unshaven, legs wide open as a head emerges and blood soaks the sheet beneath. The woman's face and upper torso are covered by another sheet. On the wall above the bed hangs a painting of a woman, wracked with agony, looking out towards the onlooker. Is it a miscarriage? Is it her own birth, emerging from her mother? I don't know, but to me it represented that moment when a woman's entire being is given over to the birth of the next generation and her own self is subsumed. I loved having my children. Even giving birth was a relatively easy process; but I remember only too well that fear that who I was was in danger of being wiped out. Frida is the only artist I know who completely understood how women long to be mothers but are terrified that 'mother' will become all they are. And men never have to suffer that erasure.

12

Sirimavo Bandaranaike

1916–2000

Imagine the awesome responsibility of being the first woman in the world to become Prime Minister of your country. A job for which you had not been trained, never expected to take on, and in a society only just in the process of developing democracy. And to shoulder that burden in a society that would be riven by increasingly violent civil strife for years to come. That's what happened to Sirima Bandaranaike in 1960 (the 'vo' was added to her first name as she rose to power, as a mark of respect).

She was born Sirima Ratwatte in April 1916 in Ratnapura, in the British colony of Ceylon, now Sri Lanka. Her father, Barnes, was a Sinhalese aristocrat who was part of the government during the colonial era. Her mother, Rosalind, was also from a leading aristocratic family. It was not uncommon for the leading families at that time to serve in government and adopt English names. Her father was named after a British governor general, as was her future husband, Solomon Bandaranaike.

Like the fathers of so many women who have recognised their daughter's intelligence and abilities and who expected that their girls would step up to the mark when it was required of them, Barnes Ratwatte wanted Sirima, the eldest of his six children, to have the best education. And that best was British; at eight years old, Sirima was sent to a convent boarding school in Colombo, the capital. She was bilingual in Sinhala and English but it was only at home that she would learn her Sinhalese culture. Her religion was Buddhism, in which she was extremely devout.

After the convent Sirima began work in the field of social welfare, often trekking for miles through the jungles and mountains of Ceylon to deliver food and medicines, set up clinics and help remote villages make a living by developing small-scale industries. She became very well known among the Sinhalese peasantry and a popular favourite. I doubt she did it with a view to electoral support in the future, as she had no personal ambitions in politics but there's no doubt the reputation she forged in these early days, as a woman who knew the meaning of hard work and had a deep understanding of the Sinhalese people, would stand her in good stead in later years.

Unfortunately, she knew nothing of the language, culture, needs and aspirations of the country's Tamil minority. The Tamils had been brought to Ceylon under British rule from India to work on the tea, coffee and sugar plantations and their religion was predominantly Hindu. This lack of curiosity, knowledge and empathy would prove disastrous in future dealings with the Tamils and fatal blunders would be made which have led to years of brutal conflict.

In 1940 Sirima married an Oxford-educated colonial government minister, Solomon (Solla) West Ridgeway Dias Bandaranaike. They were considered a perfect match: both hailed from similar, aristocratic, land-owning families and their horoscopes were found to be perfectly aligned. Rather predictably, the occasion was billed as 'the wedding of the century'. Solla was not as familiar as Sirima with the needs of the rural Sinhalese, but he seemed to have an instinctive sense of what politics could do for them, and Sirima's public role became simply that of dutiful, obedient wife.

Their eldest daughter, Sunethra, was born in 1943, followed by Chandrika, another daughter, and finally a boy, Anura, came along. Sirima was shy and methodical as a wife and mother and took no public part in her husband's political life, other than to welcome his friends to the house, listen to their heated discussions of politics and provide refreshments. Her husband's biographer, James Manor, points to Solla's sexism as the main issue in their marriage.

He recounts a story of an occasion in the couple's Colombo house when she was slow in delivering the tea to a large group of guests at a political rally. Her husband, the host, grew increasingly irritated. When tea finally appeared and Sirima had gone back to the kitchen – clearly where her husband thought she belonged – he shouted, in the most sarcastic manner possible, 'Sirima! These gentlemen drink tea with sugar. For the sugar to get into the cup, there must be some instrument. You have not put a spoon in the sugar bowl.'

Sirima, swallowing her pride, quietly brought the spoon; she put it into the sugar bowl and retired from the fray, overhearing her husband tell the gathering, 'We have to think for them too.' You might expect a cultured, educated woman to have given as good as she got and told her husband where to get off for humiliating her in front of guests. Not so. She made no complaint, and Manor says: 'No wonder the men failed to see what a forceful leader she would be – perhaps too forceful!' There may have been a hint of a more steely character when, much later, she said:

> I feel most strongly the home is a woman's foremost place of work and influence, and, looking after her children and husband, duties of the highest importance. But women also have their vital role in civic life, they owe a duty to their country, a duty which cannot, must not, be shirked.

Her husband may have expressed overt sexism in the home and in front of political colleagues but he was certainly aware of her deep knowledge of the needs of the Sinhalese population, gained as a result of her social work. As his political ambitions increased after the country's independence from Britain in 1948, and the country became the Dominion of Ceylon – it would not be the Republic of Sri Lanka until 1972 – Sirima privately became his policy adviser and confidante. In 1951, she persuaded Solla to resign from the government and the ruling United National Party (UNP); they were both exasperated by the lack of progress made since independence. Two months later he formed the Sri Lankan Freedom Party (SLFP), with democratic socialism and Sinhalese cultural resurgence as its foremost policies.

The following year's general election saw Sirima enter for the first time into the public life of an actively political wife. She campaigned on her husband's behalf in his constituency while he travelled around the rest of Ceylon to spread the message of his new party. He won with the largest majority of any candidate, although the new party gained only nine seats. But the wind was blowing in its favour. At the next election in 1956 Solla won a landslide victory, formed a left-wing coalition and became Prime Minister. The people came out in strong support of his nationalist rhetoric and policies, particularly his promise to replace English with Sinhalese as the island's sole official language. That shift was aimed at diminishing the dominance of the English-speaking elite, but it sowed the seeds of a bitter conflict with the Tamil minority.

Sinhalese ideology had been an important element in Solla's rise to power, but when in office he could not keep a check on what he'd unleashed; nationalist groups demanded more than he was able to effect quickly. In 1959 he was assassinated by a Buddhist monk, Talduwe Somarama Thero, who was motivated partly by what he described as 'the greater good of his country, race and religion'. He claimed the Prime Minister's failure to pursue nationalist reforms aggressively led to his elimination, but it was also discovered he had been persuaded to take a leading role in the conspiracy by the head priest of his order, who had been refused a shipping contract and other business deals for a company he led.

On 25 September Thero went to the Premier's house in Colombo, his saffron monk's robes giving him free access. As the Prime Minister began a routine surgery to meet members of the public, Thero waited his turn. As Bandaranaike stepped forward to greet him, Thero took out the gun he'd concealed under his robes and fired. Sirima was in the garden when she heard the commotion inside and rushed indoors to find her husband collapsed, gravely wounded, with the monk still pointing his gun at him. She flung herself at the gunman, who was shot by the Premier's bodyguards.

Solla was rushed to hospital. Despite six hours of surgery by the country's most skilled doctors, he died the following day. In a message to the nation from his hospital bed, Solla asked that the authorities show compassion to the 'foolish man dressed in the robes of a monk'. Bandaranaike had suspended capital punishment when he came to power but after his death the government restored it. Thero was hanged for committing murder but his co-conspirators received only life sentences, as conspiracy to murder was not a capital offence.

Sirima became known as 'the weeping widow' but her time for grieving was short. She was bombarded with desperate pleas from her husband's party to assume the leadership. In July 1960 she led the party to victory on a wave of public sympathy and took office as the world's first female Prime Minister. She was, of course, the first of several dynastic appointments in which young women took power after the death of a father or husband: Benazir Bhutto, Cory Aquino and Indira Gandhi, Sirimavo's friend.

Yes, she had indeed been the dutiful wife and mother, someone who in her grief wept profusely, even in public. And yes, she assumed the name of her husband as Prime Minister. But the male politicians now surrounding her severely misjudged their new leader. They were obviously unaware of her years researching the lives of the Sinhalese population, oblivious to the extent to which her husband had relied on her political instincts. 'What does she know of politics?' asked one of her husband's cousins. 'In Solla's time Sirima presided over nothing fiercer than the kitchen fire. She'll end by spoiling her personal reputation and ruining the family name.' But as many men have discovered, women such as Sirimavo and Indira Gandhi were not to be underestimated.

Mrs Bandaranaike would become one of the developing world's best-known leaders, rubbing shoulders with Indira Gandhi, Zhou Enlai, Marshal Tito and others. It was the hey-day of the Non-Aligned Movement – the group of states, established in Yugoslavia in 1961, which was not formally aligned with any major power bloc – of which she became the chair in the mid-1970s. She led numerous international negotiations, including the attempts to resolve the 1962 border dispute between China and India which, without her mediation, could have spilled into war. It was at her suggestion that the UN General Assembly declared the Indian Ocean to be a Zone of Peace, preventing it becoming an area of conflict during the Cold War. Another of her biographers, Maureen Seneviratne, said: 'If Mr Bandaranaike's stature as a politician and leader was built up over decades of campaigning, Sirimavo donned hers like a cloak that had been lying in her wardrobe for years, unworn, but which had been pressed and kept ready for wearing at any moment.'

In her first four years in power she forged ahead with the socialist reform movement begun by her husband, and went further than he may have planned. She made Sinhalese the official language, sparking fury among the Tamils. Foreign oil companies were nationalised and all government-owned businesses were transferred to the state-owned Bank of Ceylon and the new People's Bank, bringing an end to American aid. Soviet aid was sought for industrial projects, and education was reformed in favour of the Buddhist Sinhalese – another move that would disenfranchise the Hindu Tamils. It's a bit of a mystery how she managed to nationalise British and American oil companies without provoking an invasion. Her anxious successor, after the 1965 elections, rapidly came to a compensation agreement within five days.

In 1964, after the crushing of an attempted military coup and a brief coalition with the Marxist LLSP, Mrs Bandaranaike lost a vote of no confidence when some Freedom Party members crossed the floor under pressure from right-wing Buddhist leaders. The government collapsed. Her party lost the '65 election, but she was personally elected to parliament for the first time. Five years later, in 1970, she was returned for a second term as Prime Minister, winning the election with a coalition of the Freedom Party, the Marxist LLSP and the Communist Party. She had a two-thirds majority and was able to press ahead with her socialist reforms. She was, though, not fast enough for the young activists of the extreme left-wing People's Liberation Front, the JVP. They had benefited from Mrs Bandaranaike's reforms to the education system, but they couldn't get jobs, so in 1971 they launched an insurrection. It was swiftly defeated, but at the cost of more than a thousand young lives.

The government pressed on hurriedly with land reform, nationalisation of the tea estates and a new republican constitution, which changed the name of Ceylon to Sri Lanka ('resplendent island') and made Buddhism the state religion, adding more fuel to stoke the fire of Tamil resentment. Tamil political pressure for an independent homeland in the north-east of the country had come to nothing. Sirimavo said, 'The Tamil people must accept that the Sinhala majority will no longer permit themselves to be cheated of their rights.'

Mrs Bandaranaike imposed rigid state control over the economy. The result was disastrous: oil prices soared and living standards began to collapse as rationing, bureaucracy and corruption began to take hold. As a result, she was defeated at the 1977 election: her party won only eight seats and the UNP, led by JR Jayewardene, secured a crushing majority. He took this as a mandate to rip up the 1972 constitution and in 1978, he was sworn in as Executive President, head of a powerful state that paid mere lip service to democracy.

In 1976 the Tamil Tigers movement was formed. The battles between its members and Sri Lankan armed forces saw some of the worst brutality in Sri Lanka for almost half a century. There was a nationwide pogrom against the Tamils in 1983, and a full-blown civil war began. It dragged on until 2009, when the Tamils were finally defeated, amid claims of war crimes and atrocities on both sides.

As for Mrs Banadaranaike, in 1980 Jayewardene had her civic rights suspended for seven years, for what he alleged had been abuse of power. She was unable to play any public role; her main task was to try and hold her party together. Her daughter, Chandrika, together with her husband, the film star Vijaya Kumaratunga, formed their own left-wing party, one of whose principal aims was to offer an olive branch to the Tamils. As would happen so often in relations between the Sinhalese and the Tamils, attempts at friendly and co-operative relations failed.

In 1985 Mrs Bandaranaike's rights were restored and she became the Freedom Party's leader again. The intervening years had seen mounting violence in Sri Lanka, generally initiated in the early days by the government or the UNP. The civil war rumbled on; in 1987 India sent peacekeeping troops in an attempt to enforce a peace settlement. Mrs Bandaranaike, the arch-nationalist, opposed India's intervention but lacking influence in Delhi or with the Tamils she had lost all power to make a meaningful intervention.

In 1988 Chandrika's husband was assassinated and Chandrika rejoined her mother, who made another bid for power but failed to win the presidential election. The following year, in an election again marred by violence, the Freedom Party was unsuccessful but the UNP lost its two-thirds majority in parliament, securing only 50% of the vote. What finally broke the harsh UNP government, whose leaders had indeed abused their power, was the assassination in 1993 of the successor to Jayewardene, Ranasinghe Premadasa.

In 1994 Chandrika became leader of the party, though her brother had also wanted the job – much is suspected and little known of their mother's role in the sibling rivalry. She campaigned brilliantly for the Freedom Party, won the presidential election and appointed her mother prime minister. But the real power lay in Chandrika's hands and in 2000, at the age of eighty-four and after forty years in public service, Sirimavo stepped down shortly before parliament was due to be dissolved. Chandrika perhaps had a wider concept of Sri Lankan society than her mother; she had been strongly influenced by her husband's ideals in seeking peace with the Tamils. Tragically, she was caught in a blast from a Tamil suicide bomber and was blinded in one eye not long before her mother's death. Her attempts at reconciliation had come to nothing.

Mrs Bandaranaike died of a heart attack on election day, 10 October 2000, shortly having cast her vote. Her daughter praised her mother effusively: 'She put us on the world map.' The Sri Lankan poet, Yasmine Gooneratne, wrote that she was 'the most formidable and charismatic leader the country has ever seen'. *The Economist* said, 'Sirimavo Bandaranaike did undoubtedly believe she was doing good.' Many praised her for helping Sri Lanka shrug off its colonial legacy. Others queued up to hurl abuse: 'This woman is the source of all the evils we see today in Sri Lanka', wrote one commentator on a *Guardian* article.

I have no doubt that 'this woman', launched into a political position she had never sought, in a country newly emerging from colonial control and exploitation, wanted nothing more than to restore the Sinhalese majority to its rightful place, as she saw it. She had, after all, spent much of her youth meeting and helping the people over whom she would rule. Her tragedy is that she lived before we began to understand how a civilised country should treat its minorities. She was a Sinhalese chauvinist, proud of her culture, but with a mind that was closed, like most of her fellows, to the needs of the Tamils. As the *Guardian*'s obituary said in 2000, 'If a country may be judged by how it treats its minorities, the failure to treat them properly in Sri Lanka has carried a fearsome price, which even yet has not been fully paid.'

13

Toni Morrison

1931–

Toni Morrison was not Toni Morrison from birth. She was born Chloe Ardelia Wofford, in Lorain, Ohio. The 'Toni' came from her choice, at the age of twelve, to take the baptismal name Anthony – Saint Anthony of Padua – when she became a Roman Catholic. She told me during an interview in 1992, just before she was awarded the Nobel Prize for Literature, that she'd taken the name Morrison when she married Harold Morrison, a Jamaican architect, in 1958. It was what women were expected to do.

She intended to use her own name, Toni Wofford, when she published her first novel, *The Bluest Eye*, in 1970, but she forgot to tell the publisher in time. The cover had already been designed and printed. She was stuck with the name of a husband from whom she'd been divorced for six years. Morrison has never really revealed why she left her husband but has hinted that he had hoped for a more subservient wife. 'He didn't need me making judgments about him,' she once said, 'which I did. A lot.' She has never married again.

Morrison was the great-granddaughter of a North American Indian and the great-granddaughter of Alabama slaves. She grew up among tales of the legacy of racial slavery in America. Her grandmother told her about the response of her great-grandfather to the announcement in 1863 of the emancipation of slaves. He was a boy of five when he heard that 'the emancipation' was coming. Imagining it to be a terrible monster, he ran and hid under the bed. Morrison's own father was haunted by the sight of two lynchings he'd witnessed as a boy. His telling of the story had a profound effect on Toni. In an interview with Public Radio in America she remembered: 'My father saw two black men lynched on his street in Cartersville, Georgia as a child. And I think seeing two black businessmen – not vagrants – hanging from trees as a child was traumatic for him.'

She described the family's life in Lorain, Ohio, as happy on the whole, and surprisingly integrated. It was a small working-class steel town that had no 'black' neighbourhoods. There was one high school and all the children played together:

Everybody was either somebody from the South or an immigrant from East Europe or from Mexico. And there was one church and there were four elementary schools. And we were all, pretty much until the end of the war, very, very poor.

My neighbours were from – my mother's neighbours who brought her stuffed cabbage – what used to be called Czechoslovakia. So that I'm not at all a person who has been reared or raised in a community in which these racial lines were that pronounced. Occasionally, as children, we might figure out how to call somebody a name, and they would figure out how to call us. But . . . it was so light. It was so fluffy. I didn't really have a strong awareness of segregation and the separation of races until I left Lorain, Ohio.

She was not entirely unaware of racism in Ohio, though. On one occasion, when Toni was around two years old, her parents couldn't find the money to pay their landlord. He responded by attempting to torch their house while they were still inside. 'It was this hysterical, out-of-the-ordinary, bizarre form of evil', she said:

> If you internalized it you'd be truly and thoroughly depressed because that's how much your life meant. For four dollars a month somebody would just burn you to a crisp. So what you did instead was laugh at him, at the absurdity, at the monumental crudeness of it. That way you gave back yourself to yourself . . . You distanced yourself from the implications of the act. That's what laughter does. You take it back. You take your life back. You take your integrity back.

Even now, late in her life, she laughs often and loudly. She still finds that a sense of humour can be a 'life saver for a person who is often depressed and finds much to be depressed about'. She frequently tries, she said, to pass her sense of humour on to her characters. *Song of Solomon*, her third novel, published in 1977, opens with an explanation of how a street in the city of Mercy got its name. A century ago, the city's only black doctor had moved there, so his patients naturally began referring to it as Doctor Street. Later, more African Americans lived there and the mail they received had Doctor Street as their address. Much to the disdain of the city's white legislators, it had almost become official. So these jobsworths declared that the street was 'Mains Avenue' and that it would never be anything else. If the street could not be Doctor Street what then could people do? Well, soon the local post office would begin to take delivery of letters addressed to Not Doctor Street.

It was her maternal grandmother, Ardelia Willis, who brought Toni's mother's family out of Alabama and into Ohio. Her husband had to travel to Birmingham to find work, leaving his family behind on the farm in Greenville. Ardelia realised, as the months passed, that the white boys in the area were 'circling'; her girls were getting towards the age where they might be sexually abused or raped. Sending a message to her husband that they could no longer stay put, in the dead of night Toni's grandmother took her children and got on the first train they could find that would take them away.

The fear of sexual abuse of young black girls troubled Morrison's father, even in Ohio. He threw a white man down the stairs in their apartment building because he was afraid the man was coming to rape his daughters. Morrison described what happened:

> I think his own experience in Georgia would have made him think that any white man bumbling up the stairs towards our apartment was not there for any good. And since we were little girls, he assumed that. I think he made a mistake. I mean, I really think the man was drunk . . . the white man was – he survived . . . [and] the real thing for me was I thought – I felt profoundly protected and defended. I was not happy because, after my father threw him all the way down into the street, he threw our tricycle after him. That was a little bit of a problem since we needed our tricycle.
>
> But that made me think there was some devilry, something evil about white people, which is exactly what my father thought. He was very, very serious in his hatred of white people. What mitigated it was my mother, who is exactly the opposite, who never rejected or accepted somebody based on race or colour or religion . . . Everybody was an individual whom she approved of or disapproved of based on her perception of them as individuals.

She learned something very important from watching her father throw the white man down the stairs. It boosted her confidence in herself to learn 'that my father could win . . . that it was possible to win'.

Morrison was, of course, a witness to the early civil rights movement, but not an active participant. 'I was not in favour of integration', she said. 'But I couldn't officially say that because I knew the terror and the abuses of segregation. But integration also meant that we would not have a fine black college or fine black education.'

In 1953 Toni graduated from Howard University in Washington DC with a BA in English. At Howard she had wanted to write a paper on the role of black characters in Shakespeare, but her professor thought it 'low class' to read and research black life. The eventual subject of her thesis was suicide in the writings of Virginia Woolf and William Faulkner. She felt uneasy and was deeply disappointed that at Howard skin colour appeared to work as a caste system, something she had, so far, only read about. In Washington, for the first time, she had encountered lunch counters at which she could not sit, fountains from which she was not allowed to drink and shops where her money seemed not to be good enough.

After college and graduate school at Cornell, she eventually returned to Howard to teach. She married and had a son but when she was a few months into her second pregnancy, her marriage fell apart. She decided to go back to Lorain to work out what to do next. In the back pages of the *New York Review of Books* Morrison found an advert for an editor in the textbook division of Random House. She applied and got the job, so she and her two young sons moved to Syracuse, New York. She spent the next eighteen years editing the work of other writers while working on her own novels. It was a pretty tough schedule for a lone working mother; she rose at 4am to write. 'That was when I first began to write, and finally, after all these years of reading books, editing books, working in libraries, I thought, "Wait a minute, there's no book in there about me!" So if I wanted to read it, I would probably have to write it', she said.

Unsurprisingly, Morrison's writing has always been rooted in the identity of a people who were forcibly removed from their own culture, treated as less than human by the society that enslaved them and, once free, struggled to find their place as free citizens of that same society. *The Bluest Eye* came first; the story of a young African American girl who longs for white skin and blue eyes. Confronting racism, rape, incest and paedophilia in poetic prose, critics compared it to the work of William Faulkner. *Sula* was next, a tale of friendship and betrayal which puts a less than pleasant spin on the idea of sisterhood. It was nominated for the American Book Award.

In 1977 she published *Song of Solomon*, about an African-American man on a quest to discover the truth about his family history and the story of a relative who escaped slavery. It was the first book by a black writer to be a main selection of the Book of the Month Club since 1940. It received the National Book Critics Circle Award, the American Academy and Institute of Arts and Letters Award, and Morrison was awarded the title 'distinguished writer' by the Academy. It was, at last, no longer considered 'low class' to read about or study black life as had been the case at Howard University. People wanted to read about the lives of her characters and the literary establishment recognised her as a great writer. She would never again be dismissed as a novelist with too limited a palette to attract a huge audience of readers.

Beloved, published in 1987, launched Morrison into the literary stratosphere. It was inspired by a newspaper cutting she found while editing an African-American history anthology, *The Black Book*. The chapter was based on the true story of a runaway slave, Margaret Garner, who rather than give up her children when her former owners come looking for her, cut her daughter's throat. It's a deeply disturbing story, set in post-civil war Ohio, and it's certainly not written in an easy-to-read style. It weaves together realist, modernist and supernatural elements and even Oprah Winfrey, who became enough of a champion of the novel to make it into a film in which she played the lead role of Sethe, admitted to Morrison that she had not completely understood *Beloved*. Morrison simply replied, 'Read it again.'

Beloved is one of my favourite novels of all time, but I confess I did feel some sympathy with Oprah's view on my first attempt at reading it. The plot is phenomenally complex and the cast of characters huge. The novel works in a double timeframe; the present is where Sethe lives with the ghostly figure of a manipulative young woman, Beloved, believed by all the characters to be the spirit of the daughter Sethe killed to save her from slavery; the past is the story of Sethe's attempts to escape from slavery. Morrison's descriptions of the brutality and sexual violence Sethe suffered are almost unbearable. There are moments in the book that still make me gasp with horror, and I've read it three times: the moment where Sethe cuts her daughter's throat with a handsaw; the moment where one of her fellow slaves, Paul D, is forced to wear an iron bit in his mouth. It's a difficult book for all kinds of reasons, technically and emotionally but it's well worth the effort.

Beloved did not win the National Book Award, although it had been expected to take the prize. In 1988 a collective of forty-eight black writers and intellectuals, including Maya Angelou and Alice Walker, published a signed statement in the *New York Times* upbraiding the publishing industry for its failure adequately to honour Morrison. 'Despite the international stature of Toni Morrison', they wrote, 'she has yet to receive the national recognition that her five major works of fiction entirely deserve. She has yet to receive the keystone honours of the National Book Award or the Pulitzer Prize.'

Two months later, she was awarded the Pulitzer. A few years later, in 1993, she was awarded the Nobel Prize for literature. At the time of writing she is the only living African-American writer to be so lauded. (The poet Derek Walcott, also a black Nobel Laureate, defines himself as of Caribbean, not American, origin.)

It was in 1992, when she was Professor of Literature at Princeton University in New York, and had just published *Jazz*, that Morrison came to London and to the *Woman's Hour* studio. *Jazz* is a bittersweet love story set in the 1920s. In the now familiar Morrison style, it explores in flashbacks the background of the characters in the American South in the mid-nineteenth century. I hadn't read anything of hers that was set in a city; Morrison's work is generally played out against the rural background with which she's familiar; she had never lived in the centre of a city herself. So what difference had the urban setting in New York's Harlem made to the way she described the place in which her characters worked and played, and suffered the violence of the inner city? Her answer was exactly what a writer's dismissal of a slightly stupid question should be. Imagination, of course. It was because she *hadn't* lived in Harlem in the 1920s that she was well placed to talk about the romance and excitement of what she imagined the city used to be.

Jazz is built on history, memory and imagination. Morrison has been very open, particularly with the students she teaches, about how great literature should consist of those three elements. She tells them she doesn't think much of those modern fiction writers who constantly reference their own lives instead of inventing new material; she told the creative writing students, 'I don't want to hear about your little life, OK?' Morrison explained her ambition as a writer to me:

I think the history of African Americans has been ill thought through and probably not properly imagined. Well documented, but not well imagined. Novels, fiction, can re-imagine the past, showing that there was agency. There were opportunities for African Americans, in slavery and afterwards, to exercise a lot of imaginative control over their interior lives as well as their exterior ones.

The title *Jazz*, I thought, would lead people to expect jazz clubs, seedy bars and singing stars, but she had completely ignored the music as a theme and concentrated on a small domestic story. Why? 'Well, for two reasons', she explained:

Jazz was a music that was for the people and of the people, not the retrospective stars, not the celebrities and also I wanted to demystify that whole jazz era. That is to talk about the people who lived through it, but did not know they were part of a Harlem renaissance, but were everyday people and not the ones who history and time have selected out for us to recall.

As in *Beloved*, love is very much the central theme of *Jazz* and particularly the difficulties of love. What was she trying to resolve in this?

I wanted to find out how it is possible to love under duress. It's what we were born for, loving and knowing, and I also wanted to explore what people can do whose bodies have literally been owned so the body was not yours. In *Beloved* that was one aspect – what it meant to love your children that much. In *Jazz* there are people whose parents, but not themselves, until recently were owned, physically owned. So part of freedom is freedom to fall in love, to choose whom you love, to inhabit your body, to express things through the body and it may appear, as it did in the Jazz Age, to be a little naughty and perhaps in some instances illegal, but it is the way in which many people who came to the large cities were able to say 'We are now free!'

The most extraordinary element of *Jazz* is its use of language; used in the same way as a jazz musician might create music. That was exactly what Morrison was trying to do, even though, on occasion, the plot, the character and the engaging of the reader in their lives is to some extent sacrificed:

> I was trying to recreate the improvisational quality of jazz. As much argument as there is about that music and about the concept of jazz – what is true jazz, what is not – the one thing that everybody agrees on is that it is inventive, that the musician practises, practises so that he can appear effortless and to riff and to seem to lose control, but at the same time exercise enormous discipline so the language for me had to exercise this amazing suggestion of control, plot and planning and use the narrative as a sort of melody. It's easily the most difficult book I've ever written technically. It has an appeal, probably not to the visceral responses people expect from some of my writing. Jazz and this book after all is art, it's artifice.

She had described the use of language as an intricate malleable toy. And she suggested it may, in the case of this novel, be more accessible to African-Americans because it is:

> BY African Americans. Organised, invented and created through the culture so that they will leap over the difficulties another culture has. It is deceptively simple and it is intricate. It leaves you a little bit hungry, but you don't dance to it. Really you have to listen and the most important thing, you have to be willing to surrender.

Alongside *Jazz*, Morrison had published a series of lectures called *Playing in the Dark*, in which she argued that American critics have ignored the use made by classic American authors of a shared history. I asked her to explain how African-Americans have informed classic American literature:

There is no topic in the US that does not involve black Americans, whether you're talking about neighbourhoods or schools or money or government or healthcare. It all has a silent partner or an overt one which is how to respond or how to handle or how to govern African-Americans. Writers from Poe to Melville to Faulkner all lived in the world and they being artists responded to that presence. There are moments in practically every one of those books where the presence is there. They didn't ignore it, but the critics have and have erased it. I'm only saying that part of American literature must include African-Americans.

Toni Morrison is still active at the age of eighty-seven, with eleven novels to her name. She holds the highest honour that can be bestowed in America, the Presidential Medal of Freedom, which she received from President Barack Obama. Her life seems almost charmed. There has, though, been tragedy in her later years. Her house by the river in New York burned down some twenty years ago. A spark from the fire had nestled in a cushion; the fire started while one of her sons, Slade, was at home alone. He escaped unhurt, but papers and precious belongings were completely destroyed, as was the house.

It's rare for Toni Morrison to draw directly from incidents in her own life in her novels. *God Help the Child*, published in 2015, is set in the present day and is about Bride, a beautiful woman who's successful in the cosmetics business but has, we learn, been tragically damaged by her light-skinned parents' refusal to show her any love. And that's because her skin is very black. Her mother, Sweetness, describes breastfeeding her baby as 'having a pickaninny sucking my teat'. When Bride begins her 'You Girl' line of make-up she says it's 'for girls and women of all complexions from ebony to lemonade to milk'. Colourism, as it's now known, has been an important theme for Morrison; here she goes back to ideas explored in *Beloved*, where the shades of colour of a woman's skin and the experiences she has as a child or young woman shape the life of the adult. At the end of the novel a close friend of Bride's, Queen, the aunt of her lover, Booker, returns to her home, and a bonfire in her yard sparks and burns the house down. Queen dies in hospital, after being rescued from the house by Booker and Bride. I suspect Morrison's experience of relief at Slade's survival of the fire played on her mind and had to be exorcised in her writing. She could so easily have lost him.

She wears a small pendant these days around her neck. It's a heart carved from butterstone, hanging on a gold chain. She touches it frequently. She explained in an interview for the *Daily Telegraph* that it had a connection with Slade, who died in 2010 from pancreatic cancer. He was only forty-five. 'There is no closure on stuff like that', she has said. 'Not with a child. A child's supposed to bury you. I think about him all the time.'

As for her writing, she is dismissive of those critics who find her subject matter too focused on the experience of the African American, especially the women who often suffered at the hands of both white and black men: 'Of course I'm a black writer . . . I'm not just a black writer, but categories like black writer, woman writer and Latin American writer aren't marginal any more. We have to acknowledge that the thing we call "literature" is more pluralistic now, just as society ought to be. The melting pot never worked.' And, more to the point, why should she be asked the question in the first place? As she has said: 'My choice was as effortless as Dostoyevsky's, and, if no one could ask him why he "only" wrote about Russians, why ask me why I "only" write about black people?'

14

Margaret Eleanor Atwood

1939–

Some of the first words Margaret Atwood ever said to me were 'Women don't have to be gooder!' It was 1988, and the first time I'd encountered this really rather terrifying, super-clever Canadian, with a famously dry wit and an impressive catalogue of bestselling, prize-winning novels, the most famous of which was, of course, *The Handmaid's Tale*, published three years earlier. I was not alone in being afraid of her. She now recognises her ability to inspire fear. 'I was certainly very scary to people in my 20s; I think younger women with talent are scary.' Frankly, she still is!

I was familiar with that stunning dystopian story and firmly convinced of Atwood's absolute commitment to the feminist cause, creating as she did a society in which men held absolute power and women were either wives, who served the purpose of running the household, cooks, cleaners or handmaidens, who existed only for breeding purposes. So I'd been a little surprised when I then read *Cat's Eye*, the novel we were to discuss that day. It was as far from a portrayal of the sisterhood which we were all then convinced lay as close to the root of female friendships and, indeed the women's movement itself, as it was possible to be.

The central theme of the story is of a disastrous relationship among a group of schoolgirls. At the centre of the group are

Elaine and Cordelia. Cordelia joins Elaine and her two 'best friends', Grace and Carol. She wins over Grace and Carol and the three begin to bully Elaine, destroying any self-esteem she may have had. They even, in the midst of a Canadian winter, throw Elaine's hat into a ravine and leave her to climb alone out of the chasm, terrified and half-frozen. Later in life the tables are turned. Elaine is a successful artist and Cordelia a depressed young woman held in a mental home. She asks for Elaine's help and is refused. Hence my question about being surprised at the famous feminist writer so effectively undermining the popular concept of sisterhood and her cool response that 'Women don't have to be gooder.'

Atwood refused to be drawn on the extent to which the novel is autobiographical, except to acknowledge that she and Elaine shared a background in Toronto, a deep knowledge of the Canadian landscape and fierce weather, and a father who was an entomologist. Whether she had been bullied in such a way as a child she never acknowledged, but, although she had begun *Cat's Eye* in 1964, she put it away until the 1980s, when her own daughter was a teenager and Margaret had the opportunity to observe girls' friendships from an adult's perspective.

In her book *Curious Pursuits* Atwood describes her relationship with her father in a chapter entitled 'Writing the male character':

> My father was a forest entomologist and fond of children, and incidentally not threatened by women, and many were the happy hours I spent listening to his explanations of the ways of the wood-boring beetle, or picking forest tent cater-pillars out of the soup because he had forgotten to feed them and they had gone crawling all over the house in search of leaves. One of the results of my upbringing was that I had a big advantage in the schoolyard when little boys tried to frighten me with worms, snakes and the like.

As for what she was keen to pass on when it came to creating a male character, she was typically dry but perhaps more reasonable than you might expect from reading her novels:

> When people ask you if you hate men, the proper reply is 'which ones?' – because, of course, the other big revelation of the evening is that *not all men are the same.* Some of them have beards. Apart from that, I have never been among those who would speak slightingly of men by lumping them all in together. I would never say, for instance – as some have – 'Put a paper bag over their bodies and they're all the same'. I give you Albert Schweitzer in one corner, Hitler in another.

That mordant wit runs through everything she writes and, as I've discovered myself during a number of encounters, her every conversation. Of her life she once wrote in a letter to the Contact Press editor Peter Miller: 'I don't have a very promotable one, as am not in possession of anything picturesque like a beard or Unemployment Insurance. Have never been a lumberjack or a janitor. Had unfortunately a happy childhood. Am (alas) educated, but you'd better soft-pedal that as it's not fashionable.' No intention of soft pedalling that one, Margaret, as indeed I very much doubt you would really want me to. It's been my experience, of all the women whose lives I have researched and attempted to promote, that education is in almost every case the one thing that unites them. If we do live in an era where it's considered non-U to show off about it, it's time for those of us who value what our parents, in many instances our fathers, made possible for us to be shouting it from the rooftops, not playing it down.

Margaret Atwood was born in Ottawa to Margaret Dorothy Killam Atwood, a former dietician and nutritionist, and Carl Edmund Atwood, an entomologist. She spent a great deal of her early life in the Canadian bush with her parents, and it's obvious that she learned a great deal from her mother, who was often engaged in chasing away bears. It was from her mother that she acquired her disregard for conventional gender roles. In *Margaret Atwood: A Biography*, Nathalie Cooke records Atwood as saying: 'When I think of my mother, I don't think of lipstick and feathers or the little woman or furniture polish or even five-course dinners. Because of her, I didn't grow up feeling that being female needed to mean having your feet bound.'

When they were out in the wilds her mother taught Margaret and her brother Harold in the mornings. They had very little to entertain themselves with other than books and imaginative games. They drew their own comics, making up their own characters and tales, and Margaret's favourite reading material was ghost stories. Her first experience of formal school was at the age of eight in Toronto and she said 'I was now faced with real life, in the form of other little girls – their prudery and snobbery, their Byzantine social life based on whispering and vicious gossip.' Ah yes, *Cat's Eye*!

Margaret found it difficult to adjust to going to school all year round. But having been used to only winter school, she found she advanced quickly because she'd discovered it was possible to plough through the entire year's curriculum in a month. She began to write poetry at high school and said she realised, while walking home across the football field, that she would be a writer. She told her school friends about her ambition and they wrote in the high school year book that it was 'Peggy's ambition to write the "Great Canadian novel"'. When she told her parents, they worried that she might never manage to make a living and were surprised that their daughter should be leaning towards the arts; everyone else in the family was a scientist.

Atwood began her university education in Toronto, taking a degree in English, writing all the while and reading her poems at a coffee house in the city. She was encouraged to go to Harvard for postgraduate study and had her first collection of poems published. She said 'nothing has since matched the thrill of opening the acceptance letter'.

A couple of two-year stints at Harvard sandwiched a time at Canadian Facts Marketing, rich source material for her début novel *The Edible Woman,* published in 1969. It told the story of Marian, who works in a market research firm. She has a boring boyfriend called Peter, develops an aversion to eggs, cake and vegetables, and eventually realises Peter is set on devouring her. She called it a proto-feminist rather than a feminist novel.

Atwood worked so hard on her writing that she became ill, losing weight and developing spinal neuritis. Of her condition, and how it's reflected in the novel, Nathalie Cooke reports that Atwood said:

> I had never had or even heard of anorexia – in 1964 it was not yet fashionable – so Marian's eating disorder had its genesis in speculations that were symbolic rather than personal or medical. However, the result for me was a marked queasiness in the face of my morning egg . . . writing fiction is a two-way street. If the author gets too bossy, the characters may remind her that, though she is their creator, they are to some extent her creator as well.

Margaret did not fit easily into Harvard. In a course she took in her first years, Victorian Humour, there was a break during the class in which the female students served tea and biscuits. Women were not allowed into the Lamont Library, where all the modern poetry and records were kept.

She later spoke about her student years in an interview with Joyce Carol Oates:

> I always felt a little like a sort of wart or wen on the great male academic skin . . . I felt I was there on sufferance. Harvard, you know, didn't hire women to teach in it . . .

> There was a joke among the woman students that the best
> way to pass your orals was to stuff a pillow up your dress,
> because they would all be so terrified of having parturition
> take place on the Persian rug that they would just ask you
> your name and give you a pass.

As far as the teaching was concerned, she learned that only two women writers between 1630 and 1900 were worthy of consideration: Ann Bradstreet and Emily Dickinson. For a woman who planned on being a writer it was 'like saying you were going to pee in the men's washroom: either daring or in bad taste'. She never finished her PhD.

Atwood began to attract attention as a writer. She won the prestigious Canadian Governor General's award for her first full-length collection of poems, *The Circle Game*, and was asked to attend the official ceremony to collect her prize. She had never fussed too much about what she wore but her flatmates were determined she should not make her first appearance in public looking like someone from the backwoods. One did her hair, another found her a dress, and they insisted on a new pair of shoes. As soon as she was out of the house they threw away the comfortable but inelegant Hush Puppies she always wore.

She became engaged twice. In 1967, she married an American writer, Jim Polk, after 'five years of equivocation'. She never changed her name to his, sticking with Atwood, as was becoming acceptable for a married woman for the first time. Alongside her writing, Atwood taught first in the University of Montreal, followed by Alberta and then Toronto. As happens so often when a couple marry young and the woman is ambitious, rather than committed to cooking, cleaning and being what's expected of a wife, her marriage to Polk began to fall apart. In 1973 the novelist Graeme Gibson came into her life; together with his two sons they moved to a farm in a small community in Alliston, Ontario. Three years later they had a daughter, Eleanor 'Jess' Atwood

Gibson, for whose sake they moved to Toronto, 'to spare Jess from spend[ing] about four hours a day on the school bus. It was a shame: but on the other hand farming was a hell of a lot of work.' Atwood and Gibson are a happy couple, although they have never married. When a fellow writer wrote that 'every woman writer should be married to Graeme Gibson' Margaret had her comment printed on a T-shirt. She is clearly considerably more successful than he, with four Booker nominations and one win, for *The Blind Assassin*, and a shower of honours and awards all over the world.

It appears that the scientific background of her childhood has begun to influence her work ever more strongly as she's grown older and more worried about the environment. The first of her works of science fiction was *Oryx and Crake*, which was shortlisted for the Booker prize. In it, Atwood imagines a horrifying dystopian future, but here genetic engineering, online pornography, computer games and medicines produced to defy the ageing process have created a world in which it's all but impossible for human beings to exist.

Atwood does not, though, see her most recent novels as science fiction. In an interview on the BBC's *Breakfast* she described science fiction as 'talking squids in outer space'. Thus, one can assume she intends that her work should not be science fiction with 'monsters and spaceships', but 'speculative fiction, which could really happen'. As one critic said of her, 'In the manner of humourists since antiquity, Atwood is a moralist who expertly reconciles the double function of literature: to entertain and to teach.'

It seems to me, though, that despite all her humanitarian work and indeed the strange (environmentally motivated) invention of the LongPen – a device which allows a person to write in ink remotely anywhere in the world via a touchpad and the Internet – it is for her terrifying dystopian novel, *The Handmaid's Tale*, that she will always be best-known. It's been a novel, a film, an opera and, in 2017, a successful television series that inspired a new generation of young women to really understand what feminism means and employ the word proudly. I remember a time in the 70s and 80s when it was the 'f-word', with all the shock and derision that the other 'f-'word' inspired. Women would often say, 'Well, I'm not a feminist, but . . .' , going on to explain that their husbands had never so much as changed a nappy or boiled an egg! It was not uncommon, if you called yourself a feminist, to be accused of being a dungaree-wearing man-hater. It's taken a long time to dispel that notion and make it plain that feminism is really about men and women enjoying equal rights and opportunities.

Margaret Atwood's *The Handmaid's Tale* has had a huge influence on young women in America who have not only embraced the term, but adopted the costumes worn by the handmaids in the television series for feminist protests, wearing the scarlet robes and puritanical white bonnets to attend demonstrations against proposed restrictions on abortion rights. The image of crowds of young, twenty-first-century women dressed in this way made a powerful impression all around the world.

It was to mark the twenty-fifth anniversary of the publication of *The Handmaid's Tale* that we spoke in 2010. First, in her cool and rather chilling voice, Atwood read her description of 'The Ceremony', in which the wife reclines on the bed, while the Handmaiden lies between her legs and is mounted by the Commander. We discussed why she had decided to make female reproduction central to the way the regime in Gilead controlled its female subjects:

> Every totalitarianism that we know anything about has always made it central in one way or another because all governments, totalitarian or not, are always worried about population numbers in relation to available resources. They've all done it. Napoleon did it. Look at Romania who made it mandatory for women to have four children

because they felt population was getting too low. Look at China who feel their population is too high and want to control their numbers. This regime, because fertility has fallen, they're interested and because of their totalitarianism which is pyramid shaped and those at the top get the most goodies and rare and desirable things and now fertile women are rare and desirable things, of course they want them. It is, of course, based on the biblical passage, Rachel and Leah having a baby contest using, in fact, their slaves. So the slaves would have the babies, but the babies would belong to Rachel and Leah. So it's a kind of forced biological motherhood which has a lot of precedents in history.

I pointed out that the book had come long before the Taliban in Afghanistan took away any rights previously enjoyed by women there, so what influenced her to write the book when she did?

If you look back in western culture not very far you will find that similar things have gone on in it and have been going on for many hundreds of years. If you go back to the early church fathers you'll find them debating whether or not women have souls. So it goes through centuries of history. It's by no means a straight road with way stations marked along it. It's very much a twisting, winding road with sometimes things getting better for women, sometimes getting really quite a lot worse.

So, how much was she conscious of working in the tradition of novels such as Huxley's *Brave New World*, or Orwell's *1984*?

I was entirely conscious of writing in that tradition because I had done a lot of reading of nineteenth-century utopians, turn-of-the-century dystopians and twentieth-century dark visions. But the other thing I was thinking was Puritan seventeenth-century New England and the book is set there for a reason. Schoolchildren are told the Puritans went there to set up a democracy, which is almost entirely false. They went there to set up their own theocracy, which is what they did. So that's why it's set in Massachusetts.

I told Margaret I remembered reading the novel when it first came out in 1985 and being absolutely chilled when the central character, Offred, has her credit card taken away, and is told she has no right to money or a job. What chills her most about her story?

Well, it's based on my travels around Soviet socialist satellite countries around the time I was writing the book and one of the things was you couldn't talk to anyone. If you were going to talk to them you had to go way out into a park. They wouldn't talk in their cars or their hotel rooms. They felt that at any time there might be surveillance. They had to trust you not to go back to the West and blather on about what they had said to you. So people who live in a fairly open society just don't understand that part. Some people said to me why don't these women go on marches? Why didn't they protest? I said read German Nazi history and figure out what would happen to people who did that. And what chilled me most about it was probably the impetus for writing the book. It was people who would blithely say 'It can't happen here.' And that was the most chilling statement because it can happen anywhere given the right amount of social disruption and turmoil.

We went on to talk about the character of Serena Joy, the Commander's wife, who is portrayed as having been a right-wing advocate of traditional women's roles. How much is she the cautionary centre of *The Handmaid's Tale*?

Well, quite simply it was then and it still is. There are a lot of women in the United States who make a career out of telling women they shouldn't have careers. And you think, well if you're really serious about this why aren't you home baking the buns? Why are you having this career which seems to pay you quite well and gives you a lot of publicity? If you really think women should be in the home, why aren't you in it?

I was interested in Atwood's depiction of life before the creation of Gilead, when women had been free to make their own choices about the way they lived their lives. She does, though, make clear in the novel that the world before Gilead saw the proliferation of pornography, prostitution and violence against women, and the pollution that led to the decline in women's fertility. Why had she been keen to point to the failures of modern life?

We do not live in a perfect world. You may have noticed that. [Laughs] Utopias and dystopias are always placed against where we are now. So the Utopia will tell us how crummy our world is and how much better we can do it if we only follow the following pattern and the dystopia will diverge from where we are, take a path that we are on and show us how much worse things can be. So it's all set against our present position and the ideology of the powers that be in Gilead is to say 'We have improved things for women, but look how much worse they were then.' And the women's movement in its many, many different branches and varieties always takes off from the same place as well – look how bad things are. We can make them better if only we . . . fill in the blank, whatever it may be. And it is a cleft stick, because if you just accept things the way they are they only get worse and, if you try to improve them in a radical way, heads inevitably roll. So, what are we to do?

It was not long after the publication of the book that a radical Islamist group, the Taliban, took over Afghanistan, following the expulsion of the Soviets. It spelt catastrophe for women there: those who had in the past worn short skirts, attended university and worked in the professions were now forbidden from leaving the house unless fully covered by a *burqa* and in the company of a male relative. I remember talking to women there who had no work, no money and no way of feeding their children. How prescient did Atwood feel she had been?

> In a way that's a bit of a side issue – a diversion. We're always trying to displace our own problems and failures with other societies, are we not, so, rather than thinking what we ourselves are doing we look at what somebody else is doing and say that is terrible. Which it is. But it doesn't let us off the hook. So, prescient/not prescient. The stuff was already going on. If you recall the Iranian return of the Ayatollah had already occurred when I was writing that book. I was in Afghanistan six weeks before Amin was assassinated [in 1979], so I saw it at the last possible moment when you could see the old Afghanistan before the astonishing amount of destruction that has taken place there occurred. I was in Iran eight months before the Shah was toppled and you could feel something was about to happen. You could just feel it. Because that was no picnic either.

We moved on to the world as it was in 2010 and the way things had changed so dramatically since 9/11 and the attacks in New York and Washington. How dangerous a book is *The Handmaid's Tale* in the current climate?

> Let me put it this way. In 1989–90 when the Cold War wall came down everybody thought that in the race between *1984* and *Brave New World*, *Brave New World* had won and

that what we were gonna get was everyone would go shopping and they did! And you had people writing books called *The End of History*, which was silly to begin with. But now, since 9/11, I would say that *1984* is now very much back in the running and Big Brother is in fact watching you from every traffic crossing in London. This place is just covered with surveillance cameras now and it always comes in as 'It's for your own protection.' It's always like that. It's always fear-based. People accept it because they're afraid. And it's fine until somebody decides they're going to use this astonishing amount of apparatus for their own purposes.

Given my interest in women's history, it's not surprising that my last question went something like this: 'There's a very strong argument in the Postscript of the novel for the recording of women's history. Why did you end there?'

The idea is important for a couple of reasons. One is that it lets us know that regime did not last for ever, so it's an optimistic thing. Gilead is over. It's now gone where regimes like that go when they're over. They go to academic conferences and people write papers about them and that is what has happened to this one. And the other reason for doing it is – the central character in the book who is our only narrator has no access to an overview. She doesn't have any historian's knowledge of how the regime really came about and how it was implemented. She doesn't know too much about its rationale, although she sees a lot of its propaganda. So it's also a way of letting the reader in on the background to that particular regime.

As always, despite my fear of the sharp wit and greatly superior intellect I confronted in every encounter with Margaret Atwood,

I was overwhelmingly impressed by her vast knowledge of history, culture and the human condition. I have been, I'm afraid, one of those who read the book when it was first published and said, 'Great dystopian and feminist story, Margaret, but it could never happen here.' I have changed my mind in the light of subsequent events, particularly in Afghanistan, Iran and other parts of the Middle East. I have often discussed her work in my speeches around the country to warn of how women's rights are rarely set in stone and we must continue to be vigilant to ensure we do not allow the ones we've gained to be rolled back. I suspect I now might be tempted to be one of the questioners she describes here:

> Once upon a time when I was doing public events people would ask me, 'What do you think about the arts?' 'What do you think of the role of women?' 'What do you think of men?' 'What do you think of all these things?' And now they ask one thing and that one thing is this: 'Is there hope?'

15

Wangari Maathai

1940–2011

It often seems that women who make their way to the top in the difficult climate of a developing country do it as part of a dynasty, following a father, a husband or even a brother. Wangari Maathai had none of those privileges. She was a simple country girl who, partly through good luck, but mostly through intelligence and hard work, rose to become a significant player in her country's democracy movement, an environmentalist whose influence spread across the world and the first African woman to be awarded the Nobel Peace Prize. She was only too aware of how rare an achievement hers was:

> I should have known that ambition and success were not to be expected in an African woman. An African woman should be a good African woman whose qualities should be coyness, shyness, submissiveness, incompetence and crippling dependency. A highly educated African woman is bound to be dominant, aggressive, uncontrollable, a bad influence.

Wangari Muta (Maathai an adaptation of her husband's name) was born in 1940, on April Fool's Day. When we met for the second time, in 2008, after the publication of her autobiography

Unbowed, she explained that she'd always looked on this inauspicious start in life as rather amusing, given the struggles she faced.

Wangari was born in a village called Ihithe, which lies in the central highlands of Kenya. Her family was Kikuyu, the largest ethnic group in the country. They had long roots in that area, but when she was three the family relocated to a white-owned farm in the Rift Valley, where her father had found a job. There was no school near the farm and she, her mother and brothers went back to Ihithe when she was seven. I asked her how she, a girl, had managed to achieve the education she had when it was virtually unknown for a girl from her background to go to school at all in the 1940s:

> Well, I owe my fortune to my father, to my parents, actually, and my eldest brother because my father was aware of the value of education. He himself barely went to school but wanted his children to go to school. So he sent us back to the village so that his sons could go to school.
>
> In a way it was an accident that I went back to where my father had come from so that my brothers could go to school, but it was my eldest brother who asked my mother why I wasn't going to school like him and, thanks to my mother, bless her heart, she said I could go to school with them. And that was how I went to school at a time when girls were not going to school.
>
> So I was very lucky. And I owe a lot to my brother, although he asked that question innocently. Fortunately she did not respond by saying 'Oh! I need her to carry or fetch firewood and go with the younger siblings to fetch water for me.' She said, 'No, go to school with the others.' So, thank you, mother.

When I asked Wangari what she best remembered from her childhood, her clearest memory was of something that, later in life, would inspire her passion for the environment:

When I look back and especially what's been happening to our planet and to our region, I remember the green countryside and the forests. I lived very close to the forests and the mountains and it was just like a carpet of green, and I remember very clean rivers from which we would fetch water and drink it. We didn't have to boil it because it was so pure. And I remember plenty. Plenty of food, plenty of firewood. It was a very calm childhood.

When Wangari was eleven she started at a Catholic boarding school in Nyeri, where she learned to speak English fluently and converted to Catholicism. As a result of being away from home she largely avoided the horrific impact of the Mau Mau uprising of the 1950s against the white British colonialists, being only briefly arrested for the 'crime' of being a Kikuyu schoolgirl. Her mother was not so lucky and was forced out of her homestead into a village where her family would be safe.

When Wangari completed her studies at the Mission in 1956 she came top of her class and was admitted into the only Catholic High School for girls in Kenya. The end of East African colonialism was drawing closer. In 1960, the then Prime Minister of the UK, Harold Macmillan, made a speech in Cape Town in South Africa in which he said: 'The wind of change is blowing through this continent. Whether we like it or not, this growth of national consciousness is a political fact.' It was a clear signal that the Conservative government had no intention of blocking the independence aspirations of countries Britain had colonised.

Kenyan politicians were already proposing ways to make western education available to their brightest students. Senator John F Kennedy, who would later become President of the United States, agreed to fund a project – known as the Kennedy Airlift – through the Joseph P Kennedy Jr Foundation. Three hundred Kenyans were selected to study in the US in September 1960. Wangari Maathai was one of them.

She won a scholarship to study biology, chemistry and German in Kansas, and went on to Pittsburgh to study for a Master's degree in biology, funded by the Africa-America Institute. While in Pittsburgh she worked with local environmentalists on ridding the city of air pollution, her first step into the work that would dominate her life.

In January 1966, Wangari returned to Kenya with an MSc in biological sciences, and found a job as research assistant to a professor of zoology at the University College of Nairobi. When she arrived at the university to begin work she was told the job had been given to someone else. She was convinced she had suffered discrimination as a result of her sex and from a bias against her tribal background. Eventually she found another job as a research assistant in the microanatomy section of the new Department of Veterinary Anatomy in the School of Veterinary Medicine at the University College of Nairobi. Her professor, a German scholar named Reinhold Hofmann, encouraged her to study in Giessen and Munich for a PhD in veterinary anatomy in the late 1960s. In the spring of 1969 she returned to Nairobi as an assistant lecturer and married Mwangi Mathai, who had also studied in America. By December 1971 she had a son and a daughter, and had become the first East African woman to be awarded a PhD, from the University College of Nairobi.

Politically things were changing in Kenya. Mwangi Mathai stood for a seat in parliament but lost. During the election campaign, Tom Mboya, the politician who had been instrumental in arranging for Kenyan students to study overseas, was assassinated and President Kenyatta effectively ended multi-party democracy in the country.

Wangari rose through academia, becoming chair of the Department of Veterinary Anatomy in 1976 and associate professor in 1977. She worked with several charitable organisations, including the Red Cross, the National Council of Women in Kenya and the Environment Liaison Centre. It was becoming clear to her that environmental degradation was an ever more damaging problem in her country. As she explained to me, inspiration for her work in conservation came from what she saw around her when she first returned from America:

When I came back we had just become an independent country. Jomo Kenyatta had just become President and he was constantly saying to the people work hard and build a new country. I wanted to rise high at the university and I embarked on research that took me to the countryside and I was shocked by my observations, especially when it rained. The rivers would be brown with silt. That is something a lot of us see in Africa, but many of us don't realise that brown colour is tons of top soil that is disappearing into the sea and lakes, but for me, because I grew up in the countryside where water was clean and there was no cultivation along the hillsides or near the river banks, that bothered me. I thought this is a disaster for the livestock industry, more so than the disease I was trying to investigate, so that started me thinking we have got to stop this erosion. Then I discussed with other women in preparation for the United Nations conference in Mexico and they were talking about how there was no clean drinking water. There was no good food, there was no firewood, there was no income, especially for women. This was not the countryside I remembered as a child. So I told them, well, maybe we could plant trees.

That small suggestion led to a huge change. In 1977 she founded the Green Belt Movement. Its stated aim is to 'work at the grassroots, national and international levels to promote environmental conservation; to build climate resistance and empower communities, especially women and girls; to foster democratic space and sustainable livelihoods'. Wangari's own motto was 'When we plant trees, we plant the seeds of peace and hope.' How did she manage to organise it and get it done?

> Well, it took time. I must say I did not have a plan of action. I knew that we needed to plant a lot of trees and we started with the National Council of Women in Kenya. I did not envisage a huge movement. We started by approaching local foresters, then we realized the local forester was planting only exotic trees and I realised local diversity was being lost. I realised when I was growing up there were a lot of indigenous trees and they were disappearing and the exotics – especially the pines and eucalyptus – were dominating the countryside. Slowly by moving from one step to another it became necessary to not only organise women in groups, but also to ask women to teach others and give them an incentive. For every tree that would survive when planted at the farms, on school compounds, on the side of rivers we gave women a financial incentive and that became important in the campaign.

As the Green Belt Movement expanded, charitable support was forthcoming, and was used for the most basic and practical purchases. A significant amount came from the British telethon *Comic Relief*; Green Belt used the money to buy wheelbarrows. Why had that been such a significant move forward?

> The Green Belt Movement is able to provide tools for the women and these tools are very important for the communities because many agricultural communities don't have tools to deal with simple tasks. Wheelbarrows and spades become extremely useful. The minute you put wheelbarrows there even the men come to be a part. They want to be involved in the work. As soon as you have a wheelbarrow you hear men say, 'Ah, this is fantastic.'

Life was never easy for this determined African woman. Wangari's third child was born in 1974, but in 1977 she and her husband separated and two years later he filed for divorce. He complained that his wife was 'too strong-minded for a woman' and that he was 'unable to control her'. In court, he called her cruel and accused her of infidelity. The judge ruled in his favour. In an interview with a magazine Wangari described the judge as either incompetent or corrupt. As a result she was charged with contempt of court, found guilty and sentenced to six months in prison. She was released after only a few days, but the cost of the divorce and loss of her husband's wages meant she had to take a second job that paid better than the university. She joined the United Nations Development Programme, which meant constant travelling, and she still held her post as a professor. She had to send her children to live with their father.

She made several attempts to get into parliament, knowing that it was only with political influence could she pursue her environmental ambitions to best effect. On several occasions she was simply not allowed to stand; again, Wangari saw the spectre of discrimination against her sex and her tribe at work, blocking her progress. Her attempt to stand for her home region of Nyeri in 1982 became something of a 'Catch-22'. In order to campaign, she was required by law to resign her post at the university. She did. The courts decided she was ineligible to run for office because she had not re-registered to vote in the previous presidential election in 1979. She fought the decision in court, but the judge disqualified her from running on a technicality. She asked for her job back but was denied and, because as a staff member she'd lived in university accommodation, she was evicted.

Discrimination deprived her of her home and her income, so she moved into a tiny house she had bought years before and threw herself into the Green Belt and the pro-democracy movements. Her protests against government plans, such as the construction of buildings in Uhuru Park, led to frequent clashes with President Daniel arap Moi, who told her to be a 'proper woman in the African tradition and respect men and be quiet'. There were attempts to close down the Green Belt Movement; in January 1992 the names of Wangari Maathai and other pro-democracy campaigners were found on an assassination hit list. She was arrested and charged with sedition and treason and spent time in jail. A number of international organisations and US senators, including Al Gore, put pressure on the government and the charges were dropped. Through the 1990s she campaigned for democratic government and for environmental causes, facing frequent arrest, harassment and, on at least two occasions, physical violence. In 2002 she won a seat in parliament and was appointed Assistant Minister in the Ministry for the Environment and Natural Resources.

In 2004, this extraordinarily determined, courageous and resourceful woman was awarded the ultimate international accolade for the phenomenal work she had done and for the recognition of the deprivations she had suffered to achieve her aims. She received a call to tell her she had been awarded the Nobel Peace Prize for 'her contribution to sustainable development, democracy and peace'. The Nobel Committee issued a statement commending Maathai for standing up 'courageously against the former oppressive regime in Kenya. Her unique forms of action have contributed to drawing attention to political oppression – nationally and internationally. She has served as inspiration for many in the fight for democratic rights and has especially encouraged women to better their situation'.

In that last interview, in 2008, three years before her untimely death from ovarian cancer, I asked her what it was that had made her so determined to fight for what she believed in the face of so much violent opposition. How had she coped with constant uncertainty throughout her life?

I think I was very lucky. I was twenty when I went to America during the sixties and you will remember

America was going through the civil rights movement led by Martin Luther King and that experience of being a black young person in America in the sixties was very interesting and empowering to me. I had never seen anything like that. There was nothing like that, despite some of the Mau Mau experience, in Kenya. It gave me a very different perception of what human rights is all about and I also came to understand you have to struggle to make things better.

It didn't come on a silver plate. I saw men sitting in a café and having ketchup poured on their heads and they wouldn't move because they were using non-violent means. That really transformed me. When I went back to my country I was ready to promote a democratic space and I knew I was doing the right thing.

For me Wangari Maathai embodies everything I admire about women who begin their lives with zero advantages, face overwhelming opposition and carry on because they know they are doing the right thing, not just for themselves, but for the benefit of everyone around them, particularly the other women who are struggling too. Her influence has cascaded around the world.

Other women have also been prominent in the environmental movement. Rachel Carson wrote *Silent Spring*, her warning against the dangers of synthetic pesticides and a chemical industry that was careless with the truth about the impact its products might have. Vandana Shiva, in India, worked to protect the diversity of native seeds. Sylvia Earle, the ocean explorer, advised us all to 'Hold up a mirror and ask yourself what you are capable of doing and what you really care about. Then take the initiative – don't wait for someone to ask you to ask.'

Wangari Maathai didn't wait for someone to ask but I'm not sure how I would have managed to bounce back after the knockbacks she faced. How do you deal with such eye-watering sexism from the mouth of the President of your country, who dared to say she should be a 'proper woman' and shut up? Then there's the husband and father of her children who accused her of being 'too strong-minded for a woman'. She survived it all to make her mark; a mark that can be seen throughout Kenya. The current tally of trees planted there, through networks of rural women, is fifty-one million. In her memory, we should all bear in mind the Chinese proverb: 'The best time to plant a tree was twenty years ago. The second best time is now.'

16

Hillary Rodham Clinton

1947–

Hillary Clinton came closer than any other woman to breaking through what she herself described as the highest and hardest glass ceiling. In 2016 she stood as the Democratic Party's chosen candidate to become President of the United States, an office that, for all the changes across the globe, is still the most powerful position in the world. On that fateful election day – 8 November – she failed, losing the election to Donald Trump.

Although she won the majority of the popular vote, she didn't make it through America's rather strange system of electoral colleges. The system of electing a US President is a two-step affair: first the electorate goes to the polls, but each state is worth a set number of Electoral College votes. In most states, the winner of the popular ballot gets all that state's electoral college votes, unless, of course, members of the electoral college choose not to vote for them. There are 538 members of the college; 270 electoral votes are needed to win. Trump won 46.1% of the popular vote and Clinton 48.2%. In the electoral college Trump had 304. Clinton only 227. Democracy in America. Fact!

I watched Hillary Clinton throughout the campaign. She often looked uncomfortable in front of large crowds; she is not a natural orator. She frequently appeared to be intimidated by an overbearing Trump, particularly during those crucial head-to-head television debates towards the end of an exhausting, long and bitter battle. 'He was literally breathing down my neck', she said. 'My skin crawled.'

Quite how Clinton endured the barrage of insults she faced I shall never know. Trump consistently referred to her as a 'criminal' or 'such a nasty woman', with absolutely no evidence with which to back up his claims. The current British Foreign Secretary, Boris Johnson, compared her to 'a sadistic nurse in a mental hospital', and a Republican pollster said, 'She reminds most men of their first wife – or mother-in-law.' The misogyny came thick and fast. No wonder she said: 'There are times when all I want to do is scream into a pillow.'

She was not unaware of the impression she seemed to create: that of an aloof or cold or unemotional being. As Clinton explained in a magazine article, she:

> . . . had to learn as a young woman to control my emotions . . . you need to protect yourself, you need to keep steady, but at the same time you don't want to seem 'walled off' . . . if I create that perception, then I take responsibility. I don't view myself as cold or unemotional and neither do my friends. And neither does my family.
>
> I'm not Barack Obama. I'm not Bill Clinton. Both of them carry themselves with a naturalness that is very appealing to audiences . . . And that can be very difficult for a woman. Because who are your role models?
>
> If you want to run for the Senate or run for the Presidency, most of your role models are going to be men. And what works for them won't work for you. Women are seen through a different lens . . . I'll go to these events and there'll be men speaking before me, and they'll be pounding the message, and screaming how we need to win the election. And people will love it. And I want to do the same

thing. Because I care about this stuff. But I've learned that I can't be quite so passionate in my presentation. I love to wave my arms, but apparently that's a little bit scary to people. And I can't yell too much. It comes out as 'too loud' or 'too shrill' or 'too this' or 'too that'.

Hillary Rodham Clinton's background is better known than most. After all, she has been on the front pages for more than twenty-five years. She was born in 1947 in Chicago to Hugh and Dorothy Rodham. They were a middle-class Methodist family; Hugh ran a small business and Dorothy was a homemaker. Hillary's first involvement in politics came in 1960, when she was only thirteen; she canvassed for the Republican candidate, Richard Nixon. In 1965 she began to re-order her leanings when she was studying political science at Wellesley College. She was President of the Young Republicans for a while but became more liberal as she encountered protests against the Vietnam War, the civil rights movement and saw the assassinations of two men she admired: Martin Luther King and Robert Kennedy.

Hillary Rodham graduated with high honours in political science and went on to study law at Yale, specialising in children's studies. It was at Yale that she met one William Jefferson Clinton. During her career as a lawyer in Washington she worked for the Children's Defense Fund and served on the House Judiciary Committee during the Watergate affair, taking part in the impeachment of the President. Ironic given that, much later in her life, she had to face the possibility that her husband might be impeached as a result of his sexual shenanigans and being economical with the truth about his affair with Monica Lewinsky. In 1975 she married Bill and, as the committed feminist she had become, chose to keep her own name, Rodham.

In 1976, the couple left Washington for Little Rock, Arkansas. He enjoyed a stratospheric political ascent to Governor, and she continued her work in the law. She was one of the founders of the

Arkansas Advocates for Children and Families, became the first woman to be appointed chairman of the Board of Directors of the Legal Services Corporation and was the first to be appointed a full partner of the Rose Law Firm, where she specialised in intellectual property law and patent infringements. These are impressive career achievements for a woman still only in her early thirties, marred only by a failed business adventure with their friends James and Susan McDougal, with whom she and Bill founded the Whitewater Development Corporation.

The Clintons had been looking for a way to supplement their income and agreed to join the McDougals in the purchase of land along the White River, build holiday homes, let them for a while and then sell the houses at a profit. The McDougals fell into debt because interest rates rose, and it was alleged that Bill Clinton used his position as Governor to pressure people into lending money to his friend. A long inquiry ensued, eventually led by the independent counsel who would surface again later in the Lewinsky scandal: Kenneth Starr. The investigation continued for several years, at a cost of some $50 million. No conclusive evidence of wrongdoing by the Clintons was found but Bill's reputation was severely dented in the early years of his presidency.

The couple's longing to have children proved difficult. Hillary suffered from a common gynaecological condition, endometriosis, but eventually, at the age of thirty-three, in 1980, she became pregnant and Chelsea Victoria Clinton, the couple's only child, was born. Hillary was of course attacked for being a career woman rather than a stay-at-home wife – why wasn't she there caring for her child and her husband? The temerity of hanging on to her own name was also too much for Bill's Arkansas electorate and she ditched it.

In 1992 Bill won the Democratic nomination for the presidency. During the campaign, the misogyny that would continue to dog Hillary was redoubled. Her husband and many of their supporters saw her as a capable professional woman, a First Lady who could share her husband's political work as an equal partner. Others saw a First Lady as nothing but a decorative hostess in the White House, who would fit the image associated with all-American apple pie. She was so pressured into attempting to match the homely aura of her predecessor, Barbara Bush that she found herself appearing on television explaining how she made biscuits and buns.

Nevertheless, Hillary took on the job of chairing the Task Force on National Health reform. It was a project that eventually failed due to of lack of support for the policy in the US legislature, although she was successful, during her husband's second term and together with Edward Kennedy and Orrin Hatch, in getting the State Children's Health Insurance Programme passed. She wrote a book: *It Takes a Village: And Other Lessons Children Teach Us*; the welfare of children was always a primary concern.

It was in 1995, at the fourth World United Nations Women's Conference in Beijing, that I first saw Hillary Rodham Clinton speak live. There was no doubting her passionate feminist credentials. Throughout her speech she emphasised her understanding that all women, regardless of colour, class or sexuality, must be included when governments responded to her demands to protect and educate women and girls and value their work, whether that be in public or private life. It was a long speech, but one section has always stuck in my mind:

> It is a violation of human rights when babies are denied food, or drowned, or suffocated, or their spines broken, simply because they are born girls . . . when women and girls are sold into the slavery of prostitution . . . set on fire and burned to death because their marriage dowries are deemed too small . . . raped in their own communities . . . subjected to rape as a tactic or prize of war . . . brutalised by the painful and degrading practice of genital mutilation . . .

denied the right to plan their own families . . . human rights are women's rights . . . and women's rights are human rights, once and for all.

It was an astonishing and brave speech, delivered in front of men and women from all over the world; a speech that touched on so many issues that even in the 1990s were barely acknowledged. I wanted to run to the stage and hug her. I didn't, of course, but there have been so many occasions when I've seen her display similar courage, whether as a result of her husband's humiliating affairs or the attacks on her deeply held and profoundly honest beliefs, that I've just wanted to let her know what an important advocate and role model for women she has been.

I can't help wishing she could have appeared to the US electorate as she had appeared to me then in Beijing, and again when I finally got to meet her for a radio interview in July 2014. The occasion was the publication of her book *Hard Choices*. In 2000, she had become Senator for New York State, having officially resumed using her own name: Hillary Rodham Clinton. She had put herself forward to become the Democratic candidate for the 2008 presidential election. On that occasion she lost to Barack Obama, withdrew, and gave him her support during the campaign.

When Obama became President he asked Hillary to become his Secretary of State. She agreed and did the job for four years until she resigned in 2013. She had decided to devote herself to the Bill, Hillary and Chelsea Clinton Foundation, focusing on early childhood development and the education of girls across the world. There was much talk of her again standing for President, but she had not yet made the final decision.

On 3 July 2014 there was great excitement in the *Woman's Hour* studio. Hillary was to be the first item in the programme. She was late for the start time of two minutes past 10am. Not her fault; her minders had underestimated the amount of London traffic her car would be likely to face. A minor panic ensued, but we had another interesting and significant story with which we could lead the programme instead.

Shirley Williams, Baroness Williams, one of the UK's best-known and best-loved politicians, had agreed to take part in the programme, together with her best friend Helga. They had been close since Helga came to the UK during the Second World War as a German-Jewish refugee. We had planned to interview the two women, now in their eighties, after Hillary, but they were happy, in an emergency, to take her place at the top of the programme. We talked about the trip they had made together to Germany, where a canal towpath had been named in honour of Shirley's mother, Vera Brittain, who had angered the British during the Second World War by writing in opposition to blanket bombing of German cities. The Germans had a different view.

Into my ear, as my conversation with Shirley and Helga came to a close, were the whispered, thrilled words of the producer: 'She's here! Hillary Clinton's here!' I thanked Shirley and Helga and, as they headed for the door, I began to introduce Hillary, who crossed to the seat Shirley had vacated.

I was ready for a tough tussle with everything from Monica Lewinsky to Benghazi on the agenda, but halfway through my introduction, mentioning the years as First Lady, the failed attempt at the presidency and her stint as America's leading diplomat, travelling more than a million miles to 112 countries, Mrs Clinton stared at me with a look of complete alarm and began to shake a handbag across the table in front of me. *Woman's Hour* is, remember, broadcast live, so every word and sound effect went out to the nation. I had no choice but to say, 'Ah! Just a moment. I don't quite know what's happening here, but Hillary Clinton is waggling a handbag in front of me.'

At this point Shirley leant over, took the bag and said, with a grateful shriek, 'Oh Hillary! Thank you so much!' In that moment the cleverest, smartest, probably most famous and potentially the most powerful woman in the world was simply one of us: an ordinary woman who had thoughtfully observed that another had got up in a hurry and forgotten a vital piece of equipment. Hillary Clinton knew that nothing is more important to a woman than her life support system, her handbag!

We began our conversation about how she'd arrived at *Hard Choices* for the title of the book. In the mix had been: *The Scrunchy Chronicles: 112 countries and it's still all about the hair.* References to her hairstyle had dogged her throughout her career but how did she manage to find it all so amusing? She had to be amused, Hillary explained, or else she would be reduced to pulling out that very hair. All part of the double standard that women in public life just have to get used to, even as we keep trying to change it and create greater participation and equality for women everywhere.

It had puzzled me for some time why she had accepted President Obama's offer of the job as Secretary of State when the campaign for the Democratic Party's presidential nomination had been a particularly bruising one, in which some rather bitter things had been said, including a suggestion that her husband, Bill, was a racist. She had, she said, resolved her differences with Obama in what she described as a long and intimate conversation before the election campaign began. She and Bill had been hurt by the things that had been said but she became convinced that the Obamas themselves had not been responsible for the backbiting. She and Bill chose to support him against the Republican opponent and canvassed on his behalf during the campaign for the presidency. She said she was delighted at the result.

She was flattered to be asked to become Secretary of State, told the President she was honoured, but had to say no as her intention was to return to the Senate as the representative for New York and get back to a more regular rhythm of life. Obama said he wasn't going to take no for an answer and, as she put it, 'he kept at it, showing his persistence when he knows what he wants'. Eventually she agreed; when she called him to tell him she would serve he said, 'Well, contrary to reports I think we can become good friends.' She described their partnership as productive and said they did indeed become friends.

Hillary Clinton was the third woman in recent years to act as America's Secretary of State. She followed Madeleine Albright and Condoleezza Rice, and I wondered what impact that powerful female presence had had on the way women are perceived across the world. It was not, she thought, such a big deal when she came to a country like the UK, but in other parts of the world it was a key factor. She, Madeleine and Condoleezza would often kid each other over the prevailing situation because, in some places where women are denied their human rights almost from birth, the way they were treated was as 'honorary men'. Clinton was always the only woman in the room, including everyone in a secondary or service position, and she became used to it. But it remained the reason she always insisted on discussing women and girls as a key element of US foreign policy; not as a luxury, but as a necessity.

I reminded her that I'd first heard her discuss women's issues all those years ago in Beijing, and that it was not an easy or popular subject to raise, even in the late 1990s. A degree of criticism for being someone who 'banged on' had often been levelled at her. Nevertheless, no one had more experience than she in discovering the depth of discrimination and outright cruelty faced by millions of women in so many of the countries she visited, and she never ducked the important questions. Clinton thought it required courage and perseverance in some parts of the world, and frequently what she faced was not outright hostility, but indifference:

The rolling of the eyes because I started raising women's issues. Despite all of the pressing problems in the world, what I would say grabbed the headlines. I wanted to focus on what I think are the tram lines and one of those was the empowerment of women. So when I began talking about it, I could see the calculation behind male leaders' eyes, 'Oh, there she goes again. It's her hobby horse. She's gonna tell me this and then we'll move onto the important things.' But we still have countries where girls are not even registered at birth because they're so inconsequential. We have so much work to do. We need to change laws and regulations we need to protect women and all the rest of it, but we have work to do here at home. We still haven't broken through the highest glass ceiling and it's not just in politics. It's in business, journalism and academia. Everywhere.

I asked how she'd managed to deal with those glazed eyes when she was trying to raise specific cases of injustice to women and girls. Saudi Arabia was a particularly difficult environment for a female diplomat to challenge specific cases where women and girls were suffering. It was a country where she encountered no women at all in public life, a country where she was not free to go out without a head covering and a man to accompany her. She managed to make contact with women who were working to try and effect change on the ground and was alerted to concerns they hoped she might address. First, child marriage; she heard an appeal from a mother who wanted to protect her twelve-year-old daughter from abuse in a marriage she had tried to prevent. Then, of course, there were the women who were defying the law and driving their cars. How did she decide what to be assertive about and how to deal with it without embarrassing a government?

Her answer was long and wide-ranging:

That is such an important question and one I struggled with from time to time. The child marriage in Saudi Arabia, I had a behind-the-scenes intervention asking that this child, because that's what she was, be given a divorce. Her mother was being very courageous, standing up for her daughter, which many mothers in some parts of the world just don't feel they can or, frankly, they agree with marrying their children off at nine, ten, eleven or twelve.

When it came to driving, which is a political decision, which in my view needed to be taken seriously, I spoke out. But also in other settings, like Yemen, where there was a child marriage case – this brave little girl got on a bus, found a lawyer to represent her and got a divorce. Then I spoke out. You have to evaluate, is it going to help or hurt? Is it going to help the individuals or hurt them? Is it going to help the forces of change and the activists or not?

I have a lot of contact with activists around the world and they advise me. Like female genital mutilation which I took on in the 1990s. I supported grassroots groups that were going village to village in Senegal to convince the leaders – all men – not to subject their daughters to this barbaric procedure. It was slow and steady, but it gained credibility because it wasn't seen as being imposed from the outside. So making change is complex and you have to be constantly evaluating what will work.

We came eventually to the subject which has kept Hillary under unprecedented scrutiny for donkeys' years: her private life and her marriage. It's often assumed that her steadfast 'standing by her man' lost her votes during the presidential election. Donald Trump grasped every opportunity to remind her of her husband's infidelities. Rich, from a man who boasted about being able to grope any woman he wanted to, because he was a star. But he took the criticism of Hillary to a whole new level when he accused her of being 'an unbelievably nasty, mean enabler and what she did to a lot of these women is disgraceful'. He even gathered four women who claimed to have been sexually abused by Bill Clinton to appear at one of the televised debates, claiming Hillary had actively enabled her husband's affairs and rubbished those who had complained about him.

I can find no evidence that Hillary ever said anything derogatory about the women her husband had been involved with, at least not in public. What she said to him in private doesn't bear thinking about! It is instructive, though, that a woman could be criticised and humiliated for having done her best to keep her marriage and her family together, whereas a man still appears to have been rather admired for having 'put it about'. As for Trump's tactics during the election, Hillary described him as 'going low' and insisted her response would be to 'go high'. Her supporters saw it as the worst kind of vicious right-wing conspiracy.

I found her response to my questions about her marriage intelligent, loyal and thoughtful. It seems to me that she was painting a picture of what was described by Shakespeare as 'a marriage of true minds'. Yes, sexual infidelity can be hurtful and humiliating, but sex is not the only part of an intimate relationship that keeps a couple together. Here's how our exchange went:

HILLARY: Well, my husband and I have been together for more than four decades, starting as law students and I like to say we started a conversation there in law school and we've never stopped. Of course he's been very prominent as President of the US, but I have always appreciated the extraordinary support and constant interest he has given me as I have tried to reciprocate. Now he and I and our daughter run the Clinton Foundation. The work he's doing internationally is very meaningful to him. So we have never run out of projects to do or issues to discuss and we also have a lot of fun. I mean part of the reason I am so happy to be out of public office for the time being at least is because we get to spend time together and we get to do things like go for walks with our dogs which we really enjoy.

JENNI: But you know, I hate to mention this, but Monica Lewinsky's presence in London has been widely reported recently and she's described herself very openly as the most humiliated woman in the world as a result of her relationship with your husband when she was a young White House intern. How do you perceive her and your husband's role in all that?

HILLARY: Well that is something that we've moved beyond and our country has moved beyond and I have wished her well, but I think it's important to stay focused on the here and now and, for us, back in the US, we still have a lot of work to do. Our people are not recovered from the great recession. There's an enormous amount of anxiety and insecurity. Our politics is dysfunctional as you can see from over here. I am looking at the here and now and what we can do going forward.

JENNI: Just one more question about the private life. What is it about Bill that has enabled you to forgive his infidelities?

HILLARY: Forgiveness is a choice and I fully respect those who don't make that choice for whatever reason in their personal or professional lives. For me it was absolutely the right choice and for me it is something that is incredibly difficult, but I am grateful every day that that's the choice I have made. I have counselled others to see if in their own hearts they can also do that. If they can't, fine, and even if they do, but then choose a different path, fine as well. But it's not by accident that the great religions, the great writers, talk about how the person who forgives is liberated, maybe even more than the person who's forgiven.

We closed the interview with the 'billion dollar question'. It had been widely reported that vast amounts of money were being raised to support her second bid to become the Democratic candidate for the presidential election in 2016. Was she planning to stand? She was non-committal, saying that the most exciting thing in her life at that moment was becoming a grandmother in the coming autumn and she intended to be fully present for that event.

When I pressed her on the question of how important was it to her that there should be a woman in the White House, soon, her answer was unequivocal:

> It's really important. I really believe it's unfinished business . . . I have a daughter. I have fought for women's rights and opportunities for girls my entire adult life. I want to see us have a woman in the White House. Forty-nine other countries have, including yours, had a woman in the highest government position. Sooner is better, but, certainly in my lifetime, I wanna see it!

It was not to happen for her. She stood, she campaigned, she lost. Margaret Atwood best expressed the shock that was felt by so many of us when we discovered the extent of some of the outrageous critiques that had been thrown at Clinton: 'You can find websites that say Hillary was actually a Satanist with demonic powers. It's so seventeenth century that you can hardly believe it.' Hillary tried to deal with some of this lunacy in the book she published after the election. There is no rational explanation except to understand that we women have not come as far as we thought we had.

I said earlier that I wished the woman I had met at such close quarters had presented herself to the electorate in the same way she appeared to me. I witnessed a clever, compassionate, warm, funny, generous and humane woman; the most impressive I have ever met. And I have met a lot! Of her experience and knowledge of America's political landscape and position in the world, her predecessor, Barack Obama, seemed to me to have it about right: 'There has never been a man or a woman – not me, not Bill, nobody – more qualified.'

It may well be too late for her to make another stab at the presidency. She'll be seventy-three when Trump comes up for re-election in 2020 and, after two bruising attempts she would need to be quite mad, in my view, to put herself through it again. So, we, and the rest of the world, are left with Trump, who appears to run the White House in much the same way as he presented *The Apprentice*, shouting 'You're fired' at the slightest hint of disloyalty from any member of staff. His former Director of the Federal Bureau of Investigation, James Comey, has likened him to a Mafia boss.

It depresses me beyond measure that a significant number of the women of America were prepared to vote for and continue to support a man who's been proven to have behaved in the most vulgar way possible towards women, proudly claiming he could have sex with anyone in his version of 'locker room talk'. He announces foreign policy on Twitter, seems to spend an inordinate amount of time looking in the mirror to do his hair and we can only wait and see what evidence comes to light on his dealings with the Russians during the election and what lies he has and hasn't told.

We could have had a President of the United States who knew what she was doing. It's a tragedy.

17

Benazir Bhutto

1953–2007

My first encounter with Benazir Bhutto occurred on 3 April 1986. She was thirty-three years old, nervously buried in her aunt's substantial but dingy basement flat in Chelsea in London. I have never met, before or since, a young person with such a heavy weight of grief, fear and duty weighing down on her back; she seemed almost physically bowed under the burden.

She was beautiful, with long dark hair, uncovered as had been her habit at her family home and in the West, luminous skin and huge, meltingly sad eyes. Only her nose was less than perfect, and later she would have that fixed by a superbly competent plastic surgeon. But my overwhelming impression was of a woman who was barely more than a girl, steeling herself to return to Pakistan, the country of her birth, where her father, the country's former Prime Minister, Zulfikar Ali Bhutto, had been executed and she and her mother imprisoned only seven years earlier.

Her early life had seemed more than perfect. Her family home in Karachi was exquisite; the Bhuttos were wealthy and privileged. Her father studied politics in Berkeley, law in Oxford and then returned to Karachi to become a government minister. Her mother, Nusrat, was of Iranian descent and the first woman in the Bhutto clan to completely reject purdah. When she was first married she was only allowed to leave the compound once a week to visit her family. She quickly broke free from the constraints imposed upon her and would often drive the older women on shopping trips. When the new home at 70 Clifton, a walled, luxury compound in Karachi, was built there were no separate quarters for women, although Benazir's grandfather bought another house opposite in which to receive his male visitors.

In her autobiography, *Daughter of the East*, Benazir says there was no discrimination at all in her family; in fact, she, as the eldest child (there were two younger brothers and a sister) received the most attention. The girl nicknamed Pinkie, because her skin at birth was so rosy, was to receive the very best education, first in Pakistan, then America and finally at Oxford University. Her mother, once a member of the National Assembly, took care of her Islamic education, ensuring her daughter was taught about the powerful women in the life of the Prophet and in Muslim history.

Her father, Benazir wrote, was determined to bring his country and his children into the twentieth century. She once overheard her mother asking her father if it were his intention that the children should marry in the extended family, as had previously been the habit. His response, to her great relief, was that he didn't want his boys to marry their cousins and leave them behind the compound walls any more than he wanted his daughters buried alive behind some other relative's walls. Benazir's autobiography tells the tale of her horror when her mother, as was expected, covered her daughter in a burqa on a trip away from home, saying 'You are no longer a child.' Her father disagreed and told her mother it was not necessary, 'Let her be judged by her character and her mind, not by her clothing.'

Benazir learned her politics and her sophistication, she said, at her parents' knees. With them, in Karachi, she met the great leaders of her youth, including Chen-Yi and Chou En-lai from China. She travelled the world with her father, to the United

States, Moscow, France and the UK. She was interested in fashion and, for a time, rejected the conventional *shalwar kamiz* and head covering of a young Pakistani woman; her parents bought her expensive and stylish clothes at Saks Fifth Avenue. She became thoroughly westernised and discovered she could mix and converse with anyone.

In 1967 her father formed the Pakistan People's Party (PPP), whose rallying cry became 'Bread, Clothing, Shelter': fundamentals that the poorest people of Pakistan did not have. Her father travelled around the country encouraging the villagers to 'Call for democracy, where the vote of the poorest carries the same weight as the vote of the richest.' The first floor of 70 Clifton became the party headquarters and Benazir soaked up her father's ideas. As the party became popular, tension and violence, what she describes as 'the stuff of political life in Pakistan', began to seep into the house. There were death threats, an attempt at assassination and the President, Ayub Khan, had Bhutto and his supporters arrested. 'That was the way of dictators', she wrote, 'Where there is protest, crush it.' Soon after her father's release he told her that it was time for university and she left for Harvard's Radcliffe College in the United States in the autumn of 1969. Benazir completed her studies at Harvard and went on to Oxford to take the degree that has been the educational background for so many aspiring politicians: Philosophy, Politics and Economics.

As she told me, Pakistan had seemed far away when she was at Oxford. She had been seen as something of a glamorous jet-setter and said that, as her father had predicted, they were the best years of her life. 'I think student life', she said:

... is a very, very happy time because one wasn't really aware of what life really means. The parents were there to offer security and protection, the biggest problems are exams and I had some pretty exciting debates at the Oxford Union during my own time, including the farewell which was 'This house likes dominating women' [laughs]. It could be taken either way, but just to make things a little more complicated I argued from the cross benches. So neither side!

In 1976 Benazir had stormed one of the commanding heights of the British establishment when she was elected President of the Oxford Union, a position held by many aspiring politicians before her, although by very few women.

Her father progressed in his political career during her university years, becoming first the elected President of Pakistan and, in 1973, Prime Minister. At home on a visit in late 1976, Benazir attended his birthday party, where she was introduced to General Zia-ul-Haq, her father's Army Chief of Staff-designate. He was a man said to be respected by the army (then as now a key and often dominant factor in Pakistan politics), although he was rumoured to have links with a fundamentalist religious group that did not want Pakistan ruled by Bhutto and the secular PPP, but rather by religious leaders. It was Zia who would overthrow her father only six months later; Zulfikar Ali Bhutto was deposed in a military coup, arrested and charged with murder.

As we sat in that basement flat in Chelsea in 1986, inevitably we talked about Benazir's father, the impact of his execution on the country, the family and the daughter who had adored and admired him:

We had that last meeting. Of course they hadn't told us that it was the last meeting, but we guessed. It was very sad, very painful. It's so difficult to walk away knowing you will never see someone again. For my mother, for myself of course life became very unsteady and I think we have known very few moments of happiness in the last eight and a half years. But certainly we've known satisfaction and I think satisfaction is what is important in life – to know that your conscience is addressed. I would say with the coup d'état the entire people of Pakistan were politicised. It had a tremendous impact on making everyone aware of the political questions. The regime tried to show they were arresting my father on a charge of murder, but such was the degree of politicisation of society that no-one accepted it. And none of the character assassination would wash.

It was clear that Benazir had suffered terribly in recent years; in and out of prison, exile in London and hearing of the death of her brother, who died in the south of France as a result of taking poison. Benazir was convinced he'd been murdered. But martial law had been lifted and she was determined to return to Pakistan. Not, she insisted, because that was what her father would have wanted, but out of her own ambition and sense of duty.

We discussed her reason for deciding to return and what she expected to find when she arrived:

It's said democracy has been restored for my country. That means freedom for the individual, freedom of association, freedom of expression and the right to liberty and therefore I've decided to return to Pakistan and see if democracy has been restored. Let's say I'm waiting with the rest of the nation in the hope that democracy really has been restored and that no obstacles will be placed in the way of any individual with a dissenting view from the regime. I think our party people are very excited about my return and are looking forward to it. There's a tremendous momentum and a mobilisation but seeing is believing so I shall be waiting till the morning of the tenth.

Obviously, given the experiences she'd undergone at the hands of Zia-ul-Haq, I wondered how much she was afraid of what she might face when she landed in Pakistan:

Well, let's say there are always apprehensions in life and certainly there are apprehensions now in my mind, but I don't think one should ever be scared of life and I've always believed in meeting challenges head on. Of course, house arrest was not very nice, but not only have I been under house arrest, but it's been declared a sub-jail and not many people realise I don't have the facilities of a house arrest, but jail officials take over the situation. Solitary confinement isn't very nice wherever you are. Being alone by yourself with no communication with others, no-one to talk to and no knowledge of what is going on in the world is not a very happy situation and, in fact, I try not to think back to those days. It pulls me down.

There were certain things she truly wanted to change; she wanted to improve education and get rid of the Hudood Ordinances, introduced as part of Zia's Islamisation of Pakistan. These required four male witnesses to uphold a woman's claim of rape, otherwise she could be found guilty of adultery or fornication and stoned to death. She opposed, she told me, the exploitation of religion for political purposes and believed there should be equality between men and women. 'In fact I don't think there should be any discrimination on the basis of sex, race or religion and I'm afraid today there is discrimination on all three bases in Pakistan.'

She was, though, a devout Muslim and understood that, were she to stand for parliament and hope to be elected to the highest office, she would be required to wear the traditional *shalwar kameez* and cover her hair. She also told me privately that her mother insisted she could not expect to be elected as a single woman and had chosen a husband for her, Asif Ali Zardari, the son of a wealthy landowner.

As planned, Benazir returned to Pakistan. It's estimated that two million people came to see her speak at her first public appearance. In 1987, she married Zardari in Karachi, although the match was widely considered to be an unlikely one. He was handsome, but nowhere near as well-educated as his wife, and was known to be something of a wheeler-dealer. The wedding was known as the 'People's Wedding', with a lavish ceremony and celebrations including more than 10,000 people. As part of the arrangement, Zardari agreed to stay out of politics.

Benazir quickly became pregnant. The PPP made it known that their leader's due date was 17 November 1988. Zia set the date of the election for 16 November, expecting that would keep Bhutto out of the running. His best-laid plans went seriously awry. On 17 August, he was killed in a plane crash. And the projected due date had been misleading: Benazir's son, Bilawal, was actually expected in October, but came a month early, giving her enough time to regain her strength before serious election campaigning began. She won an overwhelming victory and became the first elected female Prime Minister in the Muslim world. I received a Christmas card signed by her and her husband in December 1988, and a signed copy of her autobiography.

The second time we met was in 1993, during her second term in office. This time I was filming part of a series for BBC2 on *Women in Power*. Benazir had ruled for two years, during which time her daughter Bakhtawar was born, so she became the first head of government to give birth while in office. Her government had been dismissed in 1990 by President Khan and she'd become leader of the opposition, regaining power in '93.

The woman who sat in state in front of me in the Prime Minister's residence in Islamabad was very different from the one I'd met in London years before. The surroundings were grand; she swept into the beautifully decorated room wearing an exquisitely embroidered silk *shalwar kameez* and a *hijab*, which she constantly struggled to keep on her head. It did not come naturally to her to cover herself. I felt I was faced with a woman completely torn between her aristocratic heritage, her sense of duty, disappointment at promises she'd made but failed to keep, and the promptings of the sharp mind of a clever, western feminist, who ruled a country of more than a 130 million, a country that seemed ungovernable by anyone, let alone a woman.

Men in uniform drifted in and out as we talked – the army kept a close ear on everything she said – and the husband who had failed to keep his promise of staying out of politics constantly hovered in the background. Her mother had thought Zardari would be an asset, but he had proved otherwise. He and his associates had become entangled in corruption cases and he'd become known as Mr 10 Per Cent. In 1990 he'd been arrested and imprisoned on charges the family insisted were politically motivated.

Zadari was, it's believed, responsible for Benazir's loss of power. When she returned in 1993 he was appointed Investment Minister and chief of the intelligence agency. He was not on the agenda for our interview – she wouldn't talk about him – but there's no doubt her reputation was seriously sullied by his. She had said on her marriage, 'Benazir Bhutto doesn't cease to exist the moment she gets married. I am not giving myself away.' I fear she overestimated her power to resist his influence and, I suspect, made the mistake of falling in love with him and failing to see his shortcomings.

We talked about what she felt she had achieved, particularly in relation to education, women's rights and those Hudood Ordinances. She believed she had made progress, introducing police stations staffed by women, and better funded schools and healthcare, but in nearly two years in government, very little legislation had been passed. The Hudood remained in place until 2006. Even after so many years she seemed young and inexperienced and appeared hardly to know how to present herself. Was she the vengeful daughter of a murdered father, an educated feminist with international experience, a demure wife and mother, or an imperious aristocrat with knowledge of political intrigue? I don't think she ever really knew.

By 1996 Benazir was again leader of the opposition. Then came charges of corruption, which were never proven in court, although her husband was arrested and jailed, accused of vast corruption and misuse of public funds. Benazir exiled herself to Dubai and then, in 2007, negotiated a return to Pakistan to prepare for re-election. *The Times* writer Ginny Dougary said of her:

> Bhutto represents everything the fundamentalists hate – a powerful, highly-educated woman operating in a man's world, seemingly unafraid to voice her independent views and, indeed, seemingly unafraid of anything, including the very real possibility that one day someone might succeed in killing her because of who she is.

On 27 December 2007 they did succeed. The transport on which Benazir was travelling from a PPP rally was blown up. Twenty-four people died with her that day. Only two months before her death she said:

> The forces of moderation and democracy must, and will, prevail against extremism and dictatorship. I will not be intimidated. I will step out on the tarmac in Karachi not to complete a journey, but to begin one. Despite threats of death, I will not acquiesce to tyranny, but rather lead the fight against it.

She was brave, unquestionably well intentioned, but faced an impossible task. She will always have detractors, but perhaps the most significant supporter she continues to have is Malala Yousafzai, the Pakistani schoolgirl who was shot by the Taliban for believing girls must be allowed to be educated. When Malala addressed the United Nations in 2013 she cited Benazir Bhutto as her personal idol and wore a white shawl that had once belonged to her hero.

18

Angela Merkel

1954–

I'm often asked who, after thirty years of presenting *Woman's Hour*, I would most like to interview. For a long time it was George Clooney (yes, I know, he's a man) but I ticked him off a couple of years ago. Now, only one true star continues to excite, but elude me: Angela Merkel.

For thirteen years I have watched in amazement as she has bestridden Europe like a mini-Colossus, wearing what makes her feel comfortable, having her husband firmly in the background and making no concessions to the pressure to look and be 'feminine' that have so dogged other women who've made it to the top. She has been Germany's Chancellor since 2005; the youngest person to hold the post and, of course, the first woman. Excepting 2010, she topped the *Forbes* list of 'The World's 100 Most Powerful Women' from 2007 to 2017.

Merkel was born in Hamburg, in what was then West Germany. When she was very young her father, Horst Kasner, a Lutheran minister and native of Berlin, was offered a job as pastor in Perleberg in East Germany. Her mother, Herlind, a teacher of English and Latin, was of German-Polish origin; she came from the Baltic port that was the German city of Danzig before the Second World War and became Polish Gdansk. Herlind carried her little daughter over the border from West to East in a basket;

Merkel has spoken of the echoes of the Moses story in the mode of transport, and referred to the fact that they felt almost like refugees.

In East Germany, her mother was not allowed to teach English, that 'capitalist language'. And it must have been no mean feat for her father to preach Christianity under that staunchly atheist regime, just as it must have taken calm determination and confidence for his daughter to retain her Protestant faith and yet lead a party, the Christian Democratic Union, that was traditionally Catholic. Many members of that party held to the belief that the role of a woman was *Kinder, Küche, Kirche* – children, kitchen, church – certainly not *Kanzlerin* – Chancellor.

Merkel and her two younger siblings, a brother and a sister, grew up in the countryside fifty-eight miles north of East Berlin. Construction began on the Berlin Wall when she was seven. Growing up in a repressive political atmosphere with which her parents profoundly disagreed must have been hard, particularly now we know the degree to which East Germany spied on its citizens, even to the extent of pressing children to give away their families to the authorities. It was then, at only seven years old, that this determined little girl announced to her mother and father that she would have a motto. It would be 'never show incompetence'.

In public her parents talked about East Germany as practising socialism with a human face; at home they, particularly her mother, picked apart the socialist propaganda Angela learned at school. From a very young age she was taught to question and think for herself. 'I am quite brave', she said, 'when a decision has to be made. But I need a bit of a run-up and I like – if possible – to think before I jump.' She has never hidden how much she hated the restrictions of the German Democratic Republic – always a somewhat absurd title for one of the most tightly controlled and repressive authoritarian regimes, firmly under the yoke of the old Soviet Empire – and how much unification meant to her: 'The only thing the East German system taught us was that we should never do it that way again.'

Now, as the most powerful woman in Europe, if not in the world, Merkel is known for being an arch-pragmatist, not a visionary. She failed her studies in political philosophy at school but insists on listening to experts. Her philosophy is said to be to choose simply what works to improve the economy, the welfare state and the quality of life for the people for whom she's responsible. There's an expression in Germany '*zu merkeln*', which means, in a not entirely complimentary way, to take an agonisingly long time to take a decision. Nonetheless, her habit of thinking very carefully, then making a decision and sticking to it, seems to have served her very well in Germany. There, according to her biographer Matthew Qvortrup, the electorate is not impressed by politicians who 'go off like a firecracker'. She has said herself, 'I find the tendency that certain male politicians have constantly to assert themselves unpleasant. Many people puff themselves up and try to drown out each other's voices in order to impose themselves. When that happens I feel almost physically oppressed.' Her cautious methods, Qvortrup believes, can be traced back to her childhood.

In 1968 Merkel joined the Free German Youth movement which was sponsored by the ruling Marxist-Leninist party of East Germany. It was said to be a voluntary organisation, but people who were not members found it difficult to get places in higher education. She had compulsory lessons in Marxism-Leninism but her grades in the subject were said to be only 'sufficient'. Later, at the Academy of Sciences, she became a member of the youth movement's secretariat. She's had to deny rumours that she spread Marxist agitation and propaganda; Merkel claims she was only secretary for culture and merely responsible for obtaining theatre tickets and organising talks by Soviet authors.

At school she learned to speak fluent Russian and was awarded prizes for language and mathematics. She went on to study physics at Karl Marx University in Leipzig between 1973 and 1978. Merkel's decision to study physics was made, she said, because 'the East German regime couldn't simply suspend the rules of elementary arithmetic and the laws of physics'. As her studies came to an end, she applied for an assistant professorship at a school of engineering. She was told that, as a condition of getting the job, she would be required to report on her colleagues to officers of the Ministry for State Security, the Stasi. She said no, claiming she was such a chatterbox she would never be able to keep secrets and be an effective spy. I love that she was a woman who would not land her friends and colleagues in trouble and found such a cheeky way of 'never showing incompetence'. Smart kid, and one not afraid of jockeying with the dreaded Stasi.

In 1977 she married a fellow physics student, Ulrich Merkel. She took his name and, even though the marriage lasted only five years, she has kept it. There's been no hint on her part that this was in any way a truly romantic liaison. He, when asked about their feelings for each other, said they were very much in love. Her take on it was: 'We got married because everyone else got married. This may seem stupid today, but I don't think we had thought seriously enough about it.' Straight talker and no nonsense. Love it!

Between 1978 and 1990 she worked and studied at the Central Institute for Physical Chemistry; she achieved her doctorate, for a thesis on quantum chemistry, in 1986. The fall of the Berlin Wall in 1989, on that fateful 9 November, and the reunification of Germany in 1990 provided the opening for a political career. Despite her loathing for the absurdities of the East German regime, Merkel herself was not found among the crowds who were celebrating the fall of the wall. It was a Thursday, the night she went to the sauna, and she said she hadn't bothered because she figured that if the Wall were opened, it was hardly going to close again. When she did finally cross the border, she soon returned home because she had to get up early the next morning and she'd 'already got rather too carried away by my standards'.

In 1984 she met a fellow scientist, Dr Joachim Sauer. He was married with two young sons, but on a scientific trip to Prague the two became close; on their return he supported Angela with her thesis. They talked science and politics and began to live together two years before his divorce was finalised. For nine years they were happily unmarried, but their domestic arrangements were hardly going to go down well as her political career began to advance. In 1993 Cardinal Joachim Meisner, the Catholic Archbishop of Cologne, a man close to the social conservatives in Mrs Merkel's party, told the tabloid newspaper *Bild* that 'apparently there is a female minister of the Christian faith who lives in sin'. Merkel had consistently argued that her private life was no one's business but her own. She was continuously asked by journalists about having children; her answer was that she had not concluded that she did not want to have children, but when she went into politics she was thirty-five and, having reached forty-five, it was out of the question. Her marital status was another matter. She knew she could not become a leading German politician if she were to continue to be badgered about 'living in sin'. She and Sauer married quietly, with no friends or relatives at the wedding. In January 1999, a small notice in a newspaper read: 'We have married. Angela Merkel and Joachim Sauer.' It's said Sauer bakes cakes and pies when they're at home together; his father worked in the baking business. They obviously share an interest in politics but he stays well out of her limelight, not even attending her inauguration as Chancellor.

A month after the Berlin Wall came crashing down Merkel joined a new party, Democratic Awakening. Following the first and only multi-party democratic election in East Germany, she became the deputy spokesperson of the new pre-unification caretaker government, under Lothar de Maizière. She effectively became the leading spokesperson because her boss was afraid of flying and, as a fearless and fluent Russian speaker, she became the politician who was sent to Moscow to negotiate German reunification.

In April 1990, Democratic Awakening merged with the East German CDU, Christian Democratic Union. After reunification was complete, it merged with its western counterpart. Merkel was elected to the Bundestag in 1990; within two months she was Germany's youngest-ever cabinet minister. She was on her way in a country described by a German journalist, Constanze Stelzenmüller, thus: 'Where other countries have glass ceilings for women, Germany has triple-reinforced concrete and it gets thicker the farther east you go.'

So, how did Angela Merkel smash it? She would probably admit that she was a long shot. Her friends describe her as warm and witty in private and I think it's evident from the games she played with the Stasi and her speedy resolution of the marriage question that there's a side to her that's full of fun and modern mores. But her public persona appears extremely dry, with none of the gift for a showy performance so often expected of politicians destined to lead; she speaks softly, with a slight lisp. The only time I've heard her speak English was when she addressed the British parliament in 2016. Her voice was low and slightly breathy and there was just a hint of humour at the end. She said:

> I shall never forget my first visit to London in the spring of 1990, very soon after the fall of the Berlin Wall and quite a few months before Germany's reunification. My husband had been invited by fellow scientists and I entered the Royal Institution for the very first time in my life. We walked through Hyde Park looking for Speakers' Corner, which – especially for us East Germans – was legendary, the very symbol of free speech. I hope that is not an insult to you, the members of the British Parliament.

A little joke; evidence of a rather wry and naughty sense of humour.

Merkel smashed the 'concrete ceiling' as she rose through the party's ranks during the 1990s. She became the favourite of the then Chancellor Helmut Kohl, who called her his '*Mädchen*', his 'little girl'. He hand-picked her to be Minister for Women and Youth in his reunification cabinet and, as he weeded out any men who might become his rivals, her star was in the ascendant.

When Kohl's government was defeated in the 1998 election, Merkel was appointed the party's Secretary General. In 1999, she ruthlessly stabbed her mentor in the back. Kohl had become involved in a party financing scandal and she was the only one of the potential rising stars – the others were all men – who had the nerve to have a piece, signed by her and demanding his resignation, printed on the front page of Germany's most respected conservative daily newspaper. Kohl fell; Merkel became the leader of the party and of the opposition in the Bundestag.

A profile in the *Guardian* from that time puts forward an interesting theory of how she had found the strength for 'this audacious patricide . . .':

> Her secret eastern weapon was the blandness with which the purposeful learn to cloak themselves in authoritarian systems. To it she added the physicist's appreciation of the simple elegance with which a lever may be applied to a hidden weak spot in a complex structure and, with a minimum of force, bring it all crashing down. This is a woman, after all, who on her desk in the chancellor's office keeps a framed picture of Catherine the Great: a princess from Saxony who travelled far from home to subdue a court teeming with dark and dangerous tribal rivalries, and from there to rule an alien empire.

Now she was leader of the opposition the German media stopped calling her 'a grey mouse'. They had underestimated, along with her male rivals, her determination and political abilities. They had thought her a political lightweight. None had considered her a rival. The press began to dub her 'Mistress Merciless'. When the 2005 election came Merkel won the CDU/CSU nomination as the challenger to Chancellor Gerhard Schröder of the SPD, the Social Democrats. Her campaign was not particularly impressive. During a television debate she twice confused gross and net income, and her proposals for an increase in VAT to reduce Germany's deficit did not go down well. The result was close, but Schröder made a fatal mistake. He asked: 'Do you seriously believe that my party will enter into negotiations with Mrs Merkel?', refusing any suggestion of a coalition and demonstrating that unsurprising wave of misogyny so often seen in a man who fears the rise of a female rival. His approach was that of the bare-knuckle political brawler, which she had often said was a style of doing politics that she found distasteful and unproductive. She simply looked at him with an expression that said: 'That's no way to speak to a lady.' She won the sympathy vote of the people; Qvortrup argues that she became Chancellor because Schröder lost his temper.

Merkel has never openly adopted the term 'feminist'. Early in her leadership she rather reluctantly put herself in the hands of some fashion consultants; constant media sniping about her being 'frumpy' was distracting. I'm sure that the comments of Silvio Berlusconi, who called her 'an unfuckable lard-arse' didn't cost her a second's sleep. As Constanze Stelzenmüller observed in a *Guardian* profile, she still 'wears less make-up and hairspray on the job than Silvio Berlusconi on vacation'. And if the Italian economy had crashed under Berlusconi's inept stewardship, we all know who would have had to bail it out. I rather suspect Mrs Merkel might have been quite relieved to discover that one of the most disgusting, lascivious men on the planet, with his overcooked tan and 'shamelessly trashy' (his ex-wife's words) list of candidates for the European parliament, had no desire to include her in his 'bunga bunga' parties. I have no doubt she brushed his vulgarity into the bin where it belonged, but we do have to ask ourselves why on earth any man believes he has the right to describe any woman in that way and yet an electorate is still prepared to vote for him.

I may never have met Mrs Merkel, but every instinct I have tells me she would never have allowed her fashion choices to be influenced by such a rampant slob. She is clearly perfectly comfortable in her smart suits, avoiding any of the comments on her cleavage, legs or ankles that have so dogged other women in power, and in her colourful jackets standing out from the anonymous dark-suited men who generally surround her. Not sure what she thinks of there being an Angela Merkel Barbie doll.

As far as Merkel's policies go, there is some evidence of a feminist perspective. She has overseen a liberalisation of Germany's abortion laws and introduced legislation requiring large corporations to allocate 30% of seats on non-executive boards to women. Laws, of course, are quickly changed, but culture takes much longer. Women remain grossly under-represented in the boardrooms of publicly listed companies, and German commentators point to the fact that 'the husband at work and the wife having his dinner on the table is still the more common picture than that observed in the Merkel household'. She has approached the controversial topic of the wearing of the burqa from a typically practical perspective, arguing that the full veil should be banned wherever legally possible. 'Showing your face is part of our way of life', she has said. 'Our laws take precedence over honour codes, tribal customs and *sharia*.'

She does, though, have a group of women – known as 'Mutti's Girl Camp' – credited with keeping her in power. Apparently, she has no objection to the term 'Mutti' (mother of the nation), although it was originally coined and used pejoratively by her opponents. The 'girl camp' is an entourage of right-hand women that appears to have outsmarted Germany's old boys' network, is

rumoured to have placed media stories to undermine the credibility of those known as the 'altar boys' and kept its boss in power
through what Matthew Qvortrup calls 'mean girl' tactics. The
group is so private its members are rarely photographed. It
consists of Beate Baumann, a 54-year-old Cambridge graduate,
said to be the only person, apart from her husband, whom the
Chancellor trusts without question, and the economist Eva
Christensen, who is forty-seven. She is Merkel's speechwriter,
spin-doctor and problem-solver, credited with inventing the
Chancellor's manner of speech.

Merkel is reported to have said in 1992, after her first ministe-
rial appointment, that she needed someone to look after her, and
it needed to be a woman because her male staff looked on her
with condescension. I remember Margaret Thatcher making a
similar observation when she said the members of her first Cabinet
had treated her as if she were their cleaning lady. Merkel and
Baumann have formed the strongest political partnership in
modern German history. Baumann became chief of staff in 1995.
She stays behind to run the office but the two are in constant
contact. When they are seen together they have the same discreet
dress code of trouser suits and short hair. Baumann is not, though,
as she has often been described, 'Merkel's shadow'. She's her
equal. When Merkel was under pressure during one of her first
international conferences, she appeared to be on the verge of
tears. Baumann hissed, 'Get your act together, woman.' Merkel
did as she was told. Merkel's cabinet shows that she has surrounded
herself with powerful women. Her defence minister is Ursula von
der Leyen, her education minister is Johanna Wanka, and the
CDU deputy leader and Minister of Food and Agriculture is Julia
Klöckner, a former beauty queen who's rumoured to be Merkel's
favoured successor.

Merkel's longevity and strength are remarkable. At a time of
huge global change, the financial crash, the euro crisis in Greece
and elsewhere, immigration issues throughout Europe and a

rising tide of populist nationalism, she has stood firm. But a week is still a long time in politics. In the weeks before the 2017 election, polls gave her only around 40% of the vote. In the election, her party lost numerous seats and the radical right-wing Alternative für Deutschland (AfD) entered parliament as the third largest party. Merkel began her fourth term as Chancellor only after four months of negotiation with the centre-left Social Democrats (SPD), with which she managed to form a coalition. The support for the AfD and Merkel's loss of popularity was clearly influenced by the German people's concerns about immigration; Mrs Merkel had welcomed to Germany large numbers of refugees to Germany fleeing the crisis in Syria. But she holds to her conviction that she made the right decision as the refugees, generally young people, will work hard for the German economy. So, she's there for another term, holding Europe together as the UK negotiates its departure from the European Union, and still veering between her motherly reputation as Mutti and the more ruthless title Merkievelli.

I've come across only one instance of Merkel showing real fear. Some years ago, she was bitten by a dog and ever since has been terrified of them. At one of their first encounters in Russia, President Putin brought his huge black Labrador Connie to the meeting. It's assumed he knew of her phobia and intended to intimidate the Chancellor. The photographs of the incident show Merkel looking extremely uncomfortable as Connie sits at her feet, while President Putin seems to be smirking. Their exchange, in Russian (they speak each other's language), consisted of Putin asking if the dog bothered her and Merkel replying, 'No, she doesn't eat journalists after all.' Putin has since claimed that he was unaware of her issue with dogs but Merkel seems to have got her own back. She's one of Europe's most vocal critics of Putin and has been instrumental in upholding sanctions against Russia following the annexation of Crimea in 2014. He couldn't bully her; she's now reported to be the only European leader who can deal with him. As for President Trump, her advisers said, apparently joking, that she's been doing her research and reading *Playboy* to get an insight into this mind. I guess you just don't mess with Mrs Merkel.

19

Madonna Louise Ciccone

1958–

You may remember I mentioned in the chapter on Frida Kahlo that I have a small Chihuahua, a dog, like Frida, of Mexican inheritance and, because I love Kahlo's work, I named my pup after her. Well, actually, I have three Chihuahuas. The first, Butch, is obviously a boy. His name is a bit of a joke, considering his size, but his sex precludes him from having a place in this book. The third, however, does have a right to be here. Her name is Madge, short for Madonna, and there are very good reasons for her name. In the first photograph I saw of her as a diminutive puppy she stared at the camera, preening herself and, undoubtedly saying, 'I'm ready for my close up. Just get on with it.'

Madge is not what you could call disobedient; she just has her own way of doing things and making sure her demands are met. When it's time to be dressed for going out, she hangs about until she's ready to have her coat on, to the irritation of everyone else in the family. If it's raining, she just says no. If she's out in the garden and decides she wants to be in, she barks – or should I say yaps or squeals – and scratches insistently at the door until she gets her own way. When we are out in the park everyone we meet stops in astonishment to pet her and tell her she is utterly gorgeous. Which she is. And she knows it, and she revels in it. She could not be more aptly named.

The real Madonna was born to Catholic parents in Bay City, Michigan, one of six children; three boys and three girls. Madonna, known as Nonnie, was the second born. Her father, Tony, was Italian and her mother, also called Madonna, was a beautiful French Canadian. She died in 1963, from breast cancer, when Madonna was only five. Her father quickly remarried; the family's housekeeper, Joan, became their stepmother. In an interview with *Harper's Bazaar* in 2017 Madonna said:

> I've obviously been devastated or heartbroken all my life, since my mother's death. I've had so many challenges throughout my career, however successful people perceive me to be. The only way I've been able to survive the betrayal of lovers, family members, and society is to be able to create as an artist.

Madonna described her childhood as like living in a zoo. She had to share everything and sleep in a single bed with her two sisters. She said she was a she-devil who had to try hard to be heard and would do anything, including burning her own fingers, to get attention. Her brother, Christopher, said she was spoilt from the beginning. She was her parents' favourite; aggressive, according to her brother, good-hearted, but very bossy. Her portrayal of her life as being dirt poor and deprived is not necessarily entirely accurate. Her father always had work as an engineer at the Chrysler motor corporation and their existence is described by her biographer, J Randy Taraborrelli, as healthy and middle class.

From a young age Madonna was a big fan of Hollywood films. As one of her attention-seeking activities, she would frequently leap on to a table and perform a number in the style of Shirley Temple. But at the end of her act she would lift her dress and flash her knickers. It was a naughty gesture from a little girl that made everyone laugh and applaud. An early lesson in how to please an audience.

As far as religion was concerned, Madonna described the family as strict and old-fashioned. Her grandmother took her to church regularly and taught her she must learn to love Jesus and be a good girl. Madonna said of her education, 'I grew up with two images of women: the virgin and the whore.' She also expressed serious difficulties with the emphasis on notions of guilt and forgiveness, and said they were responsible for screwing up many a Catholic:

How many Catholics are in therapy, just trying to get over the idea of Original Sin? Do you know what it's like to be told from the day you walk into school for the first time that you are a sinner, that you were born that way, and that's just the way it is? You'd have to be Catholic to understand it.

As a student Madonna was bright, but never missed an opportunity to shock, joining a dance class and learning how to move in an uninhibited way. When she was eleven, in a talent show, she scandalised the parents of the other children, as well as her own father, by go-go dancing in the style of Goldie Hawn, wearing a bikini and with her skin covered in fluorescent green paint. Elements of *Little Miss Sunshine* in her wild display! Her father was furious at her bumping and grinding and grounded her for two weeks. It wouldn't be the first time he felt ashamed of his daughter. She's often said how much she struggled throughout her career with the fact that her father disapproved of everything she did.

As a teenager Madonna was surprisingly comfortable with her body; rare in a growing girl. As an adult, she has said in interviews: 'I liked my body when I was growing up and I wasn't ashamed of it. I liked boys and I didn't feel inhibited by them. Maybe it comes from having brothers and sharing a bathroom'. Her first boyfriend, Russell Long, who was seventeen to her fifteen when they first had sex in his car, said of her, 'She didn't have a problem with people knowing we were having sex . . . She was proud of it, said that it had made her feel like a woman . . . she didn't mind being seen naked. She just seemed comfortable with all of it.' Years later though she said of those early experiences: 'Even after I made love for the first time, I still felt like a virgin. I didn't lose my virginity until I knew what I was doing.'

Her dance teacher, Christopher Flynn, gave her tremendous confidence in her abilities as a performer, and told her she was beautiful. He was the first gay man she became close to and, as well as teaching her how to move, he introduced her to the more erotic aspects of the night life in Michigan, an education she couldn't have experienced elsewhere. When Madonna was seventeen he became a dance professor at the University of Michigan School of Music, Theatre and Dance and arranged for his protégée to apply for a scholarship. She won and enrolled there in 1976. Two years later, though, she left for New York, taking a plane and a taxi for the first time in her life. 'I came here,' she said, 'with thirty-five dollars in my pocket. It was the bravest thing I'd ever done.'

She learned, she said, from growing up in the Midwest, that the world is divided into two categories: people who follow the status quo and play it safe and people who throw convention to the wind and dance to the beat of a distant drum:

> Drinking beer and smoking weed in the parking lot of my high school was not my idea of being rebellious because that's what everybody did. I never wanted to do what everybody did. And I thought it was cooler to not shave my legs or under my arms. I mean, why did God give us hair there anyways? Why didn't guys have to shave there? Why was it accepted in Europe but not in America? . . . I did the opposite of what all the other girls were doing . . . I dared people to like me and my nonconformity.

Like so many ambitious young women who've been raised in the confines of a small town, not conforming to expectations is essential as a way of getting up and going. Whether its Bay City or Barnsley – as it was in my case – being different is what gives you the confidence to aim that little bit higher, and it's the lights of the big city that lure you away. For me it was London. I remember so clearly standing by the milestone near my home – London 150 miles – wondering how long it would take me to travel that distance and be with people like me. For Madonna, New York was where other non-conformists and artists plied their trade. She couldn't wait to shimmy and shake in a world where she would be surrounded by other daring people.

New York was not quite all she'd hoped it would be, just as for me the streets of London were not paved with gold. In her first year, earning her rent by posing nude for art classes, she found life hard and lonely. Manhattan is a beautiful but at first sight terribly intimidating landscape. The buildings rise so high, way beyond human scale, the traffic is incessant and there's a sense that danger might lie around every corner. Madonna was not immune to the risks and the fear, particularly after she was held up at gun point. Then, she had no money or valuables to hand over and was spared. She faced the terror of sexual violence that so many young women have endured; she was dragged to the roof of her building with a knife at her back, and raped. She has always claimed, though, that confronting and dealing with these all too common experiences made her determined to survive.

Survive she did, earning money by whatever means possible to keep her going towards her aim of becoming an artist. She worked for a time at *Dunkin' Donuts* and performed with modern dance troupes. But it was really her voice that impressed, and her talent matched her strong determination so that by 1979 she had performed as a backing singer, met Dan Gilroy and formed her first rock band, the Breakfast Club. She played the drums. In 1980 she formed a new band, Emmy and the Emmys, and in 1981 began to market herself as a solo act. Her music quickly turned heads, catching the attention of New York DJ and producer Mark Kamins, who helped her sign a deal with Sire Records in 1982. Shortly thereafter her debut single, 'Everybody', was released, followed by 'Burning Up', both such hits that she created her debut album, *Madonna*. In 1984 she released her second album, *Like a Virgin*. She was now an international star who needed only one name – Madonna – to identify her.

And so began the Madonna phenomenon, which would make her the most famous woman in the world in the 1980s and 1990s. She was the 'Material Girl', whose every move was surrounded by controversy. She married the film star Sean Penn but they were together for only two years and divorced in 1989. An affair with Warren Beatty followed; it was said he broke her heart when he ended things. Hit records came thick and fast, as did outrageous interviews in which she explained she wore crucifixes around her neck because they were sexy – they showed a naked man. She would often say she found Jesus sexy; no doubt a calculated means of creating shock, but blasphemous to those she'd left behind in the religious community where she'd grown up. 'He was sexy to me', she said, 'but I also said it to be provocative.'

In 1992 she founded her own company, Maverick, the first of the great pop divas to take control of her music and her image. She published a book called *Sex* and starred in the film *Evita* as Eva Peron. She was pregnant during the filming with her daughter Lourdes (whose father was Carlos Leon, a fitness trainer). At every step Madonna defied expectations of how a woman could or should behave and invited criticism and admiration in equal measure.

In 1994, in her mid-thirties, she began to seek what she called 'meaning and a purpose in life' and was introduced to Kabbalah. She was accused of joining a cult and being brainwashed; she explained that she'd been talking about God and heaven and hell without feeling religious dogma was being shoved down her throat. She was learning about science and quantum physics, reading Aramaic and studying history, and was pleased to find that questions and debate were encouraged.

At the age of forty, she met the film director Guy Ritchie, the *enfant terrible* of British Indy film. My two teenage sons watched Ritchie's crime comedies, *Lock, Stock and Two Smoking Barrels* and *Snatch* endlessly but I was extremely surprised to find his mother was a minor aristocrat and his stepmother a Conservative councillor and later a life peer. He couldn't have been more a part of English polite society, despite the violence and foul language of his films.

Madonna and Guy had a son, Rocco. But they were, from the start an unlikely coupling. She didn't find living in England easy. 'Just because we speak the same language doesn't mean we speak the same language. I didn't understand that there was still a class system. I didn't understand pub culture. I didn't understand that being openly ambitious was frowned upon. Once again I felt alone.' Her marriage to Ritchie was not to last and her explanation of where it went wrong will be familiar to many a woman who's wanted her own as well as a family life. In a passionate defence of her life and choices, she described her work as being:

. . . like breathing and I can't imagine not doing it. That is one of the arguments I would get into with my ex-husband, who used to say to me, 'But why do you have to do this again? Why do you have to make another record? Why do you have to go on tour? Why do you have to make a movie?' And I'm like, 'Why do I have to explain myself?' I feel like that's a very sexist thing to say. Does somebody ask Steven Spielberg why he's still making movies? Hasn't he had enough success? Hasn't he made enough money? Hasn't he made a name for himself? Did somebody go to Pablo Picasso and say, 'Okay, you're eighty years old. Haven't you painted enough paintings?' No, I'm so tired of that

question. I just don't understand it. I'll stop doing everything I do when I don't want to it anymore. I'll stop when I
run out of ideas. I'll stop when you fucking kill me. How
about that?

Madonna is now fabulously rich, and controversy still attends her
every move, whether it's her custody battle with Ritchie over
their son or her adoption of four Malawian children: David,
Mercy, Esther and Stella. She's been criticised for whisking them
away from their own culture, no matter how poor and deprived it
was. She said she did it in the best interests of the children. She
had learned that millions of children had been orphaned by
AIDS, she has far more money than she needs and believed she
had found a way to spend it wisely. She had not anticipated that
trying to adopt children and give them a better life would land
her in:

> ... another shit storm ... Ten years later, here I am,
> divorced and living in New York. I have been blessed with
> four amazing children. I try to teach them to think outside
> the box. To be daring. To choose to do things because they
> are the right thing to do, not because everybody else is
> doing them. I have started making films, which is probably
> the most challenging and rewarding thing I have ever done.
> I am building schools for girls in Islamic countries and stud-
> ying the Qur'an.

Now she's sixty years old she is no less certain of herself than she
was as a child. And no less determined to sing and dance like a sex
goddess than she was at the start of her career. She's been dealing
with the inevitable barbs about a woman of her age acting as a
pop icon: cries of 'put it away' or 'time to retire, grandma' are
legion, as is criticism of her habit of dating younger men.
Madonna's response to the toxic combination of sexism and

ageism has provoked exactly the response I would have expected and hoped for:

> It's an outdated patriarchal idea that a woman has to stop being fun, curious, adventurous, beautiful or sexy past the age of 40. It's ridiculous. Why should men get to have all the fun until the day they leave the earth? How do we fight this? By standing up to men and standing up to social mores or standards that say we cannot. The more women that do it, it will just be a matter of time.

A number of people have asked me why I felt this 'shocking woman' deserved a place in this book. Can she really be mentioned in the same breath as Joan of Arc, Catherine the Great or Angela Merkel? A selection of endorsements and comments from younger women, interviewed by *Billboard*, who grew up with her in the 1980s and are now well-known pop stars in their own right, justifies my decision.

> When I think of greatness and what a legend is, I always think of Madonna. She does things her way no matter what and that always inspires me. She has made history.
>
> Anyone who has ever worked alongside her understands why Madonna is Madonna. She works harder than anyone. She exists in this world by her own rules; she has remained in control of her own voice, paving the way for the Taylor Swifts and Adeles of this world to do their thing in the process. Her music was the soundtrack to my preteen angst and she was my idol as a feminist and an artist.
>
> Madonna paved the way for girls to express themselves sexually, without apologising.

And me? I can't help it. As a feminist, a one-time keen dancer and lover of great popular music, I'm just a fan!

20

Anna Politkovskaya

1958–2006

On 13 October 2004 I interviewed the Russian journalist, Anna Politkovskaya, about her book *Putin's Russia* and her history of working to investigate and tell the truth about some of the most shocking incidents in the late twentieth and early twenty-first centuries. I had longed to meet her, because for me she represented everything I believed a great journalist should be. I was only too well aware that I would never have had the courage to pursue the kind of stories she had investigated since Putin came to power. Nor would I be brave enough to face the kind of danger that a Russian journalist was forced to accept came with the territory if she were prepared to question the actions of this powerful and ruthless leader. I had gasped with admiration at her determination to report to the world what had happened in the second Chechen War, the Moscow Theatre Siege and the infiltration by Islamic terrorists of the school in Beslan. Meeting her was a privilege and a delight.

Two years later she was dead, assassinated in the entrance to her block of flats in Moscow.

She was completely aware of the risks she faced. She wrote:

We are hurtling back into a Soviet abyss, into an information vacuum that spells death from our own ignorance. All we have left is the Internet, where information is still freely available. For the rest, if you want to continue working as a journalist, it's total servility to Putin. Otherwise it can be death, the bullet, poison, or trial – whatever our special services, Putin's guard dogs, see fit.

She was born Anna Mazepa in New York City. Her Ukrainian parents worked as Soviet diplomats at the United Nations. As she was born in the USA she had both American and Russian citizenship and passports from both countries, but when her parents returned to Russia she spent most of her childhood in Moscow and never left the country for more than a few weeks at a time, despite her difficulties with the Putin regime. As Helena Kennedy QC writes in her introduction to *Nothing but the Truth: Collected Dispatches*:

> Her fearlessness in the face of grave danger made her one of the few international journalists whom human rights activists and lawyers held in awe . . . here was a writer who – at great personal risk – defied state intimidation to speak truth to power . . . I remember . . . asking whether she might not think of leaving Russia, at least temporarily. She held my hand, smiling, and said, 'Exile is not for me. That way they win'.

Anna studied journalism at Moscow State University, graduating in 1980. Her final thesis was on the poetry of Marina Tsvetaeva, a Russian and Soviet poet who produced some of the greatest poems in twentieth-century Russian literature. Marina Tsvetaeva lived through the Revolution of 1917 and the Moscow famine that followed it. She sent her daughter to an orphanage in the hope it would save her from starvation, but the child died of hunger. Marina travelled around Europe in great poverty before returning to Russia in 1939. Her husband and surviving daughter were arrested on espionage charges and her husband was executed. Marina killed herself in 1941. It's clear to me why her exquisite talent with words and the valour with which she faced adversity so inspired Anna.

At university Anna met and married a fellow journalism student, Alexander Politkovsky. They had two children, Vera and Ilya, and Alexander became a successful television presenter. However, they divorced in 1999, when Anna began a series of trips to the Chechen war zone and did not spend as much time with her family as her husband believed she should. It was also obvious she was putting herself at risk simply by reporting on the war.

This was the Second Chechen War, begun by Putin to put right what went wrong first time round. The initial conflict had been instigated by Boris Yeltsin late in 1994. The dissolution of the Soviet Union three years earlier had seen countries born and reborn, and local wars break out. Chechnya was among the regions to declare itself independent of the new Russian Federation. Yeltsin's war aimed to reclaim it. The Russian press were relentless in their reporting of the conflict, eventually paving the way to a peace settlement. As Anna herself would later say, stopping the war was the media's greatest achievement of the era. At the time she was reporting on the day-to-day struggles of ordinary Russians for *Obshchaya Gazeta*, but when Putin took office and the Second Chechen War began in 1999 she was working for *Novaya Gazeta*, the newspaper where she would make her name as one of Europe's leading reporters.

Putin's Kremlin ensured life for an investigative journalist became more difficult than ever. Leveraging his background in the KGB, he pursued a policy designed to ensure that the media would not be able to embarrass him with reports on the Russian army's brutal activities in the conflict. Anna was determined to get beneath Putin's claims that his crackdown on Chechnya was merely in tune with the West's 'War on Terror'.

With the support of her newspaper, *Novaya Gazeta*, Anna made more than fifty trips to the area. She brought back stories of extrajudicial killings, kidnappings, rapes, torture and disappearances carried out by the army. She suffered a terrifying mock execution at the hands of the Russian army; an attempt to stop her from reporting in Chechnya. Anna wrote that, far from suppressing terrorism, such activities were creating and nurturing it. She also, in her descriptions of the torture methods being employed, explained that they were of the nature taught in the training manuals of the KGB, which had become the FSB. She laid the responsibility directly at the door of the former KGB agent who would soon become President of Russia: Vladimir Putin. From the outset he presented himself as a ruthless hard man, protecting Russia's borders. It was an image he was certain would appeal to the Russian people and frighten off any detractors. When Anna was criticised for her work she said only, 'What am I guilty of? I have merely reported what I have witnessed, nothing but the truth.'

Our interview began with a question about the opening to her book, *Putin's Russia*. She had written: 'This book is about Vladimir Putin, but not as he is normally viewed in the West. Not through rose-tinted spectacles.' What did she mean?

He's very strict, very aggressive, very masculine and bloody. He was absolutely unknown in Russia in 1999 when President Yeltsin presented him, saying, 'He is my so-called son in policy.' We knew about him only as the former head of the KGB and were afraid of him. But President Yeltsin wanted him to be elected as President of Russia and after that, I think, Kremlin policy makers tried to raise the second Chechen war as the best way for an election. And all the war, all the methods during this war were so bloody and so brutal after Putin's election. We had 'great success' in terrorist attacks. From 2001 to 2002, the Dubrovka hostage case in the theatre during a musical when people died with chemical weapons, then more terrorist attacks in

2003/2004 and Putin every time explained it only as international terrorist action of Bin Laden's hands, but the real reasons were absolutely the result of the methods during the second Chechen war.

Why, I asked her, would this book not be published in Russia? 'No, no, it's impossible, because we have a new epoch where it's absolutely impossible to publish anything against Putin. We have a state ideology which describes Putin as a so-called new Czar of Russia and all his steps are absolutely right without any other point of view.'

Anna was closely drawn into two of the most infamous terrorist attacks of this period, atrocities that made the news around the world. She had spent so much time in Chechnya that she was more familiar than anyone with the place itself and the motivations of the Chechen terrorists. She was convinced that her knowledge and understanding of the issues would enable her to conduct negotiations for the liberation of hostages. In the Dubrovka theatre siege the terrorists were demanding an end to the war. First, Anna attempted to bring drinks and help to the theatre hostages. Some hostages were released, but neither Politkovskaya nor other negotiators were able to prevent the storming of the theatre by Russian special forces and the deaths of hostages and terrorists from poison gas. She believed that more time for negotiation would have saved lives and felt the strong-arm tactics employed by the state were a terrible mistake.

We also discussed the Beslan school siege, where more than a thousand hostages were held by Chechen terrorists for three days. Anna had been on her way to Beslan, but claimed she had been drugged to prevent her arrival. What happened? 'On the 1st September, I tried to push the leader of the Chechen separatists to negotiate with those individuals who went to the school in Beslan. I was absolutely sure that he could have stopped the incredible movements in this moment.' She had, unusually, made her approaches to the Chechens absolutely openly, without any attempt to act in secret, because she felt action was needed quickly. She was in a hurry to make the arrangements for a trip to Beslan to begin negotiations. It was extremely rare to speak to any of her contacts over a mobile phone and discuss all the details of any plan because she knew that there would always be some-one else listening to her conversations. For two years, whenever she'd discussed sensitive information, she hadn't dared use her mobile in Russia, convinced anything she said would go straight to the authorities. And she wasn't only trying to protect herself. So, no mobile phones?

> No, no, no, no! Secret topics no, because it was very danger-ous. Not just for me, but for persons who were involved in this situation. But I had no other possibility to discuss because I had to wait in the airport and wait for the plane to Beslan. After some hours in the airport they put me in the airplane and gave me a cup of tea. I drink this cup of tea and that's all.

'Where did you end up? How did you get off the plane?'
'I returned to myself only in the hospital and after that I was in the hospital in Moscow.'
'Was there any evidence that you had been drugged?'
'It needs to be investigated, but I think we will have no result [laughs].'
As at the Dubrovka, she felt negotiations at Beslan had been deliberately thwarted by a show of strength. Three hundred and thirty-four people, including 186 children, were killed when Russian security forces stormed the building.
'I know that you've had death threats in the past and then this incident around the Beslan investigation. Why do you continue to do the job you do when it's so dangerous?'

[Laughs] I am absolutely sure that risk is the usual part of my job. Of the job of any Russian journalist. I cannot stop because it's my duty. I think that the duty of doctors is to give health to their patients, the duty of a singer is to sing, the duty of a journalist is to write what this journalist sees in the reality. It's only one duty.

And so I saw this beautiful, delicate 46-year-old woman, who had peered at me over her glasses just as I had peered at her over mine, both with a twinkling recognition of each other's similar aims and duties. For me the duties were not dangerous at all. My reputation might be at risk but not my life. For her the risk of torture and death was ever present. But I had not thought that I was seeing her for the last time.

Almost two years to the day after the encounter that had so moved and impressed me, I heard her worst fears had come true. She had been shopping and carried two bags of groceries up to her flat on the seventh floor in the tiny lift. She dropped her bags at the door and went back to get the rest of her parcels. When the lift opened on the ground floor, her killer was waiting. She was shot four times. The first two bullets pierced her heart and lungs and the third shattered her shoulder with such force that she was thrown back into the lift. Then the killer delivered what is known in Moscow as the control shot: he fired a bullet into her head from inches away. He dropped his weapon, which had had its serial number removed, and slipped away. It was a classic contract killing; even now it's not known who ordered it.

I can only repeat what the journalist Jon Snow said in her honour. Putin had tried to diminish the impact her work had had on our understanding of some of the dark forces at work in contemporary Russia but, Snow said, 'for many of us who continue to aspire to the highest standards of journalism, Anna Politkovskaya will remain a beacon burning bright, a yardstick by which integrity, courage and commitment will be measured'.

Anna is no longer here to bring to the light the politics that frighten and confuse us. She would, I know, have been the first into Syria to investigate the allegations of the bombing of civilians with chemical weapons and ask what role Putin played. She would have been to Salisbury to find out exactly what happened to the Skripals and search for where the nerve agent Novichok had been produced. It's been widely reported that Putin has said his country's enemies will be served with poison. None of this would have surprised Anna, who would have made wise observations about the potential consequences of what's being called the new Cold War. In the March 2018 presidential election the Russian people had the choice of Vladimir Putin or Vladimir Putin. Vladimir Putin won.

According to the Committee to Protect Journalists, fourteen journalists have been killed in Russia since 2006. While more died in the ten years before Anna's death, it's still shocking that the job of telling the truth to the people can be so dangerous. Most recently, in 2018, the investigative journalist Maksim Borodin died from injuries he sustained after falling from the window of his flat. The authorities classified his death as suicide. His colleagues say no; he was killed as a result of his work on crime, corruption and the recent involvement of Russian mercenaries in Syria.

Journalism in Russia is now an extremely dangerous business. It's almost as if journalists are seen as combatants in a war on words, to be wiped out. As the body count mounts, only the bravest or most foolhardy will risk their lives to report the truth. In the old Soviet Union there was total control of the press that spawned a bitterly humorous line about the two Soviet papers, *Pravda*, meaning 'Truth', and *Isvestia*, meaning 'News'. The joke went that 'Truth contained no News . . . and News no Truth.' It seems we may be going that way again.

Anna did everything she could to speak truth to power.

Power won.

21

Cathy Freeman

1973–

Whether it's the Commonwealth Games or the Olympics, there I am, glued to the television screen. Full of wonder at those strong, lithe women who wave at the crowds from the blocks, wait for the starting pistol and put every ounce of energy and power to run at top speed for longer than the human body should be expected to. I also have to confess to feeling a considerable amount of shame as someone who never won a race, always stayed in goal in hockey where minimal effort was required, and has, frankly, never so much as run for a bus.

How do they manage the years and years of getting up at dawn and training, training and more training to be the best? How do they face the pressure of an event such as the Olympics, where the whole world will be watching? How do they deal with the fear that all their hard work could go down the drain as the result of the slightest slip? As my father used to say to my son, who longed to be a professional rugby player, 'Eee, lad, do something else. You'll be one injury away from the dole queue!' And, if you represent a country such as Australia, where sport seems to be something of a religion, how would you ever live with yourself if you let your nation down?

In the opening words of her autobiography Catherine Astrid Salome Freeman describes what went through her head as she positioned herself on the blocks, got her fingers perfectly on the line, stared at the track and waited for the starting pistol. 'I'm just a little black girl who can run fast, and here I am sitting in the Olympic stadium, with one hundred and twelve thousand people screaming my name. How the hell did I get here?'

How indeed? Cathy Freeman was brought up in a small housing commission bungalow in Mackay on the coast of Queensland, Australia. She shared a room with her two younger brothers. Her parents had their own bedroom, as did her older brother. The bungalow was not in a fashionable part of the town but the posh houses owned by the white people were not far away. At the top of the hill were magnificent, brick houses that had big gardens, verandas, barbies and swimming pools. Cathy imagined all white people were rich, in fact that anyone who owned a telephone, a car or even a carpet was rich. She watched another girl she knew, also called Catherine, who lived at the top of the street, and wondered how different their lives were. White Catherine, she thought, would play with dolls and have make-up; Aboriginal Catherine was running around in the dirt with her brothers.

Cathy's family history is typical of what happened to so many Aboriginal families, victims of the government's racist policies that began at the start of British colonisation in 1788 and continued, in some parts of Australia, into the 1970s. In the earlier years thousands of Aborigines were killed in what is now acknowledged to be an attempt at genocide. In the nineteenth century, slavery was not uncommon; Aboriginal labourers were often kidnapped to work on ships in the 1860s, a practice known as 'blackbirding'.

Only recently has the world become aware of the cruel practice of removing Aboriginal children from their families and taking them miles away to harsh training camps for 're-education'. I first found out about the 'Stolen Generations' when I saw the film *Rabbit-Proof Fence* in 2002 and met the women on whom the story was based. Cathy's grandmother, Alice Sibley, was one of that generation, forcibly removed from her parents, her culture, her identity and her language when she was only eight and taken to 'The Mission', a government-controlled religious facility and penal settlement on Palm Island, off the coast of Queensland, close to the Great Barrier Reef.

It's estimated that between 100,000 and 300,000 children were taken from their Aboriginal families and either placed into institutional religious missions or fostered by white families, if their skin colour was not too dark or they were of mixed descent. The plan was to eradicate indigenous peoples by training them to live and work in white society. It was assumed that, over generations, they would marry white people and be assimilated. In the 1930s, the Northern Territory's Chief Protector of Aborigines, Dr Cecil Cook, argued that 'everything necessary [must be done] to convert the half-caste into a white citizen'. Clearly no one concerned themselves too much that the source of so many children of mixed race was the long-standing sexual exploitation of young Aborigine women by non-indigenous men.

By the end of the First World War, Palm Island had grown into the largest of the Australian government's Aboriginal Settlements. Aborigines across Queensland could be removed there for 'falling pregnant to a white man' or being born a mixed descent child. Children were separated from their parents, segregated by gender and banned from entering the 'white zones'. Everyday activity was controlled, including the imposition of nightly curfews and food rationing. All the islanders were required to work thirty hours a week and, until 1960, were not paid for their labour. The children were punished for speaking their indigenous language and incarcerated for minor misbehaviours such as swearing at a teacher.

As Cathy writes in her autobiography, her mother, Cecelia, and her uncles were not allowed to leave the island, even to go shopping, without a permit. Failure to arrive back at curfew time resulted in arrest and being forcibly taken back to the island by the police. As late as the 1950s anyone who was late for the morning roll call, even by one minute, was denied food. Cecelia's stepfather, Sonny Sibley, was one of the instigators of a strike on Palm Island in 1957; the family was banished from the island and sent to another Queensland Mission in Woorabinda.

The Queensland State Government website describes the 1957 events:

> There had been a series of disturbances on Palm Island since the settlement was established, but no organised, collective and open revolt occurred until 1957. During this period the residents of Palm Island staged a strike against the harsh conditions imposed by Superintendent Bartlam and demanded improvements to housing and rations as well as increased wages. The residents also demanded that Bartlam leave the Island and he was forced to flee his office and call for reinforcements from Townsville. Armed police arrived by RAAF launch to put down the disturbance. The 'ringleaders' and their families were rounded up and marched on board the launch at gun point before being deported in chains to other Aboriginal settlements.

Cathy doesn't mince her words when she writes about the appallingly vicious treatment her family suffered at the hands of an openly racist administration. She describes the missions as 'effectively prisons' and explains the extent to which her anger and her understanding of the pain that had been felt by her forebears was an inspiration that drove her on to great things.

The potential for further revolt did not ease the restrictions on those who were forced to live in Woorabinda. Cathy's family was never granted a permit to leave the mission but her mother met her father, Norman, there and the two young people managed to make their escape when Cecelia was twenty-one. Cathy didn't learn the full extent of her family's suffering until 2006, when she was invited to take part in the television programme *Who Do You Think You Are?* She described what happened in an interview with the *Guardian* newspaper in 2016:

> The moment I heard about what happened to my parents before I was born was the moment I realized that the right to be heard is one of the pillars of social justice . . . In 1963, about 10 years before I was born, my mum Cecelia and my dad Norman were living in Ayr. Their parents and siblings were living at Woorabinda, an Aboriginal settlement about seven hours' drive away. Living under The Act meant that my mother had to write away to the superintendent of Woorabinda for permission to visit her family for Christmas . . . I was sitting with my mother when we were going through this information and there was this letter of rejection. Her request to visit her family was denied on the basis that my parents weren't married . . . My goodness, that sort of discrimination and ignorance, it's just appalling . . . Competition and performance is often driven by emotion, no doubt. So, I wish I'd known about this back when I was competing. Who knows how much faster I could have run!

Cathy's speed on the track was identified early. Her first race was an 80-metre dash for eight-year-olds at St Joseph's Primary School. She won easily, even though she had to run with one eye closed after poking herself on a piece of wire sticking out from a steel post on her way to the start. That's determination for you! The following week she won again, against older children. With the help of the school, and her sports teacher Mrs Bauldrey, the money was raised to support her talent. It bought a pair of spikes in which to run, a shirt, and the air fare to Brisbane for the state primary school titles. She won her first gold medal and loved it. She was pretty pleased with the attention her success inspired; her mother was bursting with pride. All the adults who watched her were very excited by her speed and style on the track.

When she was fourteen the vocational guidance officer at her secondary school asked her whether she had thought about what she wanted to do when she finished high school. 'Yeah,' she said, 'I want to win a gold medal at the Olympic Games'. 'OK', said the teacher, 'but what about after the medals and the Olympics?' 'I don't care,' said Cathy.

Cathy's determination to be Australia's finest athlete was not only fired by her enjoyment of her sport. She revelled in the admiration it brought her. She was showered with attention from the tough mother who pushed her on and from her coaches. Her stepfather, Bruce Barber was her first coach, and he was the one who told her she was, indeed, good enough to run in the Olympics. But she has always said that, alongside her Aboriginal history, her primary motivation was her older sister, Anne-Marie, who had been born with cerebral palsy and was looked after in a care home. Cathy has spoken about the lessons she learned from her sister, who died in 1990, and how they fed her sporting will. 'I ran because she couldn't. I've got two arms and two legs and it's my duty to use them', she said.

Cathy's road to Olympic glory is well known. In 1987, she began to be coached professionally by Mike Danila, was awarded a scholarship to Fairholme College and made such amazing progress Danila thought about entering her for the Commonwealth Games. In 1990 she competed in Auckland in the Australian relay team and became the first Aboriginal Australian to win gold. Throughout the early 1990s she competed in the junior world championships, got a new coach, Peter Fortune, was named Young Australian of the Year and moved up the rankings.

Cathy's first big breakthrough came in 1994, when she won gold in the 200- and 400-metre races at the Commonwealth Games in Canada. For the first time, she carried the Australian and Aboriginal flags around the track in victory. In 1996 came her chance to fulfil her Olympic dream. She became the first Australian Aborigine to compete and she set an Australian record, finishing second to the French woman Marie-José Perec in the 400 metres. Her record time of 48.63 ranked her as the sixth fastest woman of all time. Gold had eluded her and silver was not enough for Cathy, but her reputation as a great Australian was growing. She was bumped up from Young Australian of the year to Australian Person of the Year. The two titles had never been before won by the same person.

The 2000 Sydney Olympics fulfilled Cathy's dream. She became the first competing athlete to light the Olympic flame. Then, with the world watching and the hopes of a nation on her shoulders, she won the 400 metres and that longed-for Olympic gold medal. Again, Cathy carried the Australian and Aboriginal flags as she ran her victory lap barefoot, having secured her status as an Australian legend in 49.11 seconds in front of a screaming home crowd.

Of course, her legendary status was not merely the result of seventeen years of hard work, constant training and fighting her way through illness, injury, disappointment and grief at the deaths of her sister and her father. It was about politics. In her autobiography she wrote: 'there had been a lot of pressure on me from some sections of the Aboriginal community to boycott the Games; they believed the world's attention could then be diverted to their fight to improve living standards in the Aboriginal communities, but the government's refusal to apologise for the stolen generation fuelled my resentment.' It also, she has said, fuelled her speed.

There were differing views of that moment when she climbed the steps to light the Olympic flame in Sydney. Some saw her as representing the hopes of Aboriginal people; others, according to press reports, saw it as tokenism. One *Guardian* article summed up that perspective: 'A last-ditch attempt by a nation still dominated by beer-swigging, dunny-inhabiting, singlet-wearing white boys to change its image in the eyes of the world. To blot over the hundreds of years of Aboriginal oppression and shirtiness to sheilas.'

Olympic opening ceremonies are a canvas on which a nation can portray itself as it wants the rest of the world to see it. Cathy's view, as expressed in her book, was this, 'As the cauldron reached the top I began to think about my race. I was so honoured and proud to have been chosen to light the Olympic cauldron. It was such a powerful statement for the Aboriginal People and for reconciliation in this country.'

In 2003 Cathy retired from athletics, having lost her enthusiasm for the sport. Quite honestly, after twenty-two years of the most punishing training schedule and coping with injuries and pressure, I can hardly blame her. It makes complete sense to bow out of a life in which you've pushed your body to its absolute limits before it begins to let you down, and find a way to live the family life you've craved. In 2009 she married for the second time. Cathy and her husband, James Murch, had their first child in 2011, but her work in reconciliation continues. In 2007 she set up the Cathy Freeman Foundation, with the aim of 'supporting Indigenous students to achieve their potential in school and acknowledging the strength and wisdom that lies within remote Indigenous communities'. She wants, she says, 'an Australia where Indigenous and non-Indigenous children have the same education standards and opportunities in life'.

A year after the start of the Foundation, in 2008, the then Prime Minister, Kevin Rudd, issued an apology to the Indigenous Australians and the 'Stolen Generations' on behalf of the Australian government. Through her sport and her determination that no Aboriginal child will ever again be denied equal chances in life, Cathy symbolises the end of Australia's apartheid. It joins countries such as South Africa and, perhaps, Northern Ireland; countries where communities have been torn apart by racism and religious conflict but have come to the conclusion that truth and reconciliation are the only way forward for humanity.

As for sport, it is so important to have role models like Cathy Freeman for girls and young women as obesity and lack of fitness become a global problem. It's worth remembering that women were forbidden to run in the Olympics in ancient Greece and married women were banned even as spectators. When the modern games began in 1896 no women were allowed to compete in track and field events. It was argued that their wombs would be damaged and they could never bear children. Not so, as athletes like Cathy have proved. In 1928, women were permitted to run for the first time. When one of them fell briefly after the 800 metres race, the International Olympic Committee ruled that such a distance was too great a strain on the female body and the event was banned. It only returned in 1960. So, you see, powering through 400 metres like Cathy Freeman, or 800 or 1500 metres like Kelly Holmes, or winning the heptathlon like Jessica Ennis-Hill or Katarina Johnson-Thompson is a profoundly feminist act. Women can do it. (Bit late for me, though!)

we're going to overturn the idea that a woman somehow has to behave better than a man. It would be lovely if all men and all women were kind and gentle, but it just ain't so and, if we're to have truly equal opportunities, we have to acknowledge that a woman can be every bit as hard and ruthless as any man.

The second phrase that will remain with me from Margaret Atwood is that question she hears from audiences after discussions about *The Handmaid's Tale*: 'Is there hope?' There can be no doubt that we can look around the world in the twenty-first century and wonder, indeed, whether there is any hope. America is ruled by a man who is a self-confessed misogynist. On the other side of what used to be the Iron Curtain, there's a leader who appears to see himself as Superman. In China, there's barely a woman to be spotted in the power structure. North Korea has played around with nuclear weapons as if Kim Jong-un were engaged in a computer game.

The treatment of women in India and Pakistan, where the rape and murder of women and girls are day-to-day occurrences, is horrific. In certain parts of the Middle East a nightmare scenario not unlike that depicted in *The Handmaid's Tale* is played out. In Syria, men, women and children live in terror of bombs and chemical warfare. Throughout Africa and Egypt hundreds of thousands of little girls are forced to undergo genital mutilation.

Hopeful? It appears not. But on the ground are women, in all these places, who are trying to do good for their sisters. In India, women with a high profile, such as the novelist Arundhati Roy, are leading the way in demanding stronger laws and a new cultural awareness that women are not the disposable playthings of any man who chooses to have them. At the grassroots, women police officers are being appointed, as they were in Pakistan under Benazir Bhutto, to make it easier for survivors to report their abusers.

In countries such as Somalia, women's groups are travelling to remote villages to speak to men and women about the horror of the genital mutilation of girls, educating them so that they know it's a cultural, not a religious practice, and persuading them to stop. In Afghanistan, where the Taliban banned women from any kind of work outside the home when they ruled the country between 1996 and 2001, there is a television station called Zan TV. Fifty women are employed to create an all-female daily mix of news, politics and lifestyle shows. *Zan* means 'woman' in Dari, the variety of Persian spoken in Afghanistan.

Then, of course, there are the 'Me Too' and 'Time's Up' movements, which have spread around the world. Rightly, there have been concerns about ideas spread through social media, where there's the constant risk of insulting and threatening trolling, and questions about whether it was entirely appropriate for the messages to be advanced by wealthy and privileged famous women in low-cut, alluring, black frocks.

We shouldn't be worried. This wildfire mass activism has given me more hope than I've had for a long time. Across the world young women have learned what feminism means. They are saying they are not going to take sexual harassment and threats to their careers if they don't go along with a powerful man's desires. If some men suffer from being exposed as bullying creeps, all well and good. This is not an attack on all men, just the bad ones. I see young men welcoming these movements with a sense of relief that, at last, they can have a conversation about what's acceptable behaviour and what's not and begin to feel free to flirt and enjoy relationships between men and women that are open and equal.

So, yes, Margaret, there is hope. And it's women who are standing up and making the changes. Like the twenty-one heroes of mine in this book they're saying: 'Troll me if you want to but listen to what I have to say. You don't scare me!'

KEY SOURCES AND SUGGESTIONS FOR FURTHER READING

Pharaoh Hatshepsut

A History of Ancient Egypt by Marc Van De Mieroop (Wiley-Blackwell, 2011)
The Woman Who Would be King by Kara Cooney (Oneworld Publications, 2015)
'The King Herself' by Chip Brown, *National Geographic*, April 2009, https://www.nationalgeographic.com/magazine/2009/04/hatshepsut/

Joan of Arc

Henry VI, Part One by William Shakespeare (Penguin Classics, 2015)
Joan of Arc: A History by Helen Castor (Faber & Faber, 2015)
Joan of Arc: The Image of Female Heroism by Marina Warner (Oxford University Press, 1991)

Isabella of Castile

Isabella of Castile: Europe's First Great Queen by Giles Tremlett (Bloomsbury, 2016)
Isabella of Spain: The Last Crusader by William Thomas Walsh (R. M. McBride & Company, 1930)

Artemisia Gentileschi

The Artemisia Files: Artemisia Gentileschi for Feminists and Other Thinking People, edited by Mieke Bal (University of Chicago Press, 2005)

Artemisia Gentileschi: The Image of the Female Hero in Italian Baroque Art by Mary D. Garrard (Princeton University Press, 1991)
Orazio and Artemisia Gentileschi, edited by Keith Christiansen and Judith W. Mann (Metropolitan Museum of Art, New York, 2001)
'Artemisia's Moment' by Mary O'Neill, *Smithsonian Magazine*, May 2002, https://www.smithsonianmag.com/arts-culture/artemisias-moment-62150147/

Catherine the Great

Catherine the Great: Portrait of a Woman by Robert K. Massie (Head of Zeus, 2016)
Catherine the Great: A Short History by Isabel de Madariaga (Yale University Press, 2002)

The Warrior Queens: Boadicea's Chariot by Antonia Fraser (Phoenix Press, 2002)

Clara Schumann

Clara Schumann: The Artist and the Woman by Nancy B. Reich (Cornell University Press, 2001)

Sounds and Sweet Airs by Anna Beer (Oneworld Publications, 2017)

'Robert Schumann and Clara Wieck: A Creative Partnership' by Anna Burton, *Music & Letters*, Vol. 69, No. 2 (April 1988), pp. 211–228, https://www.jstor.org/stable/855217?seq=1#page_scan_tab_contents

Dowager Empress Cixi

Empress Dowager Cixi: The Concubine Who Launched Modern China by Jung Chang (Vintage, 2014)

The Last Empress: The She-Dragon of China by Keith Laidler (John Wiley & Sons, 2003)

Marie Curie

Before the Fall-Out: From Marie Curie to Hiroshima by Diana Preston (Corgi, 2006)

Marie Curie: A Life by Susan Quinn (DaCapo Press, 1996)

The Madame Curie Complex: The Hidden History of Women in Science by Julie Des Jardins (The Feminist Press, 2010)

Marie Curie and Her Daughters: The Private Lives of Science's First Family by Shelley Emling (Palgrave Macmillan, 2013)

Zapped: From Infrared to X-rays, the Curious History of Invisible Light by Bob Berman (Oneworld Publications, 2018)

'Madame Curie's Passion' by Julie Des Jardins, *Smithsonian Magazine*, October 2011, https://www.smithsonianmag.com/history/madame-curies-passion-74183598/

Coco Chanel

Coco Chanel: The Legend and The Life by Justine Picardie (Harper, 2013)

Golda Meir

Lioness: Golda Meir and the Nation of Israel by Francine Klagsbrun (Schocken Books, 2017)

My Life by Golda Meir (Futura Publications, 1976)

'Golda Meir: She Lived for Israel' by Stephen Klaidman, *Washington Post*, 9 December 1978, https://www.washingtonpost.com/archive/local/1978/12/09/golda-meir-she-lived-for-israel/de317348-5121-46a3-8d1c-5608cbc73eda/?utm_term=.feded1b4f1fe

FURTHER READING

Frida Kahlo

The Diary of Frida Kahlo: An Intimate Self-Portrait, edited by Sarah M. Lowe (Abrams Books, 2006)

My Art, My Life: An Autobiography by Diego Rivera (Dover Publications, 2003)

Frida: A Biography of Frida Kahlo by Hayden Herrera (Bloomsbury, 1989)

Frida Kahlo: Song of Herself by Salomon Grimberg (Merrell Publishers, 2008)

Sirimavo Bandaranaike

The Expedient Utopian: Bandaranaike and Ceylon by James Manor (Cambridge University Press, 1989)

'Sirima Bandaranaike' by John Rettie, *Guardian*, 11 October 2000, https://www.theguardian.com/news/2000/oct/11/guardianobituaries

Toni Morrison

The Bluest Eye by Toni Morrison (Vintage, 1999)

Playing in the Dark: Whiteness and the Literary Imagination by Toni Morrison (Harvard University Press, 1992)

Song of Solomon by Toni Morrison (Vintage, 1998)

' "As an American writer" (Toni Morrison on Colbert)' by Aaraon Bady, *The New Inquiry*, 22 November 2014, https://thenewinquiry.com/blog/as-an-american-writer-toni-morrison-on-colbert/

' "I Regret Everything": Toni Morrison Looks Back On Her Personal Life', NPR, 24 August 2015, https://www.npr.org/2015/08/24/434132724/i-regret-everything-toni-morrison-looks-back-on-her-personal-life

'The Laureates's Life Song' by David Streitfeld, *Washington Post*, 8 October 1993, https://www.washingtonpost.com/archive/lifestyle/1993/10/08/the-laureatess-life-song/10d3b79b-52f2-4685-a6dd-c57f7dde08d2/?utm_term=.fc29d17d02b3

'The Radical Vision of Toni Morrison' by Rachel Kaadzi Ghansah, *New York Times*, 8 April 2015, https://www.nytimes.com/2015/04/12/magazine/the-radical-vision-of-toni-morrison.html

'The Sacred Toni Morrison' by Colleen Walsh, *The Harvard Gazette*, 20 September 2012, https://news.harvard.edu/gazette/story/2012/09/the-sacred-toni-morrison/

'Solving the Riddle' by Maya Jaggi, *Guardian*, 15 November 2003, https://www.theguardian.com/books/2003/nov/15/fiction.tonimorrison

'Who Is the Author of Toni Morrison?', *New York Magazine*, http://nymag.com/news/features/toni-morrison-2012-5/index2.html

Margaret Eleanor Atwood

The Cambridge Companion to Margaret Atwood, edited by Coral Ann Howells (Cambridge University Press, 2006)

Curious Pursuits: Occasional Pursuits by Margaret Atwood (Virago, 2006)

The Handmaid's Tale by Margaret Atwood (Vintage, 1996)

Margaret Atwood: A Biography by Nathalie Cooke (ECW Press, 1998).

Margaret Atwood: Conversations, edited by Earl G. Ingersoll (Ontario Review Press, 1990)

'Light in the Wilderness' by Robert Potts, *Guardian*, 26 April 2003, https://www.theguardian.com/books/2003/apr/26/fiction.margaretatwood

Wangari Maathai

Unbowed: My Autobiography by Wangari Maathai (Arrow, 2008)

'Can One Woman Save Africa?' by Johann Hari, *Independent*, 27 September 2009, http://www.independent.co.uk/news/world/africa/can-one-woman-save-africa-1794103.html

' "I Will Disappear into the Forest": An Interview with Wangari Maathai' by Dave Gilson, *Mother Jones*, 5 January 2005, http://www.mother-jones.com/politics/2005/01/root-causes-interview-wangari-maathai/

Hillary Rodham Clinton

Living History by Hillary Rodham Clinton (Headline, 2004)

What Happened by Hillary Rodham Clinton (Simon & Schuster, 2017)

'Hillary Clinton: "I had to learn as a young woman to control my emotions" ' by Emily Crockett, *Vox*, 8 September 2016, https://www.vox.com/2016/9/8/12851878/hillary-clinton-control-emotions-sexism-humans-new-york

'I Want Hillary Clinton to Be President' by Boris Johnson, *Telegraph*, 1 November 2007, https://www.telegraph.co.uk/comment/3643709/I-want-Hillary-Clinton-to-be-president.html

Benazir Bhutto

Daughter of the East: An Autobiography by Benazir Bhutto (Simon & Schuster, 2008)

Benazir Bhutto: Favoured Daughter by Brooke Allen (New Harvest, 2016)

Songs of Blood and Sword: A Daughter's Memoir by Fatima Bhutto (Vintage, 2011)

Angela Merkel

Angela Merkel: A Chancellorship Forged in Crisis by Alan Crawford and Tony Czuczka (John Wiley & Sons, 2013)

FURTHER READING

Angela Merkel: Europe's Most Influential Leader by Matthew Qvortrup (Gerald Duckworth & Co, 2017)
'Angela Merkel: The World's Most Powerful Woman?' by Constanze Stelzenmüller, *Guardian*, 23 August 2009, https://www.theguardian.com/world/2009/aug/23/angela-merkel-german-chancellor-profile

Madonna Louise Ciccone

Life with My Sister Madonna by Christopher Ciccone (Simon & Schuster, 2008)
Madonna: An Intimate Biography by J. Randy Taraborrelli (Sidgwick & Jackson, 2001)
'Billboard "Woman of the Year" Madonna Gives Provocative Interview on Everything from 2016 Election to Ageism' by Elizabeth Banks, Billboard, 5 December 2016, https://www.billboard.com/articles/events/women-in-music/7597392/madonna-billboard-woman-of-the-year-interview
'Madonna's Back', *Harper's Bazaar*, 4 October 2013, https://www.harpers-bazaar.com/celebrity/latest/news/a1095/madonna-interview-1113/
'Madonna's Spring Awakening' by Roxane Gay, *Harper's Bazaar*, 10 January 2017, https://www.harpersbazaar.com/culture/features/a19761/madonna-interview/

Anna Politkovskaya

Nothing But the Truth: Selected Dispatches by Anna Politkovskaya (Vintage, 2011)
A Russian Diary by Anna Politkovskaya (Vintage, 2008)
'Journalists killed in Russia since 1992', Committee to Protect Journalists, https://cpj.org/europe/russia/

Cathy Freeman

Cathy: My Autobiography by Cathy Freeman (Highdown, 2004)
'Cathy Freeman' by Homa Khaleeli, *Guardian*, 8 March 2011, https://www.theguardian.com/sport/2011/mar/08/cathy-freeman-100-women
'If I'd known my parents' story, who knows how much faster I could have run' by Cathy Freeman, *Guardian*, 18 November 2016, https://www.theguardian.com/commentisfree/2016/nov/18/if-id-known-my-parents-story-who-knows-how-much-faster-i-could-have-run
'Palm Island', Queensland government, https://www.qld.gov.au/atsi/cultural-awareness-heritage-arts/community-histories-palm-island
'Why Bradman Should Do a Freeman' by Tanya Aldred, *Guardian*, 19 September 2000, https://www.theguardian.com/sport/2000/sep/19/cricket3

ACKNOWLEDGEMENTS

My thanks, as always, to my ever supportive agent and friend, Barbara Levy, and to my editor, Sam Carter. He's everything an editor should be – erudite, attentive and unafraid to tell me when I've fallen below the high standard he expects. I'm tremendously grateful to Emily Carter for her assistance with the research on such a wide range of historical periods, countries and cultures. There was a point at which I held my head and thought 'what do I actually know about nineteenth-century Russia?' Without Emily my task would have been nigh on impossible. Thanks too to Ann Grand for copy-editing, Sophie Richmond for proofreading, and Abi Scruby and Harriet Wade for their additional research. And for my dearest Margot Weale, responsible for publicity, thank you. I'm ready for the off! It's a team that makes a book, not just an author!